THE RESCUE MAN:
A "Snafu Snatching" Rescue Pilot's Extraordinary Journey through World War II

By Henry Lowenstein, Ph.D.
Assisted by Carla Faye Grabert-Lowenstein, Esq.

Published by Van Rye Publishing, LLC
www.vanryepublishing.com

ISBN-10: 0-9982893-0-2
ISBN-13: 978-0-9982893-0-4

Praise for *THE RESCUE MAN*

"*The Rescue Man* is impressive in its sweep of WWII history that includes the key military, political and economic forces shaping the world. . . . [Lieutenant Hayes's] achievements in combat rescues are truly impressive and worthy of being told and studied."

> —Robert H. Reed, General (four-star), U.S. Air Force (Retired); Former Chief of Staff, Supreme Headquarters Allied Powers Europe (NATO)

"A remarkable story of accomplishments, frustrations and perseverance unfolds as you follow an Idaho farm boy's journey towards his ultimate goal of becoming a military aviator. . . . The reader will be enthralled by the transition of this farm boy into a stellar military pilot, eagerly following the highs and lows of the many and varied experiences he encountered during his remarkable journey."

> —J.A. "Bill" Saavedra, Colonel, U.S. Air Force (Retired); Volunteer Historian, U.S. Air Force Historical Support Division, U.S. Air Force Office of History, Washington, DC

"*The Rescue Man* is an outstanding rendition of the experience of pilots, both Navy and Army Air Force, who served in World War II accomplishing air–sea rescues in the unique Consolidated PBY Catalina 'flying boat.' . . . For our downed airmen, these 'rescue men' flying into stark danger were their salvation from a watery grave. Thousands of airmen were saved, but the story of those who saved them remained largely untold after the war. . . . This book is a must read for today's generation to never forget."

—Walter "Scottie" Scott, World War II veteran; Ensign, U.S. Navy (Retired); Former PBY Catalina pilot and flight instructor, Naval Air Training Center, Pensacola, Florida

"*The Rescue Man* tells the story of one of the 150 WWII Army Air Force pilots who also earned Navy wings. . . . These brave young airmen flew thousands of overwater search and rescue missions and are credited with saving thousands of lives. Lieutenant Frank 'Bud' Hayes's journey, from a small town in Idaho through enlistment and pilot training in two different services to a . . . crash in the Philippines, is a compelling story of bravery and devotion forged in family and community values."

—Charles Thrash, Colonel, U.S. Air Force (Retired); Former Commander, 354th Tactical Fighter Wing and A-10 pilot, Myrtle Beach Air Force Base, Myrtle Beach, South Carolina

"I spent twenty-six years of active duty in the U.S. Air Force and have always been enthralled by true and personal descriptions of the U.S. Army Air Force fighting men and women and their sacrifices and courage in our country's wars to protect our freedoms. *The Rescue Man* is one of the finest of these descriptions I have ever read. . . . I strongly recommend the book to everyone who respects those like Bud Hayes who made the ultimate sacrifice."

—Thomas "Buddy" Styers, Colonel, U.S. Air Force (Retired); Former Commander, 554th Combat Support Group, Nellis Air Force Base, Nevada

"The story of First Lieutenant 'Bud' Hayes is one of heroism, flying skill and honor. . . . First Lieutenant 'Bud' Hayes is a true American hero. His story needs to be told, and has been written wonderfully by Dr. Lowenstein. This is a must read for anyone interested in WWII or flying in general."

> —Nathan E. "Nate" Cagle, Commander, U.S. Navy (Retired); Former Mission Commander, Patrol Plane Tactical Coordinator and P-3 Orion pilot, Patrol Squadron 9, Patrol Squadron 66 and Patrol Squadron 91

"Dr. Lowenstein's book, *The Rescue Man*, is any historian's dream; a story of the Second Emergency Rescue Squadron and its operations through the eyes of one of its pilots. To have Bud's story told in vivid detail as this book accomplishes is simply amazing. Rarely do we hear the family history of those many young men who served in the Second Emergency Rescue Squadron and the tenacity and risks they took in operation. . . . I highly recommend the book."

> —James R. Teegarden, Chief Warrant Officer 4 and UH-60 Blackhawk instructor pilot, U.S. Army Aviation Center of Excellence, Fort Rucker, Alabama; Director, http://pbyrescue.com

"In this insightful and inspiring work, Henry Lowenstein not only captures the 'real life' of a GI . . . but shows us the humanity of a soldier/aviator with an ordinary Idaho small town upbringing. . . . Dr. Lowenstein's exhaustive research and extraordinary ability to effectively piece together fragments of disjointed information to build the story of Bud Hayes's life as though it were my own or someone I knew takes me back. . . . [He] has brought some sense of closure to all of us who will read this work. . . . I couldn't put it down!"

> —P.R. "Dick" Drass, Captain, U.S. Army, Ranger Division (Retired); Former Vietnam War combat veteran; Graduate, U.S. Military Academy at West Point

"While reading I was able to relive the feelings of the flow of war, especially the monotony of daily missions and the sheer adrenaline rush of actually performing what you were trained for. . . . I felt that in Bud and his feeling of duty on every page. . . . [Bud's] saving lives in battle, and my own personal experiences of war, really hit home and brought back much of the same feeling that Bud must have felt. . . . [T]hrough his actions, Bud was able to save countless generations of families."

—James Gatley, Sergeant, U.S. Army (Retired); Former 285th Air Recon Battle Group, Silver Bell, Arizona; 101st Airborne Division; Scheduler, Prescott Support Co. (air transport / cargo services)

"I started reading it over a weekend and could not put it down. I was so touched by the story I called my father, a World War II veteran. He had never talked about the war and we talked for hours of it for the first time."

—David Fink, President, Compass Associates, LLC; Lecturer in international business, Coastal Carolina University

Dedication

To
Mary Frances Hayes Grabert
in loving memory of your brother
First Lieutenant Frank Philby "Bud" Hayes
to
members of the U.S. Army Air Force
Second Emergency Rescue Squadron (1943–45)
and to
those from the State of Idaho who
faithfully served the United States in World War II

"There is nothing new in the world except the history you do not know."[1]

—Harry S. Truman (1884–1972), thirty-third President of the United States

Lieutenant Frank Philby "Bud" Hayes
(at home in Idaho, on leave, July 1944)

Contents

Preface

THIS BOOK TELLS HISTORY through a biography and presents a biography in the context of history. Its combination of history and biography provides a paradigm of millions of airmen, sailors, marines and soldiers who served in World War II—the "everyman" whom historical studies rarely capture in the shadow of larger than life generals, politicians and personalities of the era. First Lieutenant Frank Philby "Bud" Hayes represents the many young men of the United States who woke up on December 7, 1941, in their farmhouses, towns and suburbs to find their lives and destinies changed. Some went on to fight overseas, then returned home and contributed to the post-war expansion of the United States. Some returned damaged for life. Others did not return at all. This is the story of their trials and tribulations in training, waiting, war and, in some cases, demise. They all served. Their sacrificed youth and their devotion to duty saved the world.

My wife, Carla Faye Grabert-Lowenstein, was born in Twin Falls, Idaho in 1956, eleven years after the end of World War II. She grew up in Idaho's Magic Valley region on her parents' farm. Her mother, Mary Frances (Hayes) Grabert ("Mom" Grabert), moved in 1990 to a city home that her father purchased shortly after he became seriously ill. Her father eventually passed away in 1991. On our later trips to Twin Falls to visit Mom, I was always fascinated by the photos of Mom's dashing brother, a pilot named Frank Philby "Bud" Hayes, and by his military certificates that adorned the walls of her family room and bedroom.

Mom clearly adored Bud, who was two years her junior. As the photos reveal, he was extraordinarily handsome, and to this day ladies (like those at the local Costco photo counter who helped me digitize his photos for this book) "swoon" over him. Had Bud survived the war perhaps Hollywood would have grabbed him for one of those famous post-war movies. But who was Bud? Who was this Idahoan pilot of World War II and what were the times that he lived through like? And how did Idaho shape him? Now, over seventy years after the close of World War II, his story needs to be told and can finally be memorialized.

Carla had always explained that Uncle Bud had been in the U.S. Army Air Force during World War II. Family lore said he was a transport pilot who went down in a Pacific typhoon during the war and was never found. No one knew for sure though. Mom was never quite sure. And her and Bud's mother, Fay Fern Philby Jensen, never revealed all the details to anyone in the family. For decades, Bud and his story remained quite the family enigma. Now that we know his real story, it has proven to be quite different from the family lore that surrounded it.

Carla's mother, her mother's sister (the late Nedra [Hayes] Greene) and her grandmother never spoke of Bud. Neither did her cousin Carole (Nedra's daughter) who was a child at the time of Bud's service during World War II. It was not out of shame, but instead from the fact that the pain and shock surrounding the end of Bud's story had never healed. Family members could not find the emotion or strength to speak about it, and so the mystery continued to succeeding generations. The real story of this member of Idaho's "Greatest Generation" had yet to come to light.

At the time I began this writing, Carla and I had just returned from visiting Mom at her Twin Falls home. Mom, then ninety-three years old, had survived major surgery and was doing well. As during previous visits, Mom allowed me to descend into her vast basement and cull through its considerable array of boxes, bags, shelves and files, retaining what was of value and disposing of the rest—nearly a century of accumulated paper, newspapers, old magazines, holiday cards and sundry other items.

As was common of Mom's generation, which survived both the Great Depression and war rationing during World War II, people developed a habit of saving virtually everything lest it be needed at a critical future time. Mom was no different. My work in the basement was much like an Egyptian archeological dig. Among the masses of paper, bags and boxes that I sent hither to the recycle center, I recovered nuggets of family history. Such valuables as Mom's 1941 Royal Aristocrat typewriter, coins and unused postage stamps (tracing fifty plus years of postal inflation) were among the memorabilia I recovered. And photos I found elicited old memories of family and events.

Far in a back corner of the basement I discovered a sealed box containing what records remain of Mom's brother, First Lieutenant Frank Philby "Bud" Hayes, a pilot in the U.S. Army Air Force during World War II. The box contained virtually every letter Bud wrote home during the war from 1943–45, military citations, command letters and records and pre-war autobiographical papers from high school. With Mom's blessing, I brought these materials back to my South Carolina home office with the objective of summarizing the letters and writing a narrative about Bud.

As my work on Bud's story progressed over the holiday break in 2015, it became clear that his story extended well beyond our family lore, and it felt very much as if a spirit had emerged from the box to tell it. The story was to become a much broader tale of a history of sacrifice, of an Idahoan's dedication and bravery in the service of his country during World War II, of the influence of his state on him and of his yearning to return home to Idaho after the war. One could see in Bud's story the strength and experiences gained by a farm boy from Filer, Idaho who would come to master a unique Army Air Force rescue aircraft known as the PBY Catalina "flying boat," lead its crew and save many American airmen in the face of often perilous combat circumstances and conditions.

The story also drew into focus, through Bud's experiences,

the sometimes illogical acts of military planners and administrators at a time when all the nation's energies and resources were focused on victory over the Axis powers in Europe and the Pacific. The U.S. Army Air Force had sustained large combat losses, yet for months, rescue pilots like Bud were left to fly benign domestic "check" flights from obscure, rapidly-thrown-together stateside airfields while awaiting deployment. These curious circumstances proved to be the unintended consequence of an intense bureaucratic argument at the time involving the War Department's Joint Chiefs of Staff (and more specifically involving the U.S. Army Air Force and the U.S. Navy) over who would have jurisdiction over air–sea rescue missions during the war.

The war in the Pacific was heavily dependent on air power, and the U.S. Army Air Force and the U.S. Navy sustained many air losses, most of which occurred over and in water. PBY Catalina "flying boat" aircraft crews, like the one Bud piloted and commanded, were desperately needed to rescue downed airmen. Meanwhile, turf battles in Washington, at the Joint Chiefs of Staff, dragged on interminably. Ultimately, the Army Air Force and the Navy reached a compromise. Each service would have and be in control of its own air–sea rescue squadrons, but the Navy would be responsible for training all of the rescue squadron "flying boat" pilots. How many downed airmen in the Pacific would have been saved had the Joint Chiefs of Staff acted sooner in creating and deploying these rescue squadrons? That is a question left unanswered by history.

Once the U.S. Army Air Force had created its own air–sea rescue squadrons, it was able to initially deploy two such squadrons to the Pacific (one to operations under the Fifth Air Force, the other to operations under the Thirteenth Air Force) as well as one to Europe. Due to the unique nature of these rescue squadrons, which operated between air and sea, author Roscoe Creed dubbed them "The Air Force's Navy." Bud's PBY Catalina rescue crew, in particular, was assigned to the Second Emergency Rescue Squadron, Thirteenth Air Force. The squadron saw action late in the war (1944–45) in the Pacific off New Guinea, during the Borneo Campaign and in the Philippines.

Bud's story ultimately provides an example of sacrifice that is representative of the many Idaho men who served during World War II, in that era when Idaho was still a small state and each Idaho loss was felt deeply. His story is also emblematic of the thousands of "everyman" pilots whose mettle and sacrifice saved the nation and the world for later generations. Bud's story provides lessons worth preserving and repeating. Now, with his letters, with his records and with additional research, we can finally chronicle his story and celebrate his life.

Some might question why there is a need to chronicle a story after the passage of decades, in this case more than seventy years. So why do we need to tell Bud's story? There are two immediate answers. First, there is always the descendants' desire to learn about their roots and to help create pathways for future generations to do so as well. The descendants of Bud's Philby/Hayes family are no exception.

While Bud never married, his two sisters did. One sister, Nedra, married Percy Greene, a trout farmer (Greene and Blue Lakes Trout Farm) in Twin Falls, Idaho. The Greenes had two children, Carole, born in 1934, and Michael, born in 1943, both of whom had children, grandchildren and now great-grandchildren. Likewise, Bud's other sister, the aforementioned Mary Frances ("Mom") married and later divorced Marvin Peterson, having one daughter, Mary Beth, born in 1943. Mary Beth later married, had three children and now has grandchildren. Mary Frances later married Carl Grabert, a widowed Twin Falls, Idaho farmer. They had a daughter Carla Faye, born in 1956, who is now also a grandmother. Each branch of Bud's family and extended family grows. The successive generations will now have his story.

The second, and perhaps more essential, reason to chronicle a story like Bud's is the need for us all to never forget the sacrifice of those who kept the United States a free nation. The Allied victory in World War II was a decisive moment in world history, the outcome from 1938 to 1945 at times in doubt. The United States did not enter the war until December 1941. Had the Allies not achieved victory, then, as many would come to remark, part of America would be under imperial domination and speaking Japanese or German. That fate was avoided thanks to the tenacity and diligence of millions of soldiers, sailors, marines and airman—First Lieutenant Bud Hayes among them. The war became a quintessential transformative event for millions of individuals, and it reshaped America's society, culture and economy in ways lasting even to this day.

In the twenty-first century, today's generations enjoy conveniences, comforts and technology of the modern era, much of which had its origins in World War II. It is easy for these generations to take for granted the freedoms they enjoy and the bright prospects of the future. Their lives did not face hardships like the Great Depression, nor those of an era of vicious powers attempting to take over and subjugate the world.

Even the modern problem of terrorism pales in comparison to the threat posed by Hitler's German Third Reich or the horrors fostered by Tojo's Imperial Empire of Japan. Today, both of those nations, at peace, are allies, with the modern generation finding it hard to fathom a belligerent Germany or Japan. Few realize that Mitsubishi, maker of modern televisions and automobiles, once made the very airplanes that bombed Pearl Harbor. Nor do those driving the iconic Volkswagen realize it was the industrial and wartime brainchild of Adolph Hitler. Yes, the world has changed. Seventy years after World War II, the lessons from that war might have faded before ever reaching subsequent generations.

In the yearly Jewish Passover Seder (seen in the famous painting of Jesus's last supper), Jews around the world repeat the story of the Jews' flight from slavery and from Pharaoh in Egypt. For thousands of years, the tradition has been for them to tell the story to their children:

So even if we are all wise, all of us full of understanding, all of us aged and well versed, . . . it would still be our duty to tell of the deliverance from Egypt. Whoever tells the most about the departure from Egypt is worthy of praise.[1]

And as the philosopher George Santayana (1863–1952) famously said, "Those who do not learn from history are doomed to repeat it."[2]

This book uses as its primary sources Bud Hayes's pre-war writings from Filer High School (1940–41), letters Bud wrote home during his U.S. Army Air Force service (1943–45), letters from officials of the U.S. Army Air Force during that period, Bud's surviving military records, documents that the U.S. Army recently discovered (previously thought lost) and interviews with Bud's sister Mary Frances (Hayes) Grabert. Other interviews helping to form the basis of this book were conducted with Bud's living nieces and nephew and with their spouses, including with Carla Faye Grabert-Lowenstein, Michael and Dot Greene and Carole Kasel. Also interviewed for this book was Larry Leonard, who is the brother of one of Bud's co-pilots, Second Lieutenant John Leonard.

In addition, Chief Warrant Officer James Teegarden, who is the nephew of one of the founding officers of the Second Emergency Rescue Squadron that Bud served in, has been the lone keeper of nearly every surviving record related to the squadron, and he was extraordinary beyond the call of duty in providing research and records that are included in this book. Colonel Joaquin A. "Bill" Saavedra (U. S. Air Force, Retired) of the U.S. Air Force Historical Support Office also provided invaluable materials and assistance that contributed to this work. Others who assisted in this work are noted in the Acknowledgments section that appears toward the end of the book.

We acquired other information for this book from the Internet and from public records, and they are duly referenced throughout. General historical events we summarized using the *Encyclopedia Britannica* and other publicly-available reliable resources, as well as from common knowledge (for corresponding World War II events and dates). For references to monetary values in Bud's letters from the time, we translated them into present-day dollars using the online inflation calculator http://www.dollartimes.com. And the book supplements all of this content with images and information available from the Teegarden Collection (http://pby rescue.com, which is the largest archive of records about the U.S. Army Air Force's Second Emergency Rescue Squadron), from U.S. government/military records and from the Hayes/Grabert family in order to add imagery and context to Bud's story.

Bud's story now begins.

Henry Lowenstein, Ph.D.
January 20, 2017
Conway, South Carolina

Prologue

O N SUNDAY MORNING, October 7, 1945, 0630 hours, at Clark Air Base on the island of Luzon, Philippines, First Lieutenant Frank Philby "Bud" Hayes of the U.S. Army Air Force, no longer in wartime tent, was up in the base's squadron barracks donning his operation uniform in preparation for the day's mission. As he put on his long-awaited new first lieutenant bars and his U.S. Army Air Force pilot wings he pushed aside the U.S. Navy pilot wings in his kit. Everyone in Bud's squadron had long memories of the Navy's effort to block the Army Air Force from forming its own emergency rescue squadrons to save its own downed airmen. The Navy wings were quite decidedly only for use on the rarely-worn dress uniform.

After months of Bud rescuing downed airmen in New Guinea, Borneo and the Philippines, the aptly nicknamed "Snafu Snatcher's" mission that day was to be a simple pick-up and drop-off of servicemen in his PBY Catalina "flying boat" airplane. There would be no strafing, bombing or rescue peril during the mission; Bud anticipated no "snafus" of any kind. The war had ended over a month prior. The guns were silent, operations were winding down and any remaining forces were doing mop-up operations on remote islands and other similarly benign tasks. Bud anxiously awaited orders to head home to Twin Falls County, Idaho, which, not surprisingly, were delayed just like other promises of leave

1

over the years.

Bud, a strapping broad-shouldered Idaho farm boy, had naturally arisen at the crack of dawn, long a habit of his Irish ancestral family farmers. It was another hot, humid Philippines day. The base mess halls were finally preparing "real" food, erasing memories of combat rations and mystery meat from the months before. Bud headed for a hot, fresh, full breakfast. No doubt he was anticipating a return home to his Mom's fresh farm cooking and to his beloved Idaho beef and potatoes.

At the officers' mess Bud warmly greeted his new co-pilot, Flight Officer John "Jack" Leonard. Longtime navigator Lieutenant Greg Gregersen, getting a few hours extra weekend sleep, would meet them later, on the flight line. For a change they had lots of time before flight. Bud and Jack had met a couple weeks earlier, Jack being a replacement for Bud's wartime co-pilot who had rotated back to the states. The two men, twenty-one years old in years but decades advanced in life experience, hit it off immediately.

The two veteran pilots had much in common. Both had been involved in extensive and heroic combat and rescue missions in the Pacific while flying the PBY Catalina "flying boat." The "Cats," as these aircraft were sometimes called, were unusual, complex and difficult to operate, but their successful rescue missions were oh so satisfying to those who flew them. Both Bud and Jack had won the Air Medal for heroism. But on that day their orders had them acting essentially as "bus drivers." How things had changed in the month since war's end!

Bud Hayes and Jack Leonard had quite different backgrounds and upbringings. Jack came from an observant Catholic family with six children in Hackensack, New Jersey (suburban New York City). He had grown up in the cacophony of urban living: big-city-area, wall-to-wall people in multistory apartments or bungalows of close proximity and visits to the city that brought all the fast activity, menace and excitement of New York and its environs. Jack always wanted to fly, and he joined the U.S. Army Air Force after high school graduation. Proving to have those rare skills

2

sought by the Army Air Force's PBY Project, Jack, like Bud, eventually became one of less than 150 Army Air Force pilots in World War II trained to operate the Air Force's PBY Catalina with formal pilot wings from both the Air Force and the Navy.

Bud Hayes was from the other side of the American continent than Jack. He grew up in a small rural farming and ranching town in the wide expanses of Southern Idaho, in the town of Filer. Nothing could have been more remote or different from Hackensack than Idaho's Twin Falls County, which had big open land, big open skies and sparse population. Bud's family members were observant Methodists. His natural father abandoned them shortly after Bud was born, leaving Bud to be raised by a then-single schoolteacher Mom. He eventually had a stepfather, and his two older sisters both married. Bud grew up surrounded by arid farmland in cattle country. He, like Jack, always yearned to fly, and he joined the U.S. Army Air Force after high school graduation. These two young men from opposite ends of America were emblematic of the thousands of servicemen during World War II who converged with their collective talents and won the war.

As Bud and Jack ate breakfast they talked about family and home. Both were anxious for the Army Air Force to send them back to the states. But when would that occur? "Hurry up and wait" had been the bane of Bud's Army Air Force life since his enlistment. As others entered the mess, Bud and Jack shook their heads at any newly-arrived officers. "Ninety-day wonders" they called these officers, who spared no effort to get deployed there, to the Pacific, so their records would show them in a "combat" theater of operation, though they never flew a mission or experienced a bullet whizzing by. Swatting pesky tropical mosquitoes would be these new officers' most action; but no flying cross is awarded for those kills. Bud and Jack laughed at that thought and at the daily scene.

Jack was curious. He had no concept of Idaho and, perhaps like many, mistook it for "Iowa." Turning to Bud he asked, "Bud, what was it like out west in Idaho? Were you a cowboy? Did you

3

see Indians?"

Bud chuckled, "Oh boy! Nah. No Lone Ranger there. We raised cattle, rode horses across farm and ranchland, but it was no cowboy western. We farmed the land. You know, Idaho beef and potatoes. And there was a Shoshone Indian reservation nearby—peaceful people."

Jack looked on with a smile, "Then how on earth did your folks get way out there? How did you end up going from a farm to this air–sea rescue Catalina flying boat in the middle of the Pacific Ocean?"

Bud cracked his famous full smile and chuckled again. In the distance they heard mechanics' metal clanging and a few sharp words from ground crew members who were replacing rivets that had popped off a PBY Catalina and were repairing its engine. A C-47 plane popped a puff of smoke from its engines, then roared to life as it throttled up for takeoff. Men filed into the mess tent, and the buzz of voices and clatter of dishes grew.

Bud leaned back in his chair, ate another chunk of bread, took a big gulp of milk and looked wistfully across the runway. Far away in his mind's eye he could see the Snake River Canyon, the farm, his family waiting, all as it was during his prior leave in Idaho in 1944. He turned to Jack and said, "Well Jack, we have time before flight. Grab another coffee and more toast. You know, the whole war they called us 'The Rescue Men' and 'Snafu Snatchers.' I'll tell you how my journey into this war began."

CHAPTER 1

Bud Hayes's Homeland:
Filer, Idaho and the Magic Valley

TO UNDERSTAND THE METTLE of a human being, one needs to understand how his or her roots, ancestral paths, nurturing and upbringing converged with the surrounding land to build a special personality, dedication, will and strength. The land of Idaho, by its very nature, challenged the men and women who settled it to develop personal strength and determination. Those who put down roots there and farmed and ranched amid the Southern Idaho valley's heat, fertile but hard soil, droughts, pestilence and long traveling distances acquired extraordinary willpower, self-sufficiency and physical and mental strength. They arrived in Southern Idaho from the east with great optimism and with a determination to be independent and free.

So, too, do we now briefly visit Southern Idaho, Bud's homeland, in order to set the stage for Bud's story and better understand the basis of the mettle of the man who would become First Lieutenant Frank Philby "Bud" Hayes. Idaho was the origin of the special personal traits that came together in Bud's determination to fly, his aviation achievements, his service to his nation and his patriotism. And in all that, Bud's dedication to family, community and state never wavered. Coming home to Idaho was a constant goal for Bud after the war. Would he ever get that chance? Here begins Bud's tale. It is the tale of an exemplary son of the Magic

Valley of Idaho. And the story begins with his ancestry.

The State of Idaho lies in the northwestern United States, part of the expansive lands acquired by President Thomas Jefferson from France in the 1803 Louisiana Purchase. At the time it was a vast unknown wilderness. But the spot where present-day Idaho's northern edge runs along the Snake River and intersects with the Columbia River was eventually explored and mapped by the Lewis and Clark Expedition. That successful expedition famously depended on its guide, the Native American woman Sacagawea (1788–1812) of the Lemhi Shoshone tribe, located near what is today Salmon, Idaho.

In the mid-eighteen hundreds, Southern Idaho became a way station along the famous Oregon Trail. Later, small gold deposits were found there, and artisanal mining took place. The Snake River Canyon that wound its way through a valley in what would become Twin Falls County, Idaho became an important source of water, providing for travelers headed to the Oregon Territory.

Figure 1.1. Snake River Canyon, Twin Falls County, Idaho.[1]

Southern Idaho was, to be sure, made up of inhospitable arid desert, with thick walls of volcanic rock lying beneath its soil, remnants of Idaho's molten lava origins millions of years ago. As if a mighty knife sliced through the land, the Snake River cut a deep canyon through the flat valley of the Great Basin, providing valuable fresh water and ample fish, including trout, salmon and sturgeon along its falls. The river, though narrow at thirty feet wide, flows through the walls of an ancient canyon at its southern point of layered volcanic rock that is over four hundred feet deep. The river itself, calm at points, quickly becomes a "whirling and tumultuous vortex" of water.[2] Two falls (cascades) at its southern tangent formed the basis for the nascent community of Twin Falls, Idaho—a center of aquaculture, farming and cattle ranching. The Snake River Canyon's banks provided ample grasslands for grazing cattle. Nevertheless, the area remained sparsely settled, with most visitors passing onward to Oregon. After Idaho became a state in 1890, by 2014 it was the fourteenth largest state by land area in the Union at 83,642 square miles, with a population of 1.63 million people.[3] In the nineteenth century, most of its people resided in the northern and north-central part of the state.

Many early Idaho migrants arrived in South-Central Idaho as miners in search of gold. But by nineteen hundred, the lower part of Idaho became attractive to farmers and ranchers moving from Midwest regions (Nebraska, Kansas, Missouri, Iowa and Illinois, among others) in search of cheaper and larger land for farming and livestock. Events commencing around 1870 stimulated this movement of farmers, particularly those with cattle, from the Midwestern states. That movement is summarized in the following excerpt from Idaho State University.

FARMERS SETTLE THE GREAT PLAINS

Between 1870 and 1890, the biggest movement westward took place. Spreading from the railroad tracks, hundreds of thousands of settlers moved into the Dakotas, Wyoming, Montana and Idaho. The last territory settled was Oklahoma in 1889. A frantic rush took place to seize a piece of this last bit of the wilderness. The frontier was closed. There was now no dividing line between wild and settled land. How were the dry plains turned into farming land? Why did the cattlemen give way to the farmers? One reason why the cattlemen were forced out was the summer drought of 1886, when the grasslands withered and cattle starved. The winter was the worst in living memory and thousands more cattle froze to death. Many ranch owners were ruined. The other major reason for the farmers' success was the spread of new inventions that made farming possible on the Great Plains. Barbed wire began to be sold in the 1870s and large areas of land could now be enclosed cheaply and quickly. Equipment to dig deep wells became available. Most important, new machines were developed, such as the steel gang plow that could turn several furrows at once; special harrows to break up the soil; mechanical reapers and binders, and steam threshing machines. Vast areas could now be farmed far more efficiently.[4]

Among those migrating to Idaho were second generation Irish and German immigrants to America.[5] Both ethnic groups had moved to the United States for different reasons beginning in the 1840s—the Irish to escape the Irish Potato Famine, the Germans as refuge from the German Revolution (1848–49). They settled near Idaho rivers and streams (the Snake River being the largest), and established small farms, as described in the following passage:

> The little farms were extended, the sage brush land was cleared up and put into cultivation, water was introduced to the land by way of irrigation (later extensive canals). It was soon found that each man's farm would, but proper improvement and cultivation, not only make him a good comfortable home, but that the return from his crop paid as well or better than mining ventures.[6]

To those farmers and cattlemen in late-1890s Illinois, Iowa and Nebraska, the promise of that "comfortable, profitable living," as heavily promoted by western residents and land speculators alike (who probably never told of the accompanying living hardships), was appealing. And Southern Idaho was about to undergo a massive transformation thanks to new federal irrigation legislation and the foresight of a group of community leaders, including the following: Ira B. Perrine, Stanley Milner, Frank

Knox, Frank H. Buhl and Walter Filer. In 1894, Congress passed the Carey Act (Federal Desert Land Act).[7] The law allowed private companies to erect dams and irrigation systems along western rivers. Thus, in 1903, businessmen founded in what is today Twin Falls County, Idaho the Twin Falls Land and Water Company.[8]

The Twin Falls Land and Water Company proceeded, through private funding, to establish a vast irrigation system, which was supplied by the North Channel Dam (later named for aforementioned community leader Stanley Milner). Additional irrigation and dam funding resulted from President Theodore Roosevelt's and Congress's enactment of the Reclamation Act of 1902.[9] By 1905, the vast Southern Valley had been turned into fertile green farmland for harvesting and ranching. The founders sought to heavily market this new valuable land to farmers and ranchers in the Midwest under the name "Magic Valley." Farming towns along the way were named for investors, including Buhl and Filer.

New residents and farms expanded in Idaho, including in the Twin Falls community. A railroad (the Minidoka and Southwestern Railroad) connecting to the Union Pacific Main Line was constructed.[10] The Twin Falls Commercial Club began an intensive marketing campaign, particularly targeted to Irish communities in Chicago, Illinois and in Nebraska, Iowa and other farm states.[11] In addition, rapid technological advances were made at the time. Because of the hydroelectric capacity of the "twin falls," by 1912, Twin Falls, Idaho used more electricity per capita for heat than any location in the United States.[12]

Within this great migration to the Magic Valley, shortly after World War I the Philby family arrived from Southern Nebraska. The family included Bud Hayes's grandparents, mother and aunt. The Philbys were said to have descended from the Timony Family of Ireland, possibly County Donegal. Records of the early family do not exist. What we know about them comes from stories handed down through the generations.

9

Donegal is located in the northwest corner of Ireland (what is now Northern Ireland) in the Province of Ulster. It is said that the great-great Philby grandparents were among the many refugees who came to America to escape the Irish Potato Famine (the "Great Famine"), which occurred between 1845 and 1850.[13] The Great Famine hit County Donegal, Ireland around 1847.

From the skill sets the family later used in America (ultimately becoming farmers in Idaho, the land of potatoes), we can conclude that in Ireland the family members were farmers, most likely tenant farmers under absentee British landowners of the time. The Great Famine was the most catastrophic event of nineteenth century Ireland. Over one million people starved to death, having been relegated to begging for food, while others died fleeing on ships to North America.[14] By the eighteen hundreds, the Irish working class had become dependent on a single crop: the potato, which was the main staple of family diets.[15]

The scientific cause of the Great Famine was a virulent fungus (Phytophthora infestans) spread by the wind and said to have originated from North America around 1845. Potato crops rotted with shocking speed. British landlords refused to sell food, grains, vegetables and livestock meats that Americans shipped to England. Irish families who owned or rented small plots of land were left to beg, starve or flee.[16]

The Timony/Philby ancestors chose to flee Ireland, joining the over two million people who left during that era. The Philby ancestors headed for America sometime between 1848 and 1849 with what meager possessions they could carry with them onboard the ship they sailed. From our observation of the family's later birth records, we can reconstruct much of their route of settlement. It is more likely than not that the family landed in New York and, through what assistance and information were available in the Irish community there, determined their best course was to apply their agricultural skills in the expanding American Midwest where farm labor was in demand and opportunities existed.

From New York the family was referred to Irish contacts in

Chicago, Illinois, and transited there by train. Chicago, fast becoming the heart of America's expanding agricultural bread basket, had a large Irish population. The Irish community and a network of business agents assisted Irish immigrants in staffing the growing downstate Illinois agricultural communities, which contained rich soil. It is at this point where more extensive Philby family records begin, in the mid-1850s.

The earliest names are William Emanuel Philby and his wife Martha Philby (dates of birth and death unknown). They moved inland to Putnam County, Illinois, a growing agricultural area. Putnam County, county seat Hennepin, is located in North-Central Illinois along the Illinois River, approximately 115 miles southwest of Chicago. (In 2014, Putnam County was considered, "the least extensive county in the U.S.,"[17] with a population of less than six thousand.)[18]

In the 1850s, Putnam County was a hotbed of agricultural speculation by immigrants moving from the east. The Philbys, having transitioned through the Irish community in Chicago, progressed downriver to seek their livelihood there. By 1835, nearly four thousand people had moved to Putnam, and by 1844 over two hundred thousand bushels of grain were being shipped from its farms, attracting investors who formed the Illinois River Railroad in 1857.[19] In this environment the Philbys settled and began farming.

The Philby family Bible, which documents significant events in the family, begins to reference Philby lineages from around the mid-1850s. On February 18, 1856, Bud's grandfather, Benjamin Franklin "BF" Philby (1856–1934), was born. BF later married Mary Catherine Shafer of Athens, Ohio (1862–1921). BF and Mary Catherine had four children. The children's birthplaces trace the movement of the Philbys westward to larger, cheaper or more productive agricultural land. William (1882–1952) was born in Des Moines, Iowa; Blanche (1884–1953) was born in Fillmore County, Nebraska; Bud's mother, Fay Fern (1895–1979), was born in Oak, Nebraska; and Lee Owen (1899–1982) was born in

Deshler, Nebraska.

Prior to the Philbys' move to Idaho, the family at one point settled into farming along the border between Kansas and Nebraska, in Nuckolls County, Village of Oak, Nebraska.[20] In the late 1880s, Oak, Nebraska was a small rural village stop along the then Fremont, Elkhorn and Missouri Valley Railroad. "The Elkhorn," as the railroad was known, extended its service to Casper, Wyoming, and was a source of news and tales carried from both Wyoming and the budding new State of Idaho next door.[21] In Oak, on August 30, 1895, Fay Fern Philby (Bud's future mother) was born.

The Philby family later moved about fifteen miles from Oak, Nebraska to Deshler, Nebraska (in Thayer County, also along the southern border between Kansas and Nebraska). Most likely this location provided much better railroad service for farm goods, passenger service and mail, it being a stop along the large Chicago Rock Island and Pacific Railroad.[22] Beyond the references in the Philby family Bible, little is known of the family's lives or stories.

At the turn of the twentieth century, progress in agriculture and a growing demand for cattle back east stimulated a transformation of Southern Idaho, thanks mostly to dam and irrigation projects. As previously mentioned, this led to the area acquiring the name Magic Valley, which also served as an attractive marketing promotion of its vast agricultural and ranching lands to Easterners seeking to leave their crowded cities and to Midwesterners seeking to leave agricultural challenges for new life out west. Or as described in the following passage:

The name "Magic Valley" is a reference to the construction of Milner and Minidoka Dams and a series of irrigation canal systems on the Snake River during the first decade of the 20th century. In a short time these projects "magically" transformed what had been considered a nearly uninhabitable area into some of the most productive farmland in the northwestern U.S. Many cities and towns in the region were founded between 1900 and 1910 as a direct result of these projects.[23]

In the early nineteen hundreds, migrants from the Midwest, including the Philby family, were attracted to the western prospects and settled in Southern Idaho, including in Twin Falls County. The Philby family arrived there sometime around 1915 or 1916. William Philby (1882–1952), then age thirty-three, and Blanch Philby (1884–1953), then age thirty-one, each married around that time, with their own families remaining on the family farm in Deshler, Nebraska. The reasons why part of the family remained in Nebraska while father, mother and younger children headed for Idaho is lost to history.

In her late teens, Bud's future mother, Fay Fern Philby, helped on the family farm in Nebraska along with her siblings. At age twenty, Fay arrived in Idaho with the Philby family, along with her year-old daughter Nedra Naomi (1914–96), her father BF, her mother Mary and her sixteen-year-old younger brother Owen.[24]

Idaho in the 1920s was still a vast, sparsely-populated state. The 1920 U.S. Census showed the total U.S. population at 106,021,537, with Idaho ranked forty-second out of the then forty-eight states in population, with a population of 431,866 (0.4 percent of the U.S. population).[25] The population density on average was barely five people per square mile. Idaho then had roughly one-fourth of the population it would have by 2014.

The economy of the times in Northern Idaho primarily consisted of fishing, mining and logging. But in the arid lands of Southern Idaho (and of Twin Falls County, where the Philbys settled), life for residents involved farming and ranching livestock, including cattle, chickens and pigs. Water was abundant from the nearby Snake River and its dams.[26] The volcanic-based iron-rich soil there was ideal for many varieties of vegetables (including Idaho's famous potatoes), for alfalfa and for grazing livestock. Fishing, including trout farming, was present.

As the following passage describes in more detail, life in Southern Idaho was flourishing:

Even after Idaho became a state in 1890, the Twin Falls area was very sparsely populated and without significant settlements. That changed after the city of Twin Falls was founded in 1904 and Milner Dam was completed in 1905. Most of the county's other towns were established during this period as well.[27] By the 1940 census, there were over 2,717 farms (includes ranches) in Twin Falls County.[28]

Idaho historian John Hailey, writing during this period, described what was and made an Idahoan: "The people are industrious, enterprising and intelligent. They have their farms in good state of cultivation, with comfortable homes, convenient and comfortable school houses."[29]

The Philby family eventually settled in the small town of Filer. The town of Filer is located in central Southern Idaho in the north-central portion of Twin Falls County. It is approximately three miles west of the Twin Falls city limits and 110 miles southeast of Idaho's capital city Boise. Named in honor of Walter G. Filer, who served as general manager of the Twin Falls Water and Land Company, the town was established in 1906 as the terminus of the Oregon Short Line Railroad branch of Twin Falls, Idaho.[30] Similar to other communities in Southern Idaho, the Filer area was dotted with farms, ranches and churches, with the populace containing potato farmers, like the Philbys, from Ireland who passed their age-old family farming traditions to each successive generation.

Thus it came to pass in the Filer community that Fay Fern Philby met, and on December 27, 1920, married, a local farmer. He was twenty-eight-year-old Frank Harmon Hayes, with whom Fay later had two children, Mary Francis (born in 1922) and Frank Philby "Bud" (born in 1924). Frank H. Hayes was originally from Simsbury, Connecticut,[31] a small town near Hartford, Connecticut. His background, though precisely unknown, has been described in family lore as him being a "ne'er-do-well" individual and an inattentive husband and father. He abandoned the family sometime after 1925, and the family never heard from him again.[32] Fay later sought and received a formal divorce.

Fay was then left, in the mid-1920s, to support herself, her aging father and mother and her three children, including Bud, in rural Southern Idaho. At that time there existed no government safety net of unemployment insurance, government-provided food supplements or healthcare and welfare benefits. Fay had some help from family in Nebraska, from local neighbors and from church, but she also took on the task of self-development through correspondence classes, primarily through the University of Idaho's southern branch (now Idaho State University's extension programs), in order to qualify for a teacher's license.

Licensed teachers were in desperately short supply in rural Idaho, and for the local community Fay's employment was most welcome. Children in Idaho required a public education, but they were spread out over Idaho and Twin Falls County's wide distances, much as they are today, but at that time without modern roads and school bus service. In the 1920s and early 1930s, during the Great Depression, Fay made a living as an elementary school teacher (first and second grades) in Filer and Eden country schools.[33]

Figure 1.2. Bud's mother Fay Fern (left, approximate age thirty-five) and Bud's sister Nedra (right, approximate age sixteen), circa 1930–31.

This was the world, in 1924, into which Frank Philby "Bud" Hayes was born and lived his early life. In the 1930s, Fay met and married George Jensen and thereafter took his last name, becoming Fay Fern Philby Jensen. The children retained their last name Hayes. Bud's new stepfather, George Jensen, was a large stocky man of second generation Danish origin, and he made a living in contracting and building, along with cattle and farming enterprises. Family lore is that he was a hard drinker and had a temper, often being verbally and physically abusive to Fay. Consequently they later divorced in the late 1940s.[34]

Whatever had transpired late in the Jensens' marital life was apparently well kept from the children. Bud and his two older sisters, Nedra and Mary, became close, and Fay made sure they had a proper and normal upbringing in the Filer farming community. Education was important, as was Sunday school and attendance at the Methodist church. Fay gave the children chores to do at home, as well as tasks on the family farm. This included raising some of their own livestock as a way to develop self-sufficiency. Fay was an attentive and dutiful parent, but also strict.

Fay later in life taught in the Twin Falls County Schools. At that time the U.S. Department of the Interior's Bureau of Indian Affairs had major responsibilities for Indian reservations in the area and was in need of teachers. From 1956–68 Fay taught to citizens of the Duck Valley Indian Reservation (Owyhee, Nevada) where she eventually ended her teaching career.[35]

Were it not for the events of World War II to come, Bud Hayes would have been part of the next generation of Philby farmers. Farming was certainly integral to his childhood, and it helped shape the man he became and the way in which he was able to so masterfully serve his country during the war.

CHAPTER 2

Bud Hayes's Early Years

I N THE 1920s, FAY FERN PHILBY found herself a single mom again. Abandoned by Frank Hayes (Senior), she lived in Filer, Idaho raising her three children. In an autobiography that her son, Frank Philby "Bud" Hayes, wrote in high school in 1940, he tells the following story:

> I entered this world a few minutes past midnight July 3, 1924. I was duly named "Frank" for my father and paternal and maternal grandfathers. During my first years I was interested primarily in food and sleep. Measles and whooping cough gave me my first intimation of life's unpleasantries. I believe my mother was quite disappointed when I didn't talk at an early age. Both of my sisters spoke distinctly at an earlier age than I.[1]

Figure 2.1. Frank Philby "Bud" Hayes and family, 1935: Bud (left, age eleven), Bud's mother Fay Fern (center, age thirty-nine) and Bud's sister Mary Francis (right, age thirteen).

Frank Philby's nickname "Bud" appears throughout this book. According to his sister, Mary Frances, he acquired it from friends prior to high school and it stuck, both with his friends and family. It was an easy way for family members to differentiate him in conversation from other males in his family, as well as a way to help forget his namesake father, Frank Hayes (Senior), who had abandoned the family. The nickname was easy and convenient, and so it stuck.[2]

At age six, Bud wrote of family vacations of several weeks duration in Northern Idaho's Clearwater River Canyon. There the family camped out and enjoyed watching wild deer, porcupines and other wild animals at a natural spring near their camp.[3]

Bud enjoyed school, attending Poplar Hill Elementary School (grades one through five), where his mother was a schoolteacher. He also enjoyed making childhood friends with whom, in the summer, he would go swimming in irrigation canals and in Cedar Draw Lake. Winters involved skating when the lakes turned to ice. And Bud's daring caused him to find himself literally "on thin ice," as he explained: "One time I fell into a large lateral and my sister Mary, who was on the bank, fished me out after I had gone under twice. I was afraid to go home that night."[4] Later he speaks of going skiing at Rock Creek Trail (near Twin Falls), but having the trip cut short by a landslide that closed the road.[5]

Bud did not write about any financial difficulties his family might have had during his childhood. Fay Fern raised her children on her schoolteacher salary and with the help of family. When she married George Jensen, a farmer, rancher and builder, the family income became much more secure. As for Bud's sister Nedra, she married Percy Greene in Idaho Falls in July 1937.[6] Percy was later a trout farmer in the Twin Falls area.

Bud described life in Filer as involving the typical childhood adventures of a young man of the times. And it was there, in his youth, that Bud's curiosity about, fascination with and later desire for flight was kindled and soon became his passion. In the 1930s, the airplane was still a modern and fascinating invention. The Wright brothers' first flight had been barely twenty-five years prior. World War I saw the advent of the silent film *The Flying Ace* and aviation technology, which then quickly moved into mail-carrying planes, passenger flight and military advances. No doubt Bud saw the occasional crop duster biplane flying over Idaho farms.

Bud's work on his family's farm involved heavy lifting on a daily basis. A standard bale of hay weighed seventy to one hundred pounds, and Bud would later excel as a "stacker," working both his family's farm and the farms and ranches of his neighbors.[7] Bud developed a strong, stocky build which attracted him to football and baseball in school. He was later a star athlete, lettering in both of those sports at Filer High School.

For most boys Bud's age around the 1920s and 1930s, flight was a curiosity, as it was for Bud himself. Boys made paper airplanes and later wood gliders, and they saw an occasional biplane fly overhead. Crop dusting of agricultural land was in its infancy beginning in the 1920s, and it was a useful improvement for farmers in Idaho due to Idaho's vast land areas.

Bud wrote about going to Schaff's, which was a woodworking shop in Filer where the owner, a friend of the Philby family, allowed Bud and his friends to use discarded wood from shipping crates along with the shop lathe to build "balsa" airplanes. Bud produced one a week. In Bud's own words:

> The first ones were poor but I became more skillful as I continued. Last year some of my models were exhibited in the shop display at Eden High School. My grandfather was a construction contractor and both uncles on my mother's side are in that line of work, so I may, too, be a builder of something, but I would most of all like to be an aviator.[8]

The stage was set for Bud's interest in flight; his internal fire to be a pilot was kindled.

In the 1930s, American aviation hero and Virginia native Admiral Richard Evelyn Byrd made flying stops across the United States to promote his North and South Pole expeditions, as well as aviation in general. Admiral Byrd was renowned for his May 1926 feat, being the first aviator to circumnavigate over the North Pole, and later for his 1928–30 feat, leading the first successful explorations of Antarctica (the South Pole).[9] In Admiral Byrd's day he was one of the most famous American fliers, along with Charles Lindberg and Amelia Earhart. He was a pioneer, and he barnstormed America to raise awareness of and funds for his expeditions.

On November 4, 1936, Admiral Byrd appeared with the new owner of his airplane, Alton Walker, with the two of them landing at Twin Falls Air Field (now Joslin Field, also known as Magic Valley Regional Airport). Their purpose was to create interest in and raise funds for Byrd's upcoming expedition. Though Byrd was renown in the Eastern United States and internationally for his North and South Pole expeditions, in rural Southern Idaho knowledge of the North and South Poles was quite remote. The local newspaper at the time published an article about the significance of Byrd's landing in town, and also mentioned it by way of an advertisement for fifty cent rides in his plane, or one dollar for longer rides. But no other news articles focused on the event. At the time, the local people learned about such events mostly by word of mouth.

Figure 2.2. Admiral Richard Byrd on a polar expedition, 1933.

Admiral Byrd's Antarctic Airplane To Fly Here

"The Stars and Stripes," world-famous airplane used by Admiral Richard E. Byrd on both of his expeditions to the South Polar regions will be on exhibition and carry passengers from the local airport, from 2 p. m. to 9 p. m. for three days beginning on Wednesday of this week. Night flights will be featured presenting a new experience for most people. Passengers will experience the thrill of riding in the same plane that Admiral Byrd flew over the 70.-degree-below-zero ice covered regions of the South Pole.

Alton H. Walker, president of Western Airplane Distributors, Kansas City, Mo., whose company is sponsoring a two-year world tour, is here with the plane.

Forty large framed actual photographs of both Byrd Expeditions will be displayed at the airport and Mr. Walker invites the public to see these unusual pictures without obligation. Pieces of the original airplane fabric from "The Stars and Stripes" direct from the South Polar regions will be given as souvenirs to those taking flights.

On account of the plane's histor-ical career and as a permanent memorial to Admiral Byrd's sensational and dramatical experiences in the Antarctic it is expected that on completion of this tour the "Stars and Stripes" will be placed in the Smithsonian Institute at Washington, D. C.

The plane, a seven-passenger cabin Fairchild, explored over a half million square miles of frozen Antarctic territory at the rate of 4000 square miles an hour, being flown 146 hours on the first expedition and 41 on the second.

Figure 2.3. The *Twin Falls Daily News*, Tuesday, November 3, 1936, page three, announcing Admiral Richard Byrd's visit to Twin Falls County, Idaho.

Local interest in Byrd's visit spread quickly, and Byrd held over in Twin Falls County to Sunday, November 8, 1936. During the afternoon of Saturday, November 7, 1936, Mary Frances (then age fourteen) took her brother Bud (then age twelve) to Twin Falls Air Field to see the airplane everyone was talking about. The young kids were curious, and Bud was anxious to see a real airplane up close.[10]

Surprisingly, Mary and Bud arrived to find hardly anyone

around the Admiral and his aircraft. Byrd was happy to see them and he greeted them warmly, taking a keen interest in the two young people, and speaking at length about his expedition. Bud was of course fascinated with the airplane that had flown over the North Pole, a Fairchild FC-2W2 named "The Stars and Stripes" that had been specially modified for the arctic cold and renovated in 1936. For publicity purposes, the aircraft, which was black with bright orange wings and tail, had painted on its side in large bright orange letters "Byrd Antarctic Expedition."

Unlike World War I retread biplanes, the Fairchild was single-winged and thirty-one feet long with a forty-four-foot wingspan, and it held a single pilot and four people total. Powered by a single Pratt & Whitney Wasp B radial nine-piston engine of 450 horsepower, it could fly at 122 miles per hour with a ceiling of 11,500 feet. This was Bud's introduction to a real aircraft, up close. His eyes were wide with excitement, abounding with curiosity. How did it work? How do you fly it? His interest was boundless.

Admiral Byrd was impressed with the young man and his sister. With a big warm smile the great explorer asked the two young people if they would like to take an airplane ride. At no charge he took Bud and Mary up in his Fairchild aircraft on that late Saturday afternoon, near sunset; they were the only two passengers aboard. Cruising in the air at around one hundred miles per hour, Mary sat in the passenger area behind the cockpit awestruck looking at Idaho's Magic Valley below from an altitude of eight thousand to ten thousand feet, seeing the farms and her community from above for the first time.

This seminal event lit a lifetime flame of desire to fly in Bud. He was thrilled to be seated near Byrd, around the cockpit. As Byrd piloted the aircraft he described the controls and his flying maneuvers to Bud and Mary. Bud absorbed every word while the hour-long flight passed by all too quickly for him. At one point Byrd even allowed Bud to hold the controls along with him.

Bud clearly remembered this event from his young life,

writing: "Mary and I went up at night in Admiral Byrd's plane when it was at the Twin Falls Airport, four years ago." Flying gave him his biggest thrill in life.[11] Nearly eighty years later, Mary Francis also remembered the flight fondly. She said it was a clear sunny afternoon and just a bit cool.[12] And she recalled that Admiral Byrd was a very nice, kind man who spent much time with them, as they were the only ones in his airplane. He took interest in Bud and, recognizing Bud's fascination with the airplane, answered all of Bud's many questions. After the flight Bud was so excited that he could hardly leave the airfield.[13] Both Mary and Bud exceedingly enjoyed the flight. Bud was hooked on aviation from that point forward.[14]

Outside of school and family outings, life in Filer, Idaho was focused on the tasks of the day. As for the world outside of Filer, other than Admiral Byrd's visit, Bud's autobiography speaks nothing of it. The economic distress of the Great Depression and the growing clouds of conflict in Asia and Europe did not press upon Filer or his childhood at the time. Perhaps these events were present in some way; but George and Fay Fern Jensen shielded their children from them, as these were activities too remote from Filer to be of concern in the daily tasks of making a life for family.

Bud did write lovingly of life with his sister Mary, both in the activities surrounding Byrd's airplane and in daily chores around the farm:

When I was ten [in 1934], Mary and I raised some pigs. A check for $39.00 was ours when they were sold. We bought a bicycle. Fred and Ed Schaff had a bicycle too so we had more fun together.[15] Some nights we played baseball. Mary liked to play and Lindy Larson did, too. Lindy lived across the road. I guess we played baseball as much as all other games combined.[16]

Figure 2.4. Bud's sister Mary Frances (Hayes) Grabert (age sixteen), 1938.

Bud learned to drive around age twelve or thirteen (about the time of Byrd's visit). That was common in that era as young men learned at an early age to work newly-appearing mechanized farm equipment, trucks, tractors, hay balers and the like. And at some point the family moved from Poplar Hill to Eden,[17] where Fay Fern Jensen took a job as a teacher.

Bud was not happy with the move to Eden, which took him away from a convenient bus route and his close friends. But in Eden, Bud discovered new friends, like Jack Huey, who was also an avid model airplane builder. Together they built a gas-powered model airplane with a five foot wingspan. And they made sure to test the airplanes they built:

We made planes and sailed them the length of the auditorium in the school where Mother taught. Here I learned how to operate an Iron Fireman (a stoker).[18]

Bud made no mention of whether such stunts resulted in any repercussions from the school or from Mom Jensen.

While living in Eden, Bud got his first job, which was driving a stacker (hay delivery) team. He earned nine to ten dollars[19] that summer. The advent of the mechanical hay bailer created new jobs and new demands for the ranches and farms in the area. In fall, Bud dug up potatoes and screened beans around the potato stacks. He also hoed beans, but a farmer cheated him out of payment for that work.

Around 1940–41, after four years in Eden, the Jensen family moved back to Filer. Bud, now around age seventeen or eighteen, concluded his autobiography there:

Now I live at Filer, not very far from my birthplace. I enjoy being with the boys, having been separated from them for four years. I like the Filer folks and I am glad to be able to go to school in Filer.[20]

Bud seemed destined to follow the halcyon family agricultural tradition of the century before. But as it turned out, war would make his true destiny far different.

CHAPTER 3

Clouds of War Descend on Idaho and Filer[1]

I T IS SAID THAT the calmest and most tranquil place for one to be is in the center eye of a hurricane, where skies are clear and breezes and climate nearly perfect. And yet even in the eye, one is surrounded by the deadly, destructive power of rising seas and hurricane-force whirlwinds. This might well be a metaphor for life in Filer, Idaho from 1938 to 1941, at a time when Bud was of high school ages (ages fourteen to seventeen), and his close sister Mary was slightly older (ages sixteen to nineteen).

Figure 3.1. Frank Philby "Bud" Hayes (age eighteen) in his senior year at Filer High School, June 1942.

28

As life in Filer continued its relative tranquility, five thousand two hundred miles in each direction the storm clouds of war were swirling with deadly force. To the east, in Germany, Adolph Hitler's Nazi Party, military machine and megalomania were on the rise, joined by fascist associate Benito Mussolini in Italy. At the same distance to the west of Idaho, beginning in 1938, the child Emperor Hirohito of Japan, manipulated by a maniacal general and prime minister, Hideki Tojo, was on the rise and was brutally expanding Imperial Japan into Manchuria (the Korean Peninsula), China and Southeast Asia. He, like Hitler, was committing unspeakable atrocities along the way, with Japanese forces killing, torturing or enslaving millions.

In Europe, Mussolini set out to establish his vision of a new Roman Empire. Italian forces invaded Ethiopia (in 1939) and later North Africa (Libya–Tunisia regions), Albania and Greece. But Adolph Hitler's Germany became the principal world antagonist. Rising from the German Workers Party, in 1924 Hitler began systematic demagoguery against alleged abuses of Germany under the Treaty of Versailles that had ended World War I (in 1918), as well as appeals to nativism, anti-Semitism and xenophobic scapegoating. In 1933, Hitler successfully took over the democratic government of Germany, becoming Chancellor. He then began a campaign to install his National Socialist ("Nazi") regime and to "purify" Europe.

The German army began its campaign to "purify" Europe in Spain by providing proxy assistance to the Nationalists of Generalissimo Francisco Franco during the Spanish Civil War (1936–38). Two years later, in March 1938, the German army marched into Austria and annexed it to Germany without firing a shot. Likewise, Hitler and the German army later reclaimed the German Sudetenland (the western part of Czechoslovakia and its capital city Prague).

British Prime Minister Neville Chamberlain, though alarmed by Hitler's actions, refused to accept British and French ministers' calls to confront Hitler before he became too powerful.

Instead, Chamberlain flew to Munich, Germany to meet Hitler and to negotiate an agreement under which Hitler "agreed" to seek no further territory. In exchange, Chamberlin promised no British or French military action against Germany. This was known as the "Munich Agreement."

Chamberlain returned to London and proclaimed he had achieved "Peace in our time." Soon after, Sir Winston Churchill famously addressed Prime Minister Chamberlain in Parliament:

> You were given the choice between war and dishonor. You chose dishonor and you will have war. . . . If you will not fight for the right when you can easily win without bloodshed; if you will not fight when your victory will be sure and not too costly; you may come to the moment when you will have to fight with all the odds against you and only a precarious chance of survival. There may even be a worse case. You may have to fight when there is no hope of victory, because it is better to perish than live as slaves.[2]

Indeed, Hitler had no intention of abiding by the Munich Agreement. The inconvenience of paper treaties was no bar to his grand plan for world domination. The ink was barely dry on the Munich Agreement when, by 1939, Hitler's army seized the remainder of Czechoslovakia, the Baltic States and Hungary. Hitler next set his sights on invading Poland, which was a gateway for him to the communist Soviet Union (present-day Russia). At this point, future Allies (Britain and France) sent a blunt warning to Hitler that his crossing into Poland would cause war. A longstanding mutual defense treaty existed among Britain, France and Poland. The treaty stated that an act of war on one was an act of war on all. Hitler paid no heed, believing that in an era of appeasement by Chamberlain words were but empty threats.

Hitler ignored the warning. Though he harbored extreme hatred for the communists of the Soviet Union, a week prior to his planned invasion of Poland the Nazis signed the Molotov–Ribbentrop Pact with the Soviet Union. Under the pact, Hitler and the Soviet Union's Joseph Stalin agreed to divide their control of Poland. Unbeknownst to Stalin at the time, Hitler would later also move to try to take the Soviet Union.

On September 1, 1939, the full brunt of German land and air forces, in what would be known as "blitzkrieg," crossed into Poland and crushed the Polish Army. For what would be a very short period, the Soviet Union controlled Eastern Poland while Hitler's Germany controlled Western Poland. In response, Britain and France declared war on Germany and Italy. World War II had begun. Chamberlain was then defeated in elections for British prime minister, and Great Britain instead turned its hopes to new Prime Minster Sir Winston Churchill, who had long warned of Hitler's despotism.

Germany next moved quickly to invade Norway, Denmark, Belgium, Netherlands and, by 1940, France. The British Army, having unsuccessfully attempted to halt Hitler in France and Belgium, retreated to Dunkirk, Belgium. From May to June 1940, over three hundred and thirty thousand British troops were evacuated by an amazing flotilla of over eight hundred British military and civilian boats and ships of all sorts, which crossed the English Channel to rescue the stranded British and French forces. Hitler's next goal was to take England, where he was later defeated thanks in large part to Royal Air Force air defenses during the Battle of Britain.

By June 1941, Hitler's duplicity in the 1939 Molotov–Ribbentrop Pact with Stalin and the Soviet Union came to light when he launched Operation Barbarossa. On June 22, 1941, the Nazis mobilized the largest invasion force in world history, attacking and attempting a takeover of the Soviet Union. Hitler's plan was no secret, as he had outlined this precise strategy in his 1925 book *Mein Kampf*. A stunned Soviet Union was soon to join Britain as an ally against the Nazis.

The United States sat out the early years of the war (1938–41). At the time it was struggling with unemployment, the dust bowl and social and economic problems from the Great Depression. Memories of World War I were still fresh on the minds of veterans and of the population at large. The U.S. government faced a daily barrage of new personalities going on the stump, and radio mass media urged against any U.S. involvement in war in Europe.

The famous American aviator and hero Charles Lindbergh became the voice and face of the "America First Committee." While Hitler and Mussolini's nefarious actions rapidly unfolded in Europe, Lindbergh was crisscrossing the nation advocating for isolationism and even appeasement with Germany and Hitler. It was a position he would regret later in life. But in 1941, while Nazi bombs dropped on London, Lindbergh stated:

> The America First Committee is a purely American organiza-
> tion formed to give voice to the hundred-odd million people
> in our country who oppose sending our soldiers to Europe
> again. Our objective is to make America impregnable at
> home, and to keep out of these wars across the sea. Some of
> us, including myself, believe that the sending of arms to
> Europe was a mistake—that it has weakened our position in
> America, that it has added bloodshed in European countries,
> and that it has not changed the trend of the war.[3]

In the 1930s, Father Charles Edward Coughlin proclaimed in weekly radio broadcasts to over thirty million listeners nation-wide on the CBS Radio Network that Jews and Jewish bankers are the source of evil. He supported the policies of Adolph Hitler and Benito Mussolini, and therefore he too advocated for America to stay out of the war in Europe so that these dictators could continue their work there. Coughlin's broadcasts became so virulent that by 1939 CBS and the Roosevelt Administration forced him off the air.[4]

In the U.S., isolationism carried the day. Hitler was Europe's problem. Even mounting reports and evidence of the Nazis' systematic extermination of Jews, Catholics and others in Hitler's concentration camps (his "Final Solution") did not move the

Roosevelt Administration to declare war. The U.S., through its "Lend-Lease" program, provided arms to the British, French and allied forces, but did not provide American troops.

In Filer, Idaho, the faraway events in Europe must have been a curiosity from wire service stories in the local papers and from occasional news broadcasts on the radio. But there is no record of how the Hayes/Jensen family felt or reacted at that time. Bud's uncle, George Sittler, and his stepfather, George Jensen, were both veterans of World War I. We do not know if they served in combat, but they presumably must have taken interest in the looming possibility of the U.S. once again going to war.

Life in Idaho was an everyday struggle to hold home and family together. Most in the local population were familiar with Europe, their ancestors having come primarily from Ireland, Germany and the like and having settled in Idaho in the late nineteenth and early twentieth centuries. Any remaining familial ties to the old country were remote, and the families, having fled to Idaho, most likely had little interest in looking back or in having contact with the old country. Europe was far away and was not affecting daily life in Southern Idaho. Farm life carried on for Bud and his family. In the local people's struggle to make a daily living they focused more on news of crops and livestock prices than on the war in Europe. But the war did, eventually, reach Idaho.

At the other side of the world from Idaho, five thousand two hundred miles to the west (in what was known as the Far East), the Empire of Japan continued its long and brutal invasions of its Asian neighbors, expanding its imperial empire. Japan and much of Asia would have been an enigma to the residents of Southern Idaho. The only Asians known to residents of the area were probably Chinese descendants of workers who built the transcontinental railroad in the late nineteenth century. But Japan?

Perhaps some learned residents of Southern Idaho might have remembered a reference in history books to U.S. Navy Commodore Matthew Perry having sailed to Japan around 1853–54. Or maybe some local theater group put on a performance of Gilbert and Sullivan's popular Japan-based operetta *The Mikado*. But that would likely have been the extent of Southern Idaho's knowledge of Japan at that time.

There is record of some Japanese having lived in Southern Idaho at a previous time; but that preceded World War II by over thirty years, and was years before the Philby's arrival in the valley. Specifically, the Milner to Twin Falls Railroad had hired a wagonload of Japanese laborers in May 1906. They lived primarily in Buhl Township, and two even stayed on to become farmers. In contrast, the local community was quite hostile to Chinese who worked on that railroad, all of whom were run out of town by 1914.[5]

For the most part, both the nation of Japan and its people were as foreign to Idahoans as men from outer space. Japan was a faraway land, mysterious, but of no significance to the lives of those in the Magic Valley of Idaho. That would change in an instant in December 1941, when the valley's peaceful farmlands, pastures and citizens turned on end, much as things did elsewhere in the United States.

Japan is an island nation lacking in strategic natural resources. Its military acquisitions at the time were intended to secure food, fuel, rubber, steel, wood and other resources that were essential to drive its economy, its citizenry and its national ambitions. As it still does today, Japan largely depended on imports due to its lack of domestic resources. But in the 1930s, what Japan could not negotiate on its own terms it instead seized through the force of its vast army, navy and air power. In 1905, its massive battleships and military had defeated Tsarist Russia in the Russo-Japanese War. Japan was intent on being a world power, if not THE world power.

In 1931, Japanese forces seized Manchuria (the Korean Peninsula), conducting notoriously brutal mass executions of the local population and enslaving Korean women. The year of 1937 marked the beginning of Japan's equally brutal invasion of China, with one of the worst atrocities there being the infamous "Rape of Nanking" in which Japanese soldiers murdered over three hundred thousand Chinese civilians.

U.S. President Franklin D. Roosevelt and Secretary of State Cordell Hull, alarmed by Japan's expansion and its brutality against civilians, imposed a rigid trade embargo against Japan. The trade embargo further tightened with the participation of Britain and the Netherlands, later joined by France and Portugal, all of which were nations that had Asian colonial possessions containing strategic resources sought by Japan. Indonesia and New Guinea (controlled by the Netherlands); Indochina (by France); Philippines and Guam (by the United States)[6]; Macau and Timor (by Portugal); Singapore, Burma and Hong Kong (by Britain) and the like were all in Japan's sights, all being sources of strategic resources necessary for the Japanese economy and war machine.

In response to the U.S.-initiated trade embargo, Japan ordered its military leaders to plan retaliation. With such plans eventually in place, on a quiet Sunday morning, December 7, 1941, Japanese aircraft stationed on aircraft carriers under the command of Marshal Admiral Isoroku Yamamoto received a coded signal from Tokyo, "Niitaka yama nobore" ("Climb Mt. Niitaka"). This commenced a Japanese aerial attack on the U.S. territory of Hawaii, which began at 0745 hours and destroyed most of the U.S. Naval fleet and aircraft stationed at Pearl Harbor (at "Battleship Row") and the Army Air Force's Hickam Field. In all, twenty-four hundred sailors, marines and soldiers, including some native Idahoans, lost their lives from the attack. Hundreds of them remain entombed to this day in the sunken U.S.S. Arizona battleship, which is now a national memorial in the waters of Pearl Harbor.

In Filer, Idaho, at 10:45 on the morning of the attack on Pearl Harbor, memories of recent Thanksgiving family festivities were still fresh on many people's minds. The day was unremarkable weather-wise for Southern Idaho. There were relatively clear skies and temperatures in the low to mid forties pushed by the valley's cold wind whipping up the Snake River Canyon walls and across its flatlands, broken only by the leeward side of the family barn, a respite from the wind's icy fingers. The Magic Valley had seen a few inches of rain more than normal, which was welcome water that refreshed the irrigation canals of otherwise arid fields and ranches.[7] But it was otherwise just a typical Idaho early-December Sunday.

Bud was up early, as usual, and shortly after sunrise donned his farm uniform of the day, consisting of long johns underneath overalls and a flannel shirt, worn to protect against the morning chill. He buttoned up his fleece-lined winter jacket, put on his hat and gloves to prevent the icy touch of frost and headed out into the farmyard. The sounds of dogs barking and squeals from the farm pens were a world away from the anguished cries that were at that same moment emanating from Hawaii. Tending to the livestock in the early morning hours was a disciplined routine, much like his daily preparation of his aircraft crew for a long day's rescue mission would someday be.

That morning Bud returned home from chores to his mother Fay's hearty breakfast, and he then headed off to Methodist church with his family. While they prayed on that December 7 Sunday, Pearl Harbor was under attack. It would be hours, perhaps afternoon, by the time the family tuned in to the radio and heard the news; or perhaps a neighbor yelled out that Pearl Harbor had been bombed. Now, seventy-five years later, Bud's sister Mary Frances (then nineteen years old) can still remember saying, "Oh boy, those Japs!" in stark, fearful alarm upon hearing news of the attack.[8]

For those in the Magic Valley who knew little about Pearl Harbor or Hawaii or about those curious people of Japan until then, the news was startling, perplexing and fear-inducing. As more details arrived in wire services and in extra editions of newspapers, all came to know that the promised protection of isolationism was over. America was at war. War had reached even into the most remote corners of Idaho. Life would never be the same.

The following day, December 8, 1941, President Franklin D. Roosevelt addressed a joint session of Congress and the nation. He gave his well-known "Day of Infamy" speech, and he asked Congress to formally declare war on the Empire of Japan, which it did. Due to Japan's having entered into a treaty with Germany by then, the U.S. also declared war on Nazi Germany and on Italy (Germany, Italy and Japan being collectively known as the "Axis powers").

Figure 3.2. The *Idaho Times* announces the U.S. declaration of war against the Axis powers, December 1941.

News that the U.S. was at war stunned the people of Filer and Twin Falls County as much as it did the people of every other place in America. Filer's local Kohntopp family was particularly worried. Their twenty-four-year-old son Leroy Kohntopp was a sailor aboard the battleship U.S.S. Maryland, which was one of the ships hit by Japanese bombs at Pearl Harbor. But word later arrived that Leroy survived.[9] No doubt in the very small town of Filer, where everyone knew each other, that news would have quickly spread throughout.

Figure 3.3. U.S.S. Maryland at Pearl Harbor, December 7, 1941.[10] Filer, Idaho native Fire Controlman Second Class Leroy Kohntopp, who was aboard the ship at this time, survived.

America, Idaho and even the small town of Filer were under attack and had to mobilize. As was the case across the United

States, war was at Idaho's doorstep. At age seventeen, Bud Hayes's and his contemporaries' future would now be shaped by the demands, progress and events of war. The long family farming traditions in Idaho would be disrupted, perhaps never to return. But those thoughts and horizons were likely not on the minds of any seventeen-year-old in Filer or Twin Falls on the day of the Pearl Harbor attack, nor shortly thereafter. Christmas and New Years were around the corner. What the year 1942 would hold and what war with the Axis powers would mean to the young men of Filer was yet to be known.

CHAPTER 4

Bud Joins the
U.S. Army Air Force

NEW YEAR'S DAY 1942 arrived in Idaho in the wake of December's Pearl Harbor attack and the U.S. declaration of war on the Axis powers. Across the U.S. a flurry of war preparations began to take place in factories, in offices and on farms. The people of Idaho were concerned and worried, as were all Americans, about what the future would bring and what changes in their lives to expect.

News from Europe was of the continuing German Nazi march across France, Belgium, Netherlands, Scandinavia, the Mediterranean and North Africa. The Soviet Union under Joseph Stalin, having been betrayed by Hitler, began its long, deadly defense of Mother Russia against the full thrust of German forces. By the end of the war, the Soviet Union will have lost 26.6 million soldiers and civilians.[1] No doubt stories from the east trickled into Idaho of the unbelievable news of Hitler's extermination camps and atrocities. Yet Europe remained far away from the Western United States, and even more so from deep in Southern Idaho.

Those in the West turned their attentions and fears westward toward Asia and the Pacific and the catastrophic and barbarous behavior of Japan. That scene was quite at odds with the European roots of Idaho residents, with their Judeo-Christian ethics and culture. The Japanese looked and acted differently than "normal

Americans and Europeans." Stories of the atrocities Japanese invaders committed were of concern and sent fear through Americans, even in Filer.

In rapid, brutal succession, the imperial military forces of the Empire of Japan swooped down and invaded most of the Pacific Asian colonial lands, even as far as into Eastern India. Among those that the Japanese subjugated during 1942 were the long-held British colonial domains of Burma, Hong Kong and Singapore, as well as the Dutch colonies Java/Indonesia, Borneo and New Guinea. The Japanese placed the European citizens they captured in detention camps under deplorable living conditions.

Japan continued its advance into China, Malaysia, the Marshall Islands, Solomon and other Pacific islands while the U.S. held the Philippines. Japan launched attacks on the West Coast of Australia, and even on the remote Aleutian Islands of the U.S. Alaska Territory. The Japanese killed, raped, tortured and enslaved civilians, and captured British, Australian, Dutch, French and U.S. soldiers and sailors.

General Douglas McArthur (U.S. Military Commander in the Pacific), undermanned and short of supplies, was forced to evacuate his headquarters in Manila in the Philippines. But he vowed, "I shall return."[2] The remaining U.S. forces, holding the island of Corregidor under General Joseph Stillwell, as well as Wake Island, held out but were later killed or captured and brutalized in captivity by Japanese forces. In April 1942, the remaining U.S. and Filipino forces on the Bataan Peninsula surrendered, and the Japanese again committed atrocities during the forced sixty-mile Bataan Death March of their captives to Balangao. Estimates are that upwards of ten thousand died along the way.

American alarm over the barbaric proclivities of the Japanese forces reached such heights that on February 19, 1942, President Franklin D. Roosevelt issued Executive Order 9066[3] establishing "exclusionary zones" on the U.S. West Coast. This set in motion the systematic relocation of American citizens of Japanese ancestry, regardless of U.S. citizenship or patriotism, from the

U.S. Pacific coast into "detention camps" far inland, including in Idaho.[4] The people of Twin Falls, Idaho, few of whom if any had ever seen an Asian, were about to be living next door to over nine thousand Japanese Americans at newly-established Camp Minidoka that August,[5] as documented in the following passage:

> Camp Minidoka was located near Hunt, Idaho, 20 miles northeast of Twin Falls. In August 1942 the government began transporting Japanese-Americans to the camp via train. Most Minidoka residents came from Seattle and Portland and were given notice only one week before being forced to move. Ten thousand people (making Minidoka Idaho's eighth largest city) were interned in tar-paper barracks that had no insulation, running water, or interior walls, and that were heated by coal-burning stoves. Barbed wire, guard towers, armed guards, and watch dogs secured the 950-acre site.[6]

Figure 4.1. Living quarters at Camp Minidoka in Hunt, Idaho, near Eden, Idaho, 1942.

Figure 4.2. Children at Camp Minidoka in Hunt, Idaho,
near Eden, Idaho, 1942.

In addition to the realities of war in Asia, the realities of war
in Europe also eventually made their way into the Magic Valley
and the minds of its residents. German and Italian prisoners of
war (POWs) that the Allied forces had captured were a security
risk. Thus, inland Idaho proved an excellent location for their
secure detention during the war. From 1943 to 1945, Idaho was
the location of twenty-one military POW camps, each containing
living conditions far above those inflicted on Allied POWs held
by Germany and Japan. Some of the camps in Utah held nearly
twelve thousand German and Italian POWs.

In the Magic Valley, Camp Rupert (in Rupert, Idaho) became
a key maximum security camp holding Nazi S.S. soldiers and
officers guarded by heavily-armed U.S. Army troops, some of
whom manned guard towers with searchlights and machine guns.
A POW camp was even established in Filer, containing German

and Italian prisoners of a lesser threat under a Department of War program seeking to use these prisoners to supplement a wartime shortage of farmers. Screened POWs were allowed to work the farms and be paid eighty cents a day for their labor, all in compliance with the Geneva Convention.[7]

One hope for American retribution against the Axis powers arrived early in the war with an innovative plan from Lieutenant Colonel Jimmy Doolittle of the U.S. Army Air Force. Under Doolittle's daring plan, which President Roosevelt had personally approved, Doolittle worked with the U.S. Navy to train crews in sixteen specially-rigged B-25B Mitchell bombers to fly from Navy aircraft carriers and directly bomb the Japanese homeland in an effort to deter further Japanese attacks on the United States.

On April 18, 1942, Doolittle's Raiders (as the specially-trained crewmembers were called) took off from the aircraft carrier U.S.S. Hornet. In revenge for Pearl Harbor they successfully bombed the cities of Nagoya, Tokyo and Yokohama, Japan, which was a shock to the Japanese Empire and its citizenry.[8] The shock factor was sufficient, even if the damage was nominal. Japan never mounted another attack on the U.S. homeland.

For those in Idaho, a western state, though war in Europe was in the news, the news was certainly more focused on war in the Pacific. And war in the Pacific proved to be dominated by air and naval power. News about the role of air power in the form of bombers and fighters continuously made its way to Idaho.

From May 4–8, 1942, Navy Task Force Seventeen defeated the Japanese fleet in the Battle of Coral Sea. One month later, from June 4–7, 1942, U.S. Pacific Commander Admiral Chester Nimitz's fleet destroyed much of the remaining Japanese aircraft carriers and navy in the Battle of Midway. It was a victory in which the airplane Bud would someday come to pilot (the PBY Catalina) played a significant intelligence role. Each of these decisive victories owed success to aircraft and to skilled pilots. American demand for aviators and aviation support personnel meant that enlisting men for these jobs was a major priority.

Bud Hayes was in his final term at Filer High School in 1942, graduating in June of that year. He was a football star and baseball player who remained in top shape from those sports, as well as from his strenuous daily work on the family farm and on neighboring farms. He would soon be eighteen years old, in July. While Bud and his classmates were interested in the progress of the war, they did not foresee their own involvement in it quite yet. The U.S. had not at this point implemented extensive conscription of soldiers into the military. That would occur in late 1942 and would continue into 1943. As a precaution in case of potential U.S. involvement in the war in Europe, President Roosevelt and Congress had two years earlier passed the Selective Service Act of 1940.[9] It laid grounds for the first "peacetime" draft in American history, requiring draft boards to conscript qualified males who were twenty-one to thirty-six years old. However, on November 11, 1942, Congress lowered the age threshold to eighteen years of age. Bud duly registered, but the U.S. did not yet, in 1942, call on him to serve.

In Twin Falls County, the Selective Service Boards began their task of meeting designated quotas of men aged twenty-one to thirty-six years old. The initial draftees, in 1943, were the contemporaries of Bud's slightly older sisters, Nedra and Mary. With the economy of Filer and Twin Falls County heavily dependent on farming and ranching, manual labor was becoming scarce. Bud's sister Mary later recalled that Bud's services at home were suddenly in high demand, with him working in the family farming business and for more local farms than ever before, all for much-welcomed extra pay.[10] This was a tremendous contribution to his family's income. Likewise, Mary took business vocational lessons in typing. Mary, needing money to purchase a typewriter, took on extra jobs sorting apples for farmers in the area. With the money she saved she purchased a 1941 Royal Aristocrat typewriter, and she began earning money as a clerk typist.[11]

While Bud's activities were already keeping him busy working jobs on farms and ranches in the Filer area, he also enrolled in and attended courses at the University of Idaho's Southern branch during the fall 1942 semester. But the exploits of Lieutenant Colonel Doolittle of the U.S. Army Air Force, and the continuing reports of air battles from both Europe and the Pacific piqued Bud's continued fascination with, interest in and goal of becoming a pilot. He was also keenly aware that by the end of fall 1942 he would find himself in the targeted age group of the revised military draft. With the war growing, induction was a certainty.

In small-town America patriotism was high, and that was no different in the Idaho towns in Twin Falls and Jerome Counties. Bud saw friends, schoolmates and neighbors head off to war. America was on the move to defeat the "Japs" and the "Hun." Bud now knew that stacking hay and culling vegetables was not to be his future. And he did not want to wait for a draft call to detail him to a service or to a military designation not to his liking. The war was on, and Bud wanted to be a part of it from the air. Bud was determined to fly.

Just before February 18, 1943, with Bud soon approaching his nineteenth birthday, he decided to wait no longer and marched into the local recruiting office to volunteer for the U.S. Army Air Force. This was likely not an impulse decision. No doubt Bud shared the same feelings that pilot Lou Grab described, as quoted in James Bradley's book *Flyboys*:

> We were all teenagers or barely into our twenties, totally naive to the ways of the world. Our patriotic goal was to get even for Pearl Harbor. All forty-eight states were united. Aviators would be needed to defeat Japan. We were the Flyboys.[12]

Bud had clearly discovered that the Army Air Force was a volunteer service. We do not know if he discussed his plan with his parents, George and Fay Jensen, prior to volunteering; nor do we know their reaction to his decision. The Jensens, like all parents, were surely concerned seeing their son off to war. But by that time almost all parents in the U.S. were doing so. It was the duty of the time for young American men, and so it went.

As exciting as military flight service might have appeared in World War II, it was highly risky. The U.S. Army Air Force experienced a casualty rate of nearly 50 percent during the war, not counting those airmen captured as POWs.[13] The famous Eighth Air Force, operating in Europe during the war, conducted 10,631 missions during which it lost 4,145 airmen (a nearly 40 percent loss rate).[14] Those statistics might not have been known to Bud or other young men volunteering at the time. It was war, and there would be assumption of risk regardless of the service branch young men ended up in.

Although the U.S. Army Air Force was mainly a volunteer service, it was nevertheless competitive and prestigious. Pilots were given the rank of second lieutenant upon completion of training, and flight crew members and technicians received sergeant stripes. Time was of the essence to the Army Air Force. Due to time restraints, basic training, testing, classification and specific officer and pilot training were highly compressed. Bud's entry into the Army Air Force was off to a running start beginning in late February 1943.

The pace of the war against Hitler had already begun to accelerate during fall 1942. Allied forces conducting Operation Torch had landed in North Africa freeing French Morocco and Algiers, while during the Battle of El Alamein British forces defeated German and Italian forces that had occupied Libya and Egypt. Air power was playing a key strategic role on all fronts.

For relatively new enlistees, time at home in the U.S. was short, and the U.S. Army Air Force wasted no time in moving them towards war. Official U.S. Army Air Force records show that the Army Air Force sent Bud to Buckley Air Field in Aurora, Colorado from February 18 to March 2, 1943, for initial classification, then to Cedar City Air Base in Utah from March 2 to April 30, 1943, for expedited basic training.[15] These movements were so fast that Bud had no time to write home, so no letters from him exist from this time period. On April 30, 1943, he received orders to transfer to training at the Army Air Force Center in Santa Ana, California. It was there that his more focused progress toward becoming a U.S. Army Air Force pilot began.[16]

From this point forward Bud's story is chronicled, along with the events of his times, by way of his letters home to his parents in Filer, Idaho. He dutifully wrote home during this period of his life, and most of his letters have been preserved to this day. Seventy years on, Bud's writing still reflects the skills and good penmanship that his schoolteacher mother taught him. Though his letters are addressed to both George Jensen and Fay Fern Jensen, Bud was closest with his mother, and the letters express great affection from son for mother throughout the period of his writings.

CHAPTER 5

U.S. Army Air Force
Pilot Training

Santa Ana Army Air Base—Santa Ana, California

S ANTA ANA, A CITY located in Southern California outside Los Angeles, is today the heart of Orange County, near Disneyland—a bustling center of urban high-tech growth. Post-World War II the area was incorporated into Costa Mesa, California. The western part of the army air base that was at one time located there today is John Wayne Airport. But during World War II Santa Ana was far from its current urban features. Back then it was a rural farmland made up of orange groves and strawberry fields that were quickly carved out to serve as key basic training and classification headquarters for the U.S. Army Air Force. Bud, along with other volunteers, took long train and bus rides from Idaho to California to arrive at the Santa Ana Army Air Base in spring 1943.

The following excerpt from the 1943 Santa Ana Army Air Base class book describes the base at the time Bud arrived. Bud would face the nine-week basic training program and then rigorous testing to determine his fitness to be a pilot. Not just any recruit would be allowed in an airplane. Those who did not qualify would be deployed to other non-air force army units.

On 1 January 1942 the United States Army Air Corps activated Santa Ana Army Air Base and established the West Coast Air Corps Training Center at Santa Ana, California. The West Coast Air Corps Training Center at Santa Ana commanded flying training (basic, primary and advanced) at airfields in the Western United States. On 31 July 1943, it was redesignated as the Western Flying Training Command. Santa Ana Army Air Base was an air base without planes, hangars or runways.

Santa Ana Army Air Base (SAAAB) was a huge basic training camp. Plans were also made to move the entire Army Air Force administrative offices at Moffett Field to the Santa Ana area.

The master plan called for the construction of 145 buildings that would include: 79 barracks, 3 warehouses, quartermaster supply office, 4 school buildings, 10 administration buildings, 13 day rooms, 13 supply rooms, 4 cadet messes, 2 officers' quarters, a motor repair shop, post office, gasoline service station, utility buildings, theater, 2 recreation buildings, commissary buildings, chapels, dispatchers' office, officers' mess, fire station, guard house, two post exchanges, and a 151-bed hospital and all utilities. This would amount to a new city in the middle of bean and tomato fields. The construction contract for the 177 buildings at SAAAB was awarded to the Griffith Company on October 24, 1941 for $2 million. The work was to be completed in 120 calendar days.

The Base would not have a flying field as a part of its facilities. It would receive air cadets from civilian life and give them basic ground training prior to their advancement to one of the contract primary aviation schools for flight training.

The base grew rapidly as the need for pilots and air crews skyrocketed. Newly inducted soldiers, earmarked for the Army Air Forces, were given 9 weeks of basic training and then testing to determine if they were to be pilots, bombardiers, navigators, mechanics, etc. From SAAAB, they went on to other bases for training in their specialties. It planned to accommodate 2,500 to 3,000 cadets, 83 officers and 806 enlisted men, and to cost about $3,200,000 to construct.

The first group of 50 cadets arrived on February 20, 1942. On February 25, 1942 the Headquarters and Headquarters Squadron with its enlisted men and approximately 2,000 cadets arrived to begin training. By March there were 5,000 cadets on the base. Cadets lived in tents until the new barracks could be completed. Instruction began in March for a nine-week course. In May 1942 the base was organized into Wings, Groups and Squadrons. A wing consisted of ten squadrons, divided into two Groups. A squadron usually had about 180 men. This was broken into flights and then squads. The first class of 2,601 cadets graduated on July 1, 1942. By the end of 1942 the annual rate of graduates from the Pilot School was over 45,000. To carry out this program, the Air Force had recruited a faculty of over 250 well-trained and experienced high school, college and university teachers who later became officers in the Air Corps.

In the fall of 1942 SAAAB became an Overseas Replacement Depot (ORD) housing Army Air Forces personnel awaiting transportation overseas. Turnover was rapid so that by the end of the year 23,470 soldiers had passed through SAAAB. By the end of 1943 that number jumped to 57,895. The Base reached its maximum strength by the fall of 1943, with a population of some 26,000 servicemen.[1]

While Bud was in his first months of basic training at Santa Ana, President Franklin Roosevelt was making plans for an important event to be carried out to "Remember Pearl Harbor" and to signal America's commitment to the war. On April 14, 1943, U.S. Navy Intelligence learned that Japanese Marshall Admiral Isoroku Yamamoto, Japan's Naval Commander-in-Chief and architect of the attack on Pearl Harbor, was planning an inspection tour of Japanese military posts around the South Pacific. He would be traveling by transport aircraft with fighter plane escort.

President Roosevelt and Secretary of the Navy Frank Knox, upon hearing that the Japanese code covering Yamamoto's tour had been broken, ordered a secret mission to "Get Yamamoto." U.S. Commander in the Pacific Admiral Chester W. Nimitz, operating from Pearl Harbor headquarters itself, ordered a squadron of Army Air Force P-38 Lightning fighters into action for the mission. On April 18, 1943, the U.S. Army Air Force squadron over Bougainville Island (part of the Solomon Islands) found the aircraft Yamamoto was on and shot down both the Admiral's transport plane and six Japanese Zero fighter escorts. Yamamoto was dead, his plane having crashed near Buin, New Guinea.[2] Pearl Harbor, at least symbolically, had been avenged again.

Meanwhile, Bud excelled in U.S. Army Air Force basic training and its testing for pilot training selection. On June 24, 1943, Colonel W.A. Robertson, Commandant and Base Commander, sent Bud's mother Fay enthusiastic news:

> It is with great pleasure that I notify you that your son, Frank P. Hayes, has been selected by the Classification Board for Pilot training in the United States Army Air Forces. I congratulate both you and him on this achievement.[3]

The letter went on to inform that Bud would be transferred to the Army Air Force West Coast Training Center and would be given the very best and intensive training available so that he could receive his wings and "rating of pilot."[4] Colonel Robertson ended with the following lines on the importance of pilots, which are words that continue to resonate for all military pilots today:

> In either war or peace, a Pilot occupies a position that requires sound judgment, a keen and alert mind, a sound body and the ability to perfectly coordinate mind and body in the flying of

the airplane. It is imperative that the men who fly our military aircraft possess these qualifications, for upon their skill will depend in large measure the success of our war effort.[5]

U.S. Army Air Force Ryan Flying School— Hemet, California

On July 31, 1943, Bud, just past his nineteenth birthday, wrote home that he had been transferred to the Ryan Flying School in Hemet, California, and specifically to the Fifth Army Air Force Fighter Training Division, Third Squadron. Hemet is a small city located in Riverside County, ninety miles southeast of Los Angeles. During World War II, the city hosted the Ryan School of Aeronautics, which trained nearly six thousand fliers for the Army Air Force between 1940 and 1944. Hemet-Ryan Airport exists today at the site of the former flight school.[6] Hemet is part of the arid Central Valley of California where temperatures in the summer often reach into the range of 115 degrees Fahrenheit. As Bud wrote one day, "It's so damn hot I can't breathe."[7]

The Ryan Aeronautical Company was founded in 1934 by T. Claude Ryan of San Diego, California, who was previously associated with Charles Lindberg's famous "Spirit of St. Louis" aircraft. Beginning in 1938, the Ryan Company manufactured training aircraft and operated a flight training school. In 1941, Ryan received interest from, and was eventually contracted by, the U.S. Army Air Force to train pilots on Ryan's new PT-22 Recruit aircraft, which was nicknamed "The Maytag Messerschmitt." Bud's basic training was in the Recruit through 1943.[8]

Figure 5.1. A Ryan PT-22 Recruit training airplane.

History: The Ryan Recruit was the U.S. Army Air Corps' first monoplane primary trainer. Initial testing of a single RYAN S-T-A (Sport-Trainer-A) resulted in an order for 15 more aircraft, re-designated the *YPT-16*, for evaluation in 1939. Finding this tandem two-seater to be an excellent design, the USAAC ordered a production batch of 30 aircraft, designated the *PT-20*. In 1941, the Army decided a new more powerful engine was needed to endure the rigors of training new pilots. Ryan Aeronautical replaced the inline engine of the previous version with a Kinner radial engine. The resulting *PT-21* was so superior that many *PT-16s* and *PT-20s* were upgraded with the new engine, becoming *PT-16As* and *PT-20As*.[9]

Bud wrote home that his training at the Ryan Flying School would be intense and strict. The school was considered one of the best pilot training centers in the world. On the cadets' first day, officers informed them that statistics showed 40 percent would wash out of the program before completion. The PT-22 Recruit, whether by design or happenstance, was just that exacting. The

Ryan Company's aircraft were for some reason particularly difficult for one to master. There was even a saying that went, "If you
could fly Ryans, you could fly anything."

The Army Air Force strictly limited pilot trainees to one hour
in flight at a time in the Ryan Recruit. So strict was this rule, Bud
wrote home, that if anyone was as much as a minute or two over
time the Army threatened to issue a penalty of fifteen tours of
guard duty. To avoid such a penalty, Bud begged his parents to
send him a watch to keep time. Timepieces were not available on
the base, and trainees were quarantined without the ability to
access such supplies during their first fourteen days of training.
Bud wrote to his parents that the watch did not have to be fancy:
"A $1 watch would do."[10]

Flight is much a "cultivation" of air. On the Idaho farm, sea-
sonal demands of crops in the fields and daily needs of livestock
wait for no one. One tending to them must master a discipline—a
regimentation of life. The cultivator must plant seed in the spring
so as to harvest in the fall. And all the while he or she must battle
scourges such as drought, pestilence, hail and depleted soil,
among others.

Similarly, in the air, the novice pilot who plants an aircraft in
the sky ("sows" it) is trained to perfection to soar like a bird in
calm while battling perils, among them air turbulence, micro-
bursts, thermal updrafts, bird strikes or aircraft failure. Such haz-
ards are only successfully weathered by a pilot who can, through
experience and expertise, react to their effect on the aircraft. With
well over a century of Philby farming genes in Bud, and with him
having mastered the sometimes harsh Idaho farmland, could he
now also master the unrelenting forces imposed on him in the sky?

Bud eventually completed his initial basic training and pilot
ground schooling and met all necessary basic qualifications. The
day for his lifelong dream of solo-piloted flight had arrived. One
can imagine the excitement Bud felt that day as he approached
the aircraft ready to have complete control of it for the first time.
It would certainly be a seminal moment, perhaps similar to the

memory of a first kiss. This was the moment—a turning point from life on the farm to the vistas of Bud's future.

The PT-22 Recruit that Bud was to pilot that day was an open-cockpit design with the pilot (the trainee) in the front cockpit with full controls and an instructor in the back cockpit with limited controls. Even by World War II standards it had a relatively simple design. But it had its own flight idiosyncrasies—challenges requiring the pilot to maintain careful control and diligence.

Figure 5.2. A Ryan PT-22 Recruit front cockpit (some post-World War II gauges pictured).[11]

Bud gleefully entered the front cockpit donning his military-issue leather flight helmet, insulated leather flight jacket, gloves, goggles and emergency parachute. He secured his safety harness in preparation for takeoff. The stick and foot controls were manual and mechanical. Though eased somewhat by ball bearings they still required strong arms, like those an Idaho farm boy would have developed from stacking hay. (Controlling the PT-22 Recruit could be much like driving a truck without power steering.)[12]

Bud prepared for his first solo takeoff by dutifully opening a panel on the left side cowling to prime the engine and to apply a few squirts of fuel in the cylinders before takeoff. Some PT-22 Recruit models had a direct drive starter, which is a propeller rotated by hand crank located aft of the propeller and operated by a ground crewman who would turn over the engine. Other models started by hand propping, whereby a ground crewman on signal would pull down on the propeller to spin it, starting the engine. In either model Bud, when ready, would have set the switches in his cockpit then yelled to the ground crewman, "Contact!"[13] as the signal to start the engine.

A successful spin of the propeller brought the five-cylinder radial Kinner engine to life, cranking it up to eighteen hundred revolutions per minute with a sputter, crackle and pop sound. This was not the engine roar of Bud's later fighter aircraft, or even his future PBY Catalina's dual twelve hundred horsepower Wasp engines. But to this nascent pilot recruit who had for so long dreamed of flying solo, the sound nevertheless proved magical and immensely satisfying as the roar of 160 horsepower under the cowling spooled up for takeoff. With the ground crewman having removed the chock blocks and given signal, the flaps were up and the PT-22 Recruit would head down the runway at a leisurely pace, eventually achieving lift and flying skyward to cruise at 110 to 120 miles an hour.

Bud, seeing the base and the green fields of California's Central Valley disappear into specks below, remembered his prior experience with Mary, peering out the windshield of Admiral Byrd's airplane a decade earlier in Twin Falls, Idaho. But now Bud was in control. He was living his dream to fly, with air whipping past his head, the cooler temperature aloft (forty-seven degrees Fahrenheit at ten thousand feet in the air) an escape from the intense California heat and worries of the base below in Hemet.[14]

The standard hour allotted for Bud's flight would expire all too quickly, signaled by his instructor from the rear cockpit. Bud reached for the control handle near the floor to the left of his seat and ratcheted the flaps down thirty degrees for landing. The plane slowed to around sixty miles per hour. Working the knee action trunnion landing gear of the PT-22 Recruit, Bud gently glided the aircraft to the ground for as close to a feather-like landing as possible. A short taxi to the designated parking area, and switching the aircraft off, Bud's initial solo flight was complete, and he beamed while exiting the cockpit. The boy from Filer flew! Bud Hayes was now harvesting all the sky had to offer.

Figure 5.3. Cadet Frank Philby "Bud" Hayes
while part of the Fifth Army Air Force Flying Training
Detachment, Hemet, California, 1943.

Bud's next letter home included an advanced apology should there ever be a gap in his future letters home and should he have little time to write to sisters Nedra and Mary. The rigorous Army Air Force schedule left little time for writing, and even this brief letter of apology appeared rushed. He ended the letter, "Wish me luck with the Ryan."[15] It was two weeks until Bud wrote again, always on the Santa Ana base stationery paper he brought with him everywhere. The letter reveals that his parents had sent the watch he had long sought, which Bud lovingly described as, "the finest thing I have ever had in my life."[16]

The watch the Jensen's sent to Bud was far from the "$1 watch" he had asked for. Bud mentions it as a Longines brand watch which, even today, is one of the finest and most accurate Swiss watches made. It would have been quite an extraordinary expense for his family at that time. Bud's "city" buddies who crowded around to see the contents of his package from home told him the watch sold for $130.29 in fine jewelry stores in the city.[17] Longines was famous for aviators' dependence on its timepieces, counting among its clientele Charles Lindberg and Amelia Earhart. Bud's watch was probably similar to the standard Longines World War II aviator model. The family wanted Bud to be safe and to have the best. For their son's safety, they would spare no expense.

Bud was a model student, writing that he had been allowed one hour and five minutes solo flight time by the Ryan School's instructors, and that he had completed forty-five takeoffs and landings. He had finally been cleared for completely solo flight. By that time he had already logged over twenty hours behind the controls in the PT-22 Recruit alone.

Due to California's intense sun, Bud purchased a pair of Bausch & Lomb "Ray-Ban" aviator sunglasses, which were essential for flying. Around this time, as fall 1943 approached, his instructors informed him that his training was being accelerated and they would soon send him to advanced combat aircraft training. But Bud was already thinking of war's end and envisioning himself flying as a post-war career. Perhaps he saw himself crop dusting in the Magic Valley, or perhaps it was some other use of aircraft.

Bud's letters home during this period were upbeat.[18] On September 8, 1943, after an exhausting day, Bud wrote that he was in intense Link (simulator) training for the first time and was finding it difficult. As a reminder of the risks of flight, one of the cadets that day encountered an uncontrollable spin in his Ryan aircraft. The tail section of the cadet's plane fell off, but he managed to parachute to safety, with the plane crashing and becoming a total loss.[19]

By September 21, 1943, Bud had fifty-three flight hours under his belt during training. He was at that time writing letters in pencil and on line paper, which was hard to read then and even harder today, but it was all he had on the flight line. He had been told that on October 1 he would be transferred for further training, leaving out of San Francisco, but he was not able to provide any further details. Censorship of airmen's letters was present throughout the war, even when the airmen were stateside. Both Bud and his family would soon get used to it.

In this letter Bud for the first time mentioned his social life, writing that he met "a pretty girl who lives nearby and has her own car." He wrote that he was looking forward to going out, having been given a thirty-six-hour pass from base. It is not surprising with Bud's Hollywood good looks that young women near base would have sought him out. In this case her name was Dot, and Bud was taking her to the Palladium to hear the Harry James Band live. Bud gave no further details of the date, though we later learned the two spent much time together and at one point he almost considered marriage. None of this, of course, was disclosed to his conservative mother Fay back in Idaho. In those days most people were discreet and quite private about their social lives.

In his flying routine, Bud had for the first time gone into higher altitude flight, at fourteen thousand feet, but notes that it was so cold he could not sustain it. Unlike aircraft today, the Ryan trainer was not pressurized and it had an open cockpit, exposing pilots to very frigid high-altitude elements. Bud had to come down and then do it again four more times, plus "learn" to control a spin at 130 miles per hour. Bud purchased goggles to protect his eyes, at a cost of $12.50,[20] and he had to be careful with them as each replacement for a broken lens cost $1.88.[21]

U.S. Army Air Force instructors and commanders quickly recognized Bud's talent in their aircraft. He was a natural pilot and was precisely what America needed to win the war. Bud was soon off to even more advanced training.

CHAPTER 6

Advanced Pilot Training and Officer Commission

Merced Army Air Field—Merced, California

BUD'S TRANSFER FROM the Ryan Flight School occurred on schedule, in October 1943. The Army Air Force sent him to Merced Army Air Field in Merced, California, which was also part of California's Central Valley. Today it is the site of Castle Air Force Base. But during World War II Merced was home to the Western Flying Training Command of the Fourth Air Force, which provided advanced pilot training to thirty thousand pilots before war's end.

The advanced pilot training at Merced Army Air Field primarily used the venerable Vultee BT-13 Valiant trainer aircraft. During World War II, the BT-13 became a mainstay of pilot training for the Army Air Force, Navy and Marines at training facilities across the nation.

Figure 6.1. A Vultee BT-13 Valiant airplane.[1]

History: With retractable landing gear and a powerful engine, the Vultee V-54 basic combat trainer was too lavish for the cash-strapped United States Army Air Corps of 1938. So Vultee redesigned the aircraft and made it less complicated. The first order for 300 new *BT-13 Valiant*s was placed in September of 1939, and it would become the most widely-used American training aircraft of World War Two.

The Vultee BT-13 had a continuous canopy with its crew of two sitting in tandem behind dual controls. It was also equipped with blind flying instruments to teach new pilots the basics of flying at night or in foul weather. BT-13 students soon gave the airplane a nickname which described its most memorable characteristic: *Vultee Vibrator*.[2]

The Merced training schedule was certainly intense, and in Bud's first letter home, postmarked October 18, 1943, he noted that he wrote it at 1:00 a.m. after an exhausting day. His days now began at 6:00 a.m., with training often not ending until 8:00 p.m. Bud wrote that he was undergoing night flight training and was, therefore, not getting much sleep. He had also completed two days of "cross-country" flights of over six hundred miles in length.

Daytime was filled with ground school. By this time Bud had logged 110 flight hours. He wrote that by then 35 percent of the trainees who began the training program with him had washed out and transferred. Bud, having just completed instrument flying, described it: "They put you under a hood and you have to fly by instruments on takeoff and landing. The sensation of vertigo drives you crazy. You make a turn and roll out and you feel like you're still turning."[3] Bud's parents, still in Idaho, advanced five dollars[4] to carry him over to payday, but Bud returned it in his letter home. Nevertheless, due to the rather meager Army pay levels, family help with finances would be a lifeline throughout Bud's military service.

In November 1943, Bud graduated from Merced Army Flying School, sending home a postcard with a photo of the graduation. In his latest correspondence, dated December 8, 1943, he advised that he would be off to Douglas Army Air Field in Arizona for what he believed would be his last training assignment before being deployed into overseas combat.

Figure 6.2. Bud Hayes's graduating class of Merced aviation cadets, 1943. Bud Hayes is in the back row, second from right.[5]

The U.S. Army Air Force considered Bud's skills, as acquired at Merced, to exceed its expectations. He was already an exceptional pilot, but further specialized training awaited him in Douglas, Arizona.

Douglas Army Air Field—Douglas, Arizona

Douglas, Arizona, in Cochise County about 118 miles southeast of Tucson, Arizona, was about as far away and secure from the war in the Pacific and war in Europe as one could find. Located near the southeast corner of Arizona where it meets the Mexico and New Mexico borders (at the Mexican town of Agua Prieta), the area in 1943 consisted of vast remote grasslands and mountains. Founded in 1901, the town of Douglas was at one time a site where smelters serviced nearby copper mines.[6] Today it is the site of Douglas Municipal Airport.

These flatlands were the ideal place for the Army Air Force to establish an air base in 1942. Douglas Army Air Field included six operational runways, as well as ranges for training on machine guns and aircraft ordnance. The base of fifty-five hundred service-men had a primary mission to provide advanced training on two-engine aircraft, primarily bombers, and was under the command of the Western Flying Training Command of Santa Ana, California (where Bud had begun his service). Training aircraft at Douglas included the BT-14, AT-6, UC-78, AT-9, AT-17 and B-25.[7]

Douglas Air Field training was meant to qualify pilots for multi-engine aircraft. Flying with two engines, rather than with the single engine of the PT-22 Ryan Recruit or later fighter air-craft, required specialized training and piloting skills. Ultimately, Bud's preparations there would be crucial, preparing him for his future air–sea rescue work in the PBY Catalina aircraft.

. . . now the drone of whirling propellers breaks the peaceful silence of the valley . . . the azure sky is filled with the wings of aircraft piloted by flying men . . .

Figure 6.3. A Cessna UT-78, also known as AT-8, two-engine trainer at the Army Advanced Flying School in Douglas, Arizona, 1943.[8]

On December 9, 1943, Bud wrote home that he was about to be at the last stage of his advanced training. "The Army will either promote me or demote me," he wrote. Questioning if it was premature, he mentioned that the Army had already provided him with Second Lieutenant officer bars for his uniform, though he had yet to receive official promotion orders for that rank. The war was moving quickly, but military paperwork was not.

Bud was surprised at the cost of his new officer's uniform. The Army Air Force had provided a uniform allowance of $250. But with the town of Douglas being remote and away from the competition of metropolitan areas, many of the local shops near base charged airmen substantially more than their Army allowance. But a sympathetic Army Air Force Major (most likely Major McMuller, the commander of cadets) showed Bud a local dealer who would outfit him for $200.[9]

Before Bud headed into Douglas, he received a ten-day pass, and when he returned to his post began living in the officers' quarters. He hoped to get home to visit Filer in February 1944, one last time before departing for war. Meanwhile, back at Douglas Air Field, with military paperwork behind schedule, he and his colleagues ended up wearing warrant officer rank insignia until their graduation from training, despite being paid second lieutenant pay during their transition to that higher rank. Bud's description of Douglas Air Field:

> The field is a hell hole, only 4 miles from Mexico. The barracks are lousy for the tactical officers. I haven't been on the line yet so I don't know how that part is. Major McMuller is commander of cadets and is OK.[10]

As for Bud's relationship with Dot, the girl he had courted in Merced, with the physical distance between them and with Bud's departure for war looming the relationship evaporated quickly. Relationships at that time often proved fleeting. After Bud asked his parents to advance him another five dollars, and told them he was having Christmas presents sent from a store in Douglas, he explained: "I almost was going to get married at Merced, but hell, I can't support myself. What would I do with a wife? Oh Well, such is life."[11]

At Douglas Air Field Bud endured the December cold of the Arizona desert. He said he needed to wear his overcoat until noon in order to stay warm. Bud was used to the chill of Idaho, and although Arizona's chill proved much different, it was still a formidable foe.

Another formidable foe, as it turns out, was Bud's build. He was a stocky, strapping young man from years of heavy farm work and athletic training, which so far had put him at an advantage in his flying because it often required brute strength at an aircraft's controls. But it turned out that the Army Air Force found him too big to fit into the ultra-cramped cockpits of the fighter planes of the times. Bud's hopes of flying fighter aircraft were dashed.

Typical U.S. Army Air Force fighter pilot requirements of the era called for pilots who were around five feet eight inches in height, were less-than-"heavy" in weight, and had narrow shoulders. Military records show that Bud was five feet eleven inches tall and 179 pounds in weight with broad shoulders and a size ten and a half shoe.[12] Though he was handsome, with blue eyes and brown hair to match his physique, he was nevertheless too broadly built to meet U.S. Army Air Force guidelines for fighter service. Piloting larger multi-engine aircraft, which was equally important to the war effort, was to be Bud's future. Bud described the situation he found himself in: "We fly twin engine planes here so you have twice as many instruments to watch. I really put in for single engine fighters, but I was too heavy for it."[13]

HANSEN, LEONARD D.
HANSEN, MALCOLM B.
HARRISON, ANTHONY G.
HATCH, GEORGE L., JR.

HAYES, FRANK P.
HEDEEN, FRANK R.
HEINY, DEANE A.
HEIZMAN, DOUGLAS W.
HENDERSON, FLOYD E.

Figure 6.4. Bud and his squadron at Douglas Army Air Field in Douglas, Arizona, 1943. He is pictured in the back row, far left, leaning on an AT-8 aircraft engine.

The Army Air Force then began training Bud to pilot multi-engine bombers. The men at Douglas base trained on the AT-8, which is the military designation of the Cessna UT-78 Bobcat aircraft. Its various nicknames included the "Bamboo Bomber" and the "Wichita Wobbler."

Figure 6.5. An AT-8 airplane, 1943.

History: The need for a training plane to help pilots convert from single to twin-engine aircraft enabled Cessna to sell 550 aircraft for this purpose to Canada (Under the designation *Crane*), followed by 33 T-50's to the U.S. Army Air Corps under the designation *AT-8*.[14]

   As Christmas 1943 approached, war continued to slug through theater by theater in Europe and the Pacific. In Europe, General Dwight D. Eisenhower was named Supreme Allied Commander of Europe and began the complex process of planning the June 1944 D-Day invasion of that continent, code-named Operation Overlord. The Red Army of the Soviet Union had by then pushed the Nazis from Estonia. And after the Allied forces' successful April invasion of Sicily, they were bit by bit pushing back Nazi forces in Italy.

   In the Pacific, Chinese troops made headway against the Japanese in Burma, and General MacArthur's island-hopping strategy progressed, with U.S. Marines mounting an assault to take the island of New Britain. MacArthur's forces in the Southwest Pacific were in the first phases of taking Eastern New Guinea and were planning their next month's attack on Guadalcanal in the Solomon Islands. These military actions ultimately proved the high value of air power, and demand grew for well-trained U.S. Army Air Force pilots to report to duty and join the war efforts.

Nevertheless, the increased tempo of war in the Pacific and Europe was not yet reflected back at Douglas Army Air Field. Instead, by December 1944, activity at the base had ground down to minimal holiday levels. Bud wrote that he did some flying now and then but felt he was not doing anything worthwhile compared to the hectic pace of training he had experienced up to that point. But there was still some excitement in the form of one pilot he flew with who operated so dangerously that Bud refused to fly with him again. "He did everything that was ever written as being dangerous flying!" Bud wrote home. Other excitement came from listening to the radio, where Bud heard the first real-time, dramatic broadcasts by Edward R. Murrow and CBS Radio of the Royal Air Force's nighttime bombings of Nazi Berlin. Air power remained front and center in news of the war.

Bud found Douglas Air Field to be "out in the sticks" (an interesting observation considering Bud came from Southern Idaho's small, rural town of Filer). He felt that Douglas was too far out of the way of war. And he expressed having little to do during this lull period, proclaiming life at the field a "waste of time."[15] Bud's time was spent watching the flight line and participating in the few activities available to those at Douglas Air Field. "Hurry up and wait" was the U.S. Army Air Force order of the day.

Christmas presents arrived at Douglas just prior to New Year's 1944. Bud wrote home to thank his parents for gifts they sent to him, including a ring that fit perfectly and fudge that he enjoyed. (Fay Fern's homemade fudge was a family favorite for decades.) Money his parents advanced him he promised to pay back on payday, and he further promised he would write to his older sister Nedra. Bud, thinking of home, lamented that the family had to start sacrificing its cattle for the war effort. The famous Idaho beef was in short supply, and he craved that staple of his upbringing back home: "I sure wish I could get a steak. I guess they go overseas cause we never get any here."[16] Bud closed his latest letter with news of mastering instrument-flying by radio, having flown successfully back to Douglas Air Field in total fog.[17]

New Year's 1944 arrived with the war continuing in Europe and the Pacific and with Bud continuing at Douglas Air Field. The tide of the war was slowly turning toward an Allied victory, though it was as yet neither projected nor assured as the calendar turned to January. Bud's wait for his next assignment would not be long, but it was still not war.

On February 9, 1944, Second Lieutenant Frank Philby "Bud" Hayes received his formal graduation diploma from the U.S. Army Air Force Advanced Flying School at Douglas Air Field, along with his official commission as officer in the Army Air Force and his Air Force Pilot Wings. There was great excitement, celebration and pride back home in Filer, Idaho, with the news circulating amongst the Jensen/Hayes family and its friends. But there was no doubt also trepidation as Fay Fern Jensen thought about her son's next steps and his future. Would he now be sent into combat? And where might that be? The reports of Allied bombing in Europe were also replete with reported Allied losses. And the Pacific was no better. Planes downed at sea often were lost, never to be recovered. Would Bud be safe? When would they see Bud again? Would they ever see Bud again?

The family's fears subsided for a time as the U.S. Army Air Force was still not yet ready to deploy Bud into combat. Instead, the Army Air Force had other plans for taking advantage of Bud's skill at piloting multi-engine aircraft and his exceptional acumen at navigation. The Army Air Force would send him through even higher levels of training in order to lay the groundwork for his participation in a brand new division of service that was short on qualified, multi-engine pilots.

Word of Bud's new training location came two weeks later. The Army Air Force had transferred Bud to advanced navigation training at Selman Army Air Field in Monroe, Louisiana. How he actually arrived there is not known. But given the speed of the Army Air Force's decision to send Bud there, as well as Douglas Air Field's remote location from passenger rail service, it is likely that Bud hitched a ride to Selman on one of the Army Air Force's C-47 transport planes (the military version of the civilian DC-3 airplane).

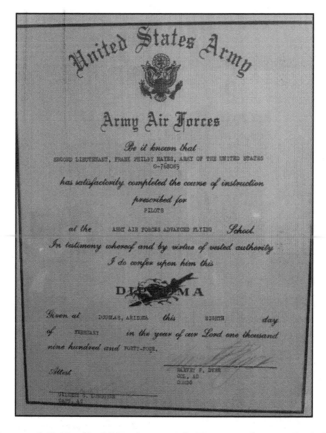

Figure 6.6. Bud's U.S. Army Air Force Advanced Flying School graduation diploma, February 1944.

73

Selman Army Air Field—Monroe, Louisiana

Monroe, Louisiana is located in the northern part of the state and is the seat of Ouachita Parish along the Ouachita River. Emerging there after his flight to Selman, Bud would have been immediately hit with a climate quite different from the deserts of his home in Southern Idaho and from his training grounds in the hot, arid climates of Central California and of Douglas, Arizona. Selman's climate was more a "jungle-like" heat, with humidity and rain (long before the availability of modern air conditioning).

Monroe, Louisiana was no stranger to aviation. In September 1928, Collett E. Woolman purchased the assets of Huff Daland Dusters, Inc. (which had been a local crop duster service) and named his new company Delta Air Service, locating its headquarters in Monroe. He then went on to create Selman Field as the company's base of flight operations. By 1930, the company, now named Delta Air Lines, was the fastest growing commercial air carrier in America, causing Selman Field to bustle with activity, including training operations for Delta pilots.[18] But in 1941, with Delta continuing to expand rapidly, it moved its headquarters to present-day Atlanta, Georgia.[19] This left Delta's excess facilities at Selman Field an ideal location for U.S. Army Air Force training operations to take place at the height of the war. Selman Field rapidly converted for the war effort, and by 1943 it was serving as a training wing of the Army Air Force Training Command.

Bud, apologizing for his delay in writing home due to the intense schedule of studying at Selman, wrote home from Selman for the first time on February 21, 1944, using officer's stationery with the heading "Officers Club, Selman Field, Monroe, Louisiana." He informed his family that he was now in advanced navigation training.[20] Selman is described in the passage that follows.

Selman Field was the largest navigation school in the United States in its time and the nation's only complete navigation course—from start to finish—during World War II. The vast majority of aircraft flown at Selman AAF were Beech C-45

Expeditors, also known as the AT-7. Of the hundreds of fields that were operated by the Army Air Forces, it was only at Selman that a cadet could get his entire training—pre-flight and advanced—and wind up with a commission and navigators wings without ever leaving the field.[21]

Figure 6.7. Students learning in-flight navigation aboard a Beechcraft AT-7, 1944.[22]

Selman was one of many military bases thrown together quickly and with minimal construction as a response to the war:

The station facility consisted of a large number of buildings based on standardized plans and architectural drawings, with the buildings designed to be the "cheapest, temporary character with structural stability only sufficient to meet the needs of the service which the structure is intended to fulfill during the period of its contemplated war use." To conserve critical materials, most facilities were constructed of wood, concrete, brick, gypsum board and concrete asbestos. Metal was sparsely used.[23]

Bud's description in letters home fits these historical accounts of the base:

I can see right now that food and quarter and cleaning are going to be the worst thing. When you are an officer, you have to wear perfect clothes or the Colonel will give you hell if he catches you.[24]

Due to his promotion to second lieutenant[25] and his need for new uniforms while awaiting his U.S. Army Air Force uniform allowance, Bud had borrowed $150[26] from his parents in Idaho. With the humid Louisiana summer approaching, he asked for a delay in paying them back as he would need to spend his next uniform allowance on required tropical-ready summer uniforms.[27]

Bud was at that time hearing that the military planned to train and deploy him in aircraft designed for anti-submarine warfare. He had been informed that he would be assigned to the "PBY Project." But he said little about what a "PBY" was, mentioning only that it was a Navy plane known as a "flying boat." At that time any knowledge of PBYs and what role they might play in the war was likely remote. In any event, Bud was told that specialized training for this new assignment of his would take place in conjunction with U.S. Navy training at Pensacola Naval Air Training Center in Florida. By now, Bud could see his deployment looming:

We will probably be overseas in about three months. In about a week we leave here for Pensacola to patrol the Atlantic for submarines. When we get enough [flight] time we go to combat to pick up fliers found down in the sea. Must close to study now. Give my love to Nedra, Mary and all.[28]

The news back home in Filer, Idaho must have again been somewhat of a relief to the Jensen family. Despite news of the inevitable deployment, George, Faye, Nedra and Mary (who was now married and working in California) no longer worried about Bud being a fighter or bomber pilot squarely in the heat of combat. Instead, Bud was going to be a rescuer (a saver of downed airmen) or a spotter of enemy U-boats. For the time being it seemed to the family that this might keep Bud safe from any direct combat harm (though they would later learn it could not keep him safe from all harm). But what was this PBY and the PBY Project? And why was Bud now being sent to train with the Navy?

Navigation and the navigation program at Selman were notoriously difficult to master during the time of World War II. So how is it that Bud was so good at navigation that he caught the eye of military evaluators who recruited him for the nascent U.S. Army Air Force PBY Project? Bud grew up as a landlocked boy in Idaho, far from the ocean. It was not an environment you might think would instill natural navigational abilities. And yet the answer does indeed lie there in Bud's Idaho upbringing.

In the vast lands of Southern Idaho in the 1930s of Bud's youth, men did not have GPS or even detailed maps, as are taken for granted today. At best a person might have a magnetic compass and use landmarks, rivers, mountains, canyons and line of sight for direction. In the evenings, Idahoans on horseback or foot learned to negotiate direction from the stars (celestial navigation). This was essential when locals managed their cattle over tens of hundreds, or even thousands, of square miles or more of ranch and farmland at twilight and nighttime. Southern Idaho indeed frequently presented big open skies with clear views of the constellations. The North Star was a bright beacon to ranchers and farmers alike.[29] Without big city lights or pollution, the stellar sky in Idaho is considered the brightest in the nation.[30]

Bud would have learned the stellar constellations both indirectly, from working outdoors, and directly, from summer camps and school. For a native Idahoan like Bud, the stars were his "roadmap." Likewise, in navigation training, stellar coordinates were the mainstay and perhaps sometimes sole guidance for any pilot finding himself over the vast, trackless oceans of the Pacific. This form of navigation was an essential skill for one to possess in the Air Force's theaters of operation. The stars were of great familiarity to Bud, and he stood out among others in mastering advanced navigation.

Bud's coveted Longines watch that his family had sent to him during his flight training in Hemet, California was invaluable during his advanced navigation training. So too was Bud's remembrance of basic transportation arithmetic taught in secondary schools even to this day, for example "Rate (speed) x Time = Distance." That calculation and others were done by hand with at best the aid of a slide ruler (with calculators and computers having not yet been invented). For one flying over the vast, open Pacific Ocean, there were few landmarks. What navigation charts existed at the time were unreliable, often remnants of eighteenth and nineteenth century Dutch, French and British traders' sea explorations.

Thus pilots had to depend on "dead reckoning" navigation (which the 1930s Army Air Corps referred to as "avigation"), described as follows:

> As commercial aviation came of age in the early 1930s, pilots recognized that the most efficient and fastest route between two points was not by following a winding road or meandering river, but by flying a straight line. The simple formula was:
>
> Speed (ground speed) x Time (since a known point) = Distance (from the same known point)
>
> By calculating the dead reckoning equation often, a pilot can

keep a record of the aircraft's course and distance from a known position. Be sure to begin counting time and gauging velocity at a known position. If you inaccurately fix your point of departure, all other calculations will be incorrect.[31]

For Bud, the superb celestial navigation skill he possessed would come into play during numerous future missions he would fly, including a heroic 1945 rescue mission in the New Guinea and Borneo Campaign in the Pacific. Bud would come to depend on good charts from his crew navigator, on star fixes and, most importantly, on the Longines watch from his parents, Fay and George Jensen. But before that came to be, a great debate was raging in the halls of the War Department in Washington, D.C., and its ultimate resolution would determine Bud's fate.

CHAPTER 7

Army versus Navy:
The Great Air–Sea Rescue Debate
and the PBY Aircraft Project

B Y 1944, AIR POWER in both Europe and the Pacific had proven to be of high strategic importance. The Pacific War, in which fliers were mostly over open seas, expanded with thousands of U.S. Army Air Force aircraft in its theaters of operation, many of which were hit or damaged and downed into the sea. Who would save the downed aircrafts' crews? As it turns out, this seemingly simple yet absolutely critical question would renew an intense interservice rivalry between the U.S. Army Air Force and the U.S. Navy, re-emerging from deep roots of animosity between the two services tracing back to the 1920s. Whatever the Joint Chiefs of Staff's ultimate answer to this "rescue question" would be, it would decide Second Lieutenant Frank "Bud" Hayes's wartime destiny.

Interservice rivalries have been the bane of militaries for centuries. The American experience has proven little different. With the advent of air power and its successes in World War I, rivalries between the then U.S. Army Air Corps and the U.S. Navy became legendary, often being intensely bitter. Each of these services had its own unique culture and strategic doctrines which put it at odds with the other, often leading to interservice clashes.

Interservice antipathy between the U.S. Army Air Corps and the U.S. Navy over the new technology of aviation traces its roots to the Colonel Billy Mitchell affair of the 1920s. Mitchell, a World War I flying hero of the U.S. Army Air Corps in 1919, was a vocal and persistent advocate for "floating air bases" (today's aircraft carriers) and of strategic use of air power to sink warships, particularly battleships. Mitchell openly criticized the Navy's conventional wisdom that wars could be won using battleships alone.

The Navy considered Mitchell's ideas on the use of air power to be extreme heresy and a significant public irritant. "How dare an Army officer question Navy strategy!" the naval military establishment would say. The Navy countered Mitchell by putting into gear its political influences to try to stop his plans from coming to fruition. Among the critics of Mitchell at the time, then Assistant Secretary of the Navy Franklin D. Roosevelt publicly denounced him as "pernicious."

In February and July 1921, Colonel Mitchell, undeterred by the Navy's counteroffensive and now even acting with approval of the Secretary of War and the Secretary of the Navy, set up a demonstration bombing of the World War I-captured German battleship *Ostfriesland*. At the time, many considered this ship to be impervious to the attack of a mere biplane bomber. On July 21, 1921, to the chagrin and alarm of Navy witnesses and adherents to its doctrine (who were watching along with foreign observers), Mitchell's bomber sank the battleship in a matter of minutes, proving air power's ability to sink floating fortresses. Mitchell's demonstration and the public announcement of its result caused the Navy to pressure President Warren Harding to order the Army Air Corps to remove him from further work on such projects.[1]

Meanwhile, a young Japanese Navy lieutenant commander named Isoroku Yamamoto, who was studying English at Harvard University, followed the 1921 news coverage of Mitchell's demonstration and the surrounding controversy with great interest. Yamamoto, a keen strategist (and poker player) brought his observations of strategic use of air power and aircraft carriers back home to Japan's Naval War College around 1921–23, when he also obtained his pilot wings and a promotion to captain.[2] By 1925, Yamamoto had been assigned as naval attaché to the Japanese Embassy in Washington, DC. Japan had emerged as a naval superpower, having defeated Tsarist Russia in war in 1906. It was now in a battleship arms race with other world powers. (Somewhat ironically, Mitchell's demonstration provided the basis for the strategies that Yamamoto and Japan put into effect during their later 1941 attack on Pearl Harbor.)[3]

Mitchell's continued exhortations on the superiority of air power over the use of battleships led President Calvin Coolidge to order the Army to court-martial him. Though evidence for the charges against Mitchell was flimsy to nonexistent, he was found guilty on December 17, 1925, and he resigned his commission a few months later. Nevertheless, Mitchell continued his public advocacy of naval air power and the use of aircraft carriers until his death on February 19, 1936.[4]

One of the judges who had voted "not guilty" during Mitchell's court-martial was then Major General Douglas MacArthur (future Allied commander in the Pacific during World War II). MacArthur would later criticize the court-martial, saying that his participation in it was one of the worst orders to serve he ever received. But although Mitchell might have lost that day, in the end his theories convinced the public, Congress and ultimately the Navy to establish aircraft carriers and naval aviation. This ultimately became a key asset for winning the war in the Pacific during World War II.[5] The Army Air Force even named B-25 bombers "Mitchell Bombers" in his honor, and eventually used them in the 1942 Doolittle Raid that avenged Pearl Harbor (as this book discussed *supra*, in Chapter 4).

Into the 1930s, General MacArthur remained one of a number of army officers still embittered by the Navy's behavior toward Army aviation and toward Colonel Mitchell in particular. Walter R. Borneman, in his book on MacArthur, states:

Many army officers, particularly MacArthur, disparaged the Navy in the 1930's for not embracing the potential of aviation, although when it did so, they criticized it for infringing on the army's turf. In many respects this sparring was a long underserved hangover from the Billy Mitchell era.[6]

In part due to MacArthur's experience in capturing Buna and Papua, New Guinea in the early months of 1943, he became an absolute adherent to the importance of air power and the Army's (his) need to control it in the Southwest Pacific area of operations. MacArthur continually advocated that his "island-hopping" strategy depended on the offensive use of combat and support aircraft along with his ground troops as a means of achieving success and reducing casualties.[7] This strategy was supported back in Washington by Chief of the Army Air Force and member of the Joint Chiefs of Staff General Henry H. "Hap" Arnold.

By 1943, the U.S. Army Air Force versus U.S. Navy interservice rivalry over aviation was rearing its head again. MacArthur's then chief of the Army Air Force, General George C. Kenney, had rapidly developed a reputation as a strategic innovator and a determined fighter whose air power tactics had proven effective in MacArthur's combat successes. In Borneman's book he notes that, "According to one Navy captain, Kenney earned a reputation as the 'biggest anti-Navy agitator' in MacArthur's headquarters, but it was hard to argue with his success in the air."[8]

Tensions over aviation between the Army Air Force and the Navy were not just confined to the top echelons of command. As Army and Navy air power increased during Pacific operations, conflict arose among pilots ostensibly devoted to the same objective of defeating Japan:

Fights between Army and Navy personnel were particularly brutal. The Navy pilots were sure they'd won the Battle of Midway, but the Army had somehow grabbed all the headlines with stories of how their B-17's had blasted the Japanese fleet. To Navy pilots who had lost friends in low-level bombing and torpedo missions, glorifying Army fliers who had dropped bombs—mostly wide to the mark—from twenty thousand feet was infuriating.[9]

A key Allied forces concern throughout 1942 and beyond was the protection of Australia. To accomplish the objective of protecting Australia, MacArthur's operations concentrated on pushing the Japanese out of New Guinea and nearby islands (the Solomon Islands and Admiralty Islands), which were all stepping stones to the Philippines and then ultimately to Japan. As *The Washington Post* reported on April 14, 1943, MacArthur made clear that he required a "sufficient concentration of land-based aviation."[10] Borneman, in his book, comments that, "If MacArthur had made his point any stronger, he might as well have said that there was not much reason for the U.S. Navy to be in the South Pacific."[11]

MacArthur (to his superiors' ire) was a master of self-promotion, making him popular back on the U.S. home front and in the press. He was determined to control his theater of war. Politically, civilian and military forces alike were hard-pressed to say "no" to MacArthur when so many thousands of sons were at war in the Pacific. Secretary of War Henry Stimson commented on MacArthur's continual friction with the Navy, saying that MacArthur's "extraordinary brilliance . . . was not always matched by his tact."[12] This proved to be a major challenge for the War Department, which still, by July 1943, held that the overall Allied strategy was "Germany first," war in the Pacific second. During this time Admiral Nimitz and General MacArthur were each receiving approximately 15 percent of total war effort resources, later increased to 30 percent.[13]

Returning to the matter of which service (Army Air Force versus Navy) would be responsible for carrying out air–sea rescues of downed aviators in the Pacific, this too led to an intense and intractable interservice rivalry. The ensuing debate was heard from Army Air Force Generals Kenney's and MacArthur's headquarters all the way to the Joint Chiefs of Staff. Antipathy had re-emerged over this issue with intense fury. When it came to war in the Pacific, the Army Air Force was determined to be independent from the Navy's control of air assets and of combat, transport and air–sea rescue missions. And the Army Air Force's demand for its own control in these areas was not without firm justification.

World War II, with its advances in technology, presented new challenges in the realm of strategic use of aviation. In the Atlantic, German U-boats caused havoc by sinking convoys of troop and supply ships that had been headed for Europe to support the war effort. Joint efforts between the U.S., Canadian and British Royal navies sought to use aircraft, such as the PBY Catalina "flying boat" that Bud would one day come to pilot, to spot and later carry attack weapons for use in anti-submarine warfare.

Especially in the Pacific theater, air operations took place mostly over open seas. And airmen launched the operations from Navy aircraft carriers or from airfields of Allied forces-captured islands in the Pacific. Land bases were primarily run by the U.S. Army Air Force, which was a necessity due to the heavy strategic bombers and supporting fighter aircraft it was using in furtherance of MacArthur's successful island-hopping strategy.

The official history of the U.S. Army Air Force in World War II indicates that by December 31, 1943, the entire Pacific theater had 4,506 U.S. aircraft operating there. In the Southwest Pacific area (MacArthur's base of operations) there were 1,297 aircraft, specifically composed of 429 bombers, 474 fighters, 234 transports and 160 reconnaissance and patrol aircraft. The other two areas of the Pacific War (the South Pacific and Central Pacific) had 1,009 bombers, 1,245 fighters, 359 transports and 596 reconnaissance and patrol aircraft, all covering the vast area of the Pacific stretching from Alaska to the Philippines.[14]

A further analysis of these figures reveals the Army Air Force's critical need for air–sea rescue assets—a need that the U.S. had come to recognize by late 1943. Assuming that half of the indicated "reconnaissance and patrol" aircraft were PBY Catalinas or related rescue aircraft, the ratio of potential rescue aircraft to the total aircraft operating in each Pacific combat area was twelve to one in the South Pacific and Central Pacific (where Admiral Nimitz operated) and was over sixteen to one in MacArthur's Southwest Pacific. Stated simply, significantly more rescue units were needed to meet the Army Air Force's needs.

At that time, in late 1943, General George C. Kenney's Army Air Force, which was engaged in operations to protect Australia by way of New Guinea as well as related campaigns, was at a disadvantage due to its sparse rescue resources while its airmen continued to be shot down over open waters. Back at the Joint Chiefs of Staff in Washington, reports of early results in Europe from the Eighth Air Force had already shown low rates of success in saving downed airmen at sea, with only 28 percent success by 1943. But with the advent of air–sea rescue in the form of the Army Air Force's First Emergency Rescue Squadron (deployed to European theaters of operation), by April 1944 the rate of successful rescues had improved to 38 percent, and by September to 90 percent.[15] The positive impact on the morale of airmen and their families stateside was immeasurable.

Air–sea rescue result rates were well known to Army Air Force command and certainly to General Kenney in the Pacific, where he needed no statistical analysis in keeping close tabs on his Army Air Force combat and support squadrons. Operations reports that were summarized at his headquarters reflected planes down and crews in need of rescue. With airmen flying over vast open ocean, it was essential for them to have confidence that they would be saved if downed at sea. Air crews' morale levels would be a key element of whether they were successful in their operations. Pacific islands were remote, and the ability of aircraft to return safely to base was often problematic. Previous U.S. experiences at both the Battle of Coral Sea and the Battle of Midway emphasized the need for air–sea rescue capabilities as a high priority for both the Army Air Force and the Navy.[16]

To be sure, the Navy in the Pacific also had a herculean task in trying to keep its airmen safe and their confidence high as it experienced an influx of naval air forces yet sparse air–sea rescue resources to support them, all over a wide ocean area. New heavy and light Navy aircraft carriers were entering service in the Pacific at a rapid rate. And, given the friction between the Army Air Force and the Navy, Army Air Force personnel believed, whether true or not, that their own needs would be secondary to those of the Navy.

Meanwhile, Admiral William F. Halsey was assigned to the Southwest Pacific theater of operation under General MacArthur. Halsey's aircraft carriers had limited patrol bomber (PBY or PBM) aircraft aboard to help rescue downed pilots. By late 1943, the increased demand for downed U.S. Army Air Force aircraft crew members to be retrieved from Pacific waters became overwhelming.

There was one additional wrinkle to the air–sea rescue dilemma that most certainly would have been on the minds of higher-ups back in Washington at this time. General MacArthur had his own specially-equipped B-17 aircraft, known as the "Bataan," in which he insisted on personally visiting frontline action to be with his troops. Had the Bataan gone done at sea, Army Air Force inability to dispatch air–sea rescue resources to retrieve MacArthur would have been costly in terms of stateside public and military morale, as well as devastating to the war effort as a whole.

America's war effort had experienced just such a close call two years earlier. World War I American aviation hero Eddie Rickenbacker, or as he was known "Captain Eddie," was head of Eastern Airlines. Secretary of War Henry Stimson asked Rickenbacker to deliver a secret message to General MacArthur in the Pacific: a message "of such sensitivity that it could not be put on paper. What the message concerned or said was never disclosed.[17]

A B-17 (similar to MacArthur's) carrying Rickenbacker left Hawaii on October 21, 1942, then overflew its previously-scheduled refueling stop at Canton Island, eighteen hundred miles away. The pilot and crew had to ditch the aircraft in the ocean. Rickenbacker and crew (some injured, one fatally) languished in life rafts for a tortuous twenty-two days, enduring starvation until two scout planes spotted them and a Navy PBY rescued them.[18] That fate was one the U.S. sought to avoid for any of its key commanders in the Pacific War, MacArthur in particular.

In any event, Army Air Force doctrine was clear that the Army was responsible for its own men! It had to act to meet its own growing air–sea rescue demands, without any hindrance from the Navy:

> The rescue of airmen forced down at sea became for the Army Air Force (AAF) a problem of increasing importance in the course of World War II. This was especially true in the Pacific, where the first desperate fighting took place and where the AAF eventually committed no less than five air forces to operations which regularly demanded over-water flight, often for great distances. In the European and North African theaters air combat more commonly occurred over land, but there, too, provision had to be made for rescue of the many American airmen who were forced down into the waters around the British Isles or into the Mediterranean Sea. The expanding activity of the Air Transport Command reinforced the need to find, sustain, and rescue airmen who were down at sea for whatever caused enemy action, want of fuel, mechanical failure, or human error.[19]

Prior to World War II, there had been a historical and clear division in the responsibility for air–sea rescue. The Army handled aviation accidents on land, the Navy handled aviation accidents at sea. But as a result of the Army Air Force's experiences in the South Pacific in early 1943, it eventually disposed of that historical demarcation, determined to be responsible for saving its own (as dictated by the traditional Soldier's Creed). On August 13, 1943, the Army Air Force created the Emergency

Rescue Branch at Army Headquarters in the Pentagon.[20]

In late 1943, the Army Air Force was steadily increasing its deployment of air power to the Pacific, mostly as a result of MacArthur's advocacy to the Joint Chiefs of Staff. Soon to be introduced to the Pacific would be the new B-29 strategic bomber. B-29s would later fly missions of over fourteen hundred miles, then even longer range missions to Japan by November 1944.[21] The Army Air Force believed that the Navy lacked the resources to provide timely air–sea rescue for the thousands of Army Air Force aircraft that were now in the Pacific. And, given the interservice friction, the Army Air Force doubtlessly feared that Navy missions would be given priority over its own. Plans were finally underway for the Army Air Force to form its own squadrons of PBY (patrol bomber) rescue aircraft, to be supported by specially-converted B-17s in performing air–rescue operations in the Pacific.[22]

World War II was a rallying point in American history where the nation pulled together in seemingly singular effort to defeat the Axis powers. Stateside, factories converted from making cars, typewriters and toasters to instead make machine guns, tanks, aircraft parts and more. Every conceivable commodity was needed for the war effort. People even tore out their homes' iron fences and donated them, as well as metal cans, all for use in the war effort. The sacrifice was unlimited.

Yet underneath this broad wave of unified patriotic effort, it was no surprise of human behavior to find bureaucratic infighting within the War Department in Washington, D.C. There, within the U.S. military establishment, an intense debate ensued over which service would control air–sea rescue during the war. This debate carried on for months on end, a possible explanation for why Bud and his colleagues were left to extended training and to "check flights" for maintaining their required pilot hours and keeping their skills sharp. The generals and admirals in Washington argued, debated and crept far too slowly toward a critical life-saving decision about air–sea rescue resources.

It remains a strange phenomenon even in civilian management today that some leaders focus too much on near-term goals rather than on long-term, big picture results. P.M. Hutt, writing about successful project management teams, identifies "turf battles" as one of the most demoralizing and counterproductive behaviors in project management:[23]

> Turf battles between departments and agencies frustrate the progress of your project team. Teams are being forced to play politics with individuals over turf issues and personal preferences. . . . This turbulent culture slows down the progress of your project and increases your team's frustration.[24]

This encapsulates the military establishment environment that the Joint Chiefs of Staff found themselves in within the U.S. War Department during the late stages of World War II. The debate there over the air–sea rescue question became intense, pronounced and lengthy. Which service branch would have control over the ever-growing number of air–sea rescue operations needed in the Pacific? Would it be the U.S. Navy, the U.S. Coast Guard (in WWII acting under command of the Navy) or the U.S. Army Air Force? The debate unfolded as follows:

> The problem of achieving some better co-ordination of effort between the Navy and the AAF, and a closer liaison with interested Allied services, had been under discussion by agencies of the Joint Chiefs of Staff since the spring of 1943. Closer integration of existing services promised savings in personnel and materiel. It was also felt that greater efforts were needed for the establishment of common rescue procedures among the several participating forces.

> But it proved easier to agree on the need for improvement than upon the best means for its achievement. The Navy argued that the rescue function should be turned over to the U.S. Coast Guard, a step that would represent a logical ex-

pansion of the latter's traditional mission and at the same time would release Army and Navy personnel for other duties. The AAF preferred to depend upon co-ordination of effort through a new liaison committee representing the several services and the Maritime Commission.

The AAF won a victory in the deliberations, [with a study committee of the Joint Chiefs of Staff] conclud[ing] that the Coast Guard, despite its enviable tradition as a rescue agency, would face insurmountable obstacles should it have to expand its responsibilities to include all air–sea rescue. Instead, the committee recommended that the Navy and the AAF continue the development of separate services but that a new agency be established in Washington for their co-ordination.

On 15 February 1944, the Joint Chiefs of Staff asked the Secretary of the Navy to establish such an agency. The new board was headed by the Commandant of the Coast Guard and included representatives of the Navy, the AAF, and the ASF. It undertook to advance pertinent research, to disseminate information that would encourage a closer co-ordination of operations and procedures, and to maintain liaison with responsible agencies in Allied countries.

Although the program of August 1943 for the creation of ultimately seven emergency rescue squadrons (ERS) had been scheduled for completion by the spring of 1944, there were only two such units in operation in the following summer. Another [the 4th Emergency Rescue Squadron] had become operational by the end of the year, in the Southwest Pacific, but the others did not achieve that status until 1945 and some of them only at the very close of the war.[25]

The Pacific War's urgent need for the Joint Chiefs of Staff to make its important air–sea rescue decision came as the U.S. recognized that victories in the Southwest Pacific were substantially due to the effective use of air power. For example, the Allies had secured Eastern New Guinea in large part due to tactical deployment of air power. And the Allies had successfully taken the Admiralty Islands (north of New Guinea) with minimal casualties, also in large part due to combat air operations. This led the Joint Chiefs of Staff to issue a directive to General MacArthur and Admiral Nimitz on March 12, 1944, with its primary goal being to have MacArthur take the Philippine island of Mindanao by November 15, 1944 (and subsequently Luzon) and for Nimitz to take Formosa (today's Taiwan) by February 15, 1945.[26]

Regardless of the interservice politics, all knew that this new directive's goals could not be accomplished without the Allies projecting substantial air power. And that air power would, in turn, require sufficient air–sea rescue capacity to save downed air crews and, more generally, to boost air crews' morale in feeling greater safety during their operations. It was this "perfect political storm" that contributed to the Joint Chiefs of Staff finally, in early 1944, formally deciding to approve the formation of an initial three Army Air Force emergency rescue squadrons, to be formed and run by the Army Air Force, subject to training by the Navy.

In early 1944, the Army Air Force went into rapid action to form and train its emergency rescue squadrons.[27] On February 6, 1944, the Army Air Force's Second Emergency Rescue Squadron had been formed and was moved from its headquarters, then at Hamilton Field, California, to Gulfport, Mississippi.[28] For the Army Air Force, finding pilots with the right skills to serve in its rescue squadrons became a high priority. From the initial transfer to Gulfport of 15 officers and 141 enlisted men, the squadron had increased by April 1944 to 59 officers and 205 enlisted men.[29] On April 1, 1944, the Army Air Force's emergency rescue squadron operations were transferred again, this time to Keesler Field in Biloxi, Mississippi. Formal training for the units was set to begin.[30]

In June 1944, the Second Emergency Rescue Squadron (then under the Fifth Air Force) was preparing to move out its initial echelon to the Pacific, specifically to the New Guinea campaign, to serve in action for the first time. The first units departed by ship on July 17, 1944.[31] (Later, in September 1944, the Second Emergency Rescue Squadron would be formally transferred to the Thirteenth Air Force.)[32]

Air–sea rescue units were in demand in the Pacific amid severe shortages of pilots due to expanded air combat operations and related losses. However, piloting the PBY Catalina "flying boat" aircraft that was needed for rescue operations there, which took place over open oceans, was far different than typical flying over land. The Pacific Ocean had few, if any, landmarks by which a pilot could visibly navigate; nor were there radio and satellite beacons of the type that are now available in our modern era. That equipment would not be invented and become standard until decades after the war. Instead, the PBY Catalina, to be effective at rescuing downed air crews in the Pacific, would require specially-skilled pilots with more than average training.

Pilots performing air–sea rescues had to be superior multi-engine aircraft fliers and tops in navigation (typically navigation by observation of moon, sun and stars, by magnetic compass and by detailed map readings). They also had to have exceptional timing and better than average mathematical calculating abilities, as used, for example, when monitoring vectors, fuel and supplies. Further required of air–sea rescue pilots was excellent visual acuity, so as to search for downed airmen's rafts, which appear as specks in a vast ocean. And all of these traits had to remain intact under intense time pressures and during intense combat, with multiple pressing priorities.

In addition, takeoff and landing of a PBY Catalina "flying boat" took particular effort at sea in the face of unpredictable swells, currents, wind, water resistance and obstacles hidden below surface. The reality of these conditions became all too apparent to the Army Air Force during a PBY Catalina incident that nearly killed Admiral Chester Nimitz, who at the time had been en route to a meeting with Chief of Naval Operations Admiral King in San Francisco. On June 30, 1942, the PBY Catalina carrying the admiral landed in San Francisco Bay and hit a log below the surface, which caused the flying boat to capsize. Admiral Nimitz, though badly shaken, remarkably emerged unharmed.[33]

The unique nature of the famed PBY Catalina "flying boat" meant that it lacked flaps and was both a boat, with a maritime hull, and an aircraft, possessing aerodynamic characteristics. Landing a PBY Catalina on land runways required use of its retractable wheels as well as a different set of procedures and skills than used when landing in the water. And the land–air–sea capabilities of the PBY Catalina meant that it had its own unique and complex controls to match these environments.

In light of the difficulties surrounding the operation of PBY Catalinas, the Army Air Force had stringent criteria for selecting air–sea rescue unit crew members. Consequently, in 1944, the Army Air Force issued Special Order fifty-eight to numerous training bases. The order required the bases to identify pilots of specific expertise and to send them to Selman Field for advanced navigation training, and eventually on to Pensacola.[34] Lieutenant Bud Hayes, with his extensive training and his fine-tuned set of skills, was identified as such a pilot and was transferred to Selman.

After Bud excelled in Selman's military navigation school, he possessed flawless navigation skills and superior skills piloting two-engine aircraft and had hundreds of hours of flight time logged, not to mention his pure physical strength for handling difficult aircraft and his budding leadership qualities. With a shortage of qualified pilots for the Army Air Force's PBY Catalina air–sea rescue missions, the time had come for Bud to fill the role. Under the new Navy/Army Air Force combined training, he was soon off to the Naval Air Training Center in Pensacola, Florida to attain a required second set of wings (in addition the Air Force wings he had already earned), representing mastery of the PBY Catalina "flying boat." The training was not for garden variety coastal patrol for German U-boats in the Atlantic. Instead, Bud was to be trained to perform complex PBY

Catalina air–sea rescue missions in the combat-heavy Pacific theater of war.

Meanwhile, the results of initial Army Air Force air–sea rescue missions taking place in the Pacific starting in July 1944 were impressive. From July 1944 to April 1945, the first echelon squadrons were recorded as having saved 1,841 downed Allied aircraft crew members. January 1945 alone saw 360 men saved. By April 1945, when air power was in heavy use and rescue pilots were in high demand, the Army Air Force quickly moved Bud and his second echelon of the Second Emergency Rescue Squadron into the Pacific war. Indeed, U.S. use of air–sea rescue pilots in the Pacific was on the rise. So much so that "when the last B-29 strike was staged on August 14, 1945, it is estimated that 2,400 men, or one-fourth of those participating in the mission, were on air–sea rescue duty."[35] The aircraft that made so many of the successful air–sea rescues possible during this period was none other than the unique PBY Catalina "flying boat," of the type Bud had begun to pilot in preparation for his deployment into the war.

CHAPTER 8

The PBY Catalina
"Flying Boat" Aircraft

A T THIS JUNCTURE in Bud Hayes's story it is useful for one to better understand the unique aircraft on which he would come to train, fly heroic missions and ultimately come face to face with tragedy. The workhorse for both U.S. Army Air Force and U.S. Navy air–sea rescue operations and specialized combat missions during the latter years of World War II was the aircraft known as the PBY Catalina, which was nicknamed "Cat" and was known as the "flying boat." Due to it having an unusual appearance, when a PBY Catalina was in flight it was often said to look like the Walt Disney flying elephant character Dumbo. As for "PBY," the P and B stood for Patrol Bombing, while Y was the designation for Consolidated Aircraft (the company that primarily designed and manufactured the aircraft beginning in 1939, with earlier versions going back as far as 1936). The following passage sheds light on the Cat's history.

History: From its introduction to U.S. Naval service in 1936, through its continued international military use into the 1970's, to the recent retirement of the last civilian fire-bomber, the Consolidated **PBY Catalina** has served a distin-guished career as one of the most rugged and versatile aircraft in U.S. history. It was created in response to the U.S. Navy's 1933 request for a prototype to replace the Consolidated P2Y and the Martin P3M with a new patrol-bomber flying boat with extended range and greater load capacity.

The Catalina was created under the guidance of the brilliant aero-engineer Isaac Macklin Laddon by Consolidated Aircraft Co. The new design introduced internal wing bracing, which greatly reduced the need for drag-producing struts and bracing wires. A significant improvement over its predecessors, it had a range of 2,545 miles, and a maximum takeoff weight of 35,420 lbs.[1]

The Catalinas also proved effective in search and rescue missions, code-named "Dumbo." Small detachments (normally of three PBYs) routinely orbited on stand-by near targeted combat areas. One detachment based in the Solomon Islands rescued 161 airmen between January 1 and August 15, 1943, and successes increased steadily as equipment and tactics improved.

The PBY Catalina was an atypical aircraft, even by modern standards. Unlike a classic "float plane" (seaplane), it was literally a "flying boat" both in its design and its construction. The underlying fuselage reflected marine engineering, with a boat hull that was sufficient to reduce water drag yet high enough to protect crew, equipment and storage areas. The wings were set high on the fuselage, directly aft of the engines for aerodynamic efficiency, with prop engines mounted high enough to avoid water damage. The nose contained a watertight anchor compartment and a forward window from which the bow gunner or bombardier could observe (with later models having an actual turret).[2] Above that level was the cockpit for the pilot and co-pilot, which included a ceiling entry somewhat resembling a modern automobile's moon roof. With the undercarriage/hull completely sealed in order to maintain buoyancy, a crew's entry was from above, by ladder, through the upper-aft side windows known as "blisters."

The PBY Catalina's interior had no flooring but rather a catwalk that passed through seven watertight bulkhead doors between compartments, precisely as would be found on a submarine or surface ship built on the same maritime theory that if one compartment was punctured it could be sealed off. The PBY Catalina had a small galley, a set of bunk beds and pantry storage for long missions, all fit for an eight-man crew.[3]

The innovative marriage of marine and aeronautical design produced a unique flying amphibious vehicle that presented extraordinary advantages as well as challenges. The PBY Catalina was a physically demanding aircraft that required pilots to use muscles more typical of athletes—certainly muscles that even fit Army soldiers rarely used. Starting the fourteen-cylinder Wasp engines proved to be an art of almost choreographic coordination among pilot, co-pilot and flight engineer.

Takeoffs from land runways required PBY Catalina pilots to use differential braking (manipulation of separate left and right brakes) to steer the aircraft since the PBY Catalina had no nose wheel steering. On water, however, the particular dynamics of the PBY Catalina required a technique known as "walking the throttles" (also known as "rocking the boat") to keep the wings as level as possible for maximum lift on takeoff. Once the aircraft left the water and its tail rudder became effective, pilots could revert to normal flying. By design, the PBY Catalina lacked flaps (a feature normally present on and essential to other aircraft) in order to allow for the reduced weight and extra fuel capacity that were necessary for its extended service distance.[4] One version of the PBY Catalina even set a record by being able to stay aloft without refueling for seventeen hours and thirty-three minutes, which was an amazing aviation feat for its time.[5]

In the World War II-era PBY Catalina models, the pilot's and co-pilot's flight controls were on the ceiling of the cockpit, minimized, with almost no gauges. This design was intentional so that the pilots would have few visual distractions from flying and from their observations during search and rescue or submarine spotting missions. The PBY Catalina was one of the first aircraft to have an on-board flight engineer, who was in control of much of the aircraft mechanicals located in the upper wing spar of the plane, between the wings.[6] The PBY Catalina's crew communicated with the pilot via an internal intercom. And a typical crew itself consisted of up to seven to nine airmen with a pilot, co-pilot, radioman, navigator, flight engineer/mechanic, bow turret gunner, waist gunners (x 2) and ventral gunner.[7]

Figure 8.1. A PBY Catalina (OA-10A) "flying boat" airplane in flight, 1945.[8]

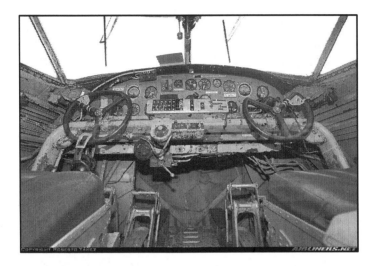

Figure 8.2. A PBY Catalina cockpit, displaying modern-day gauges.[9]

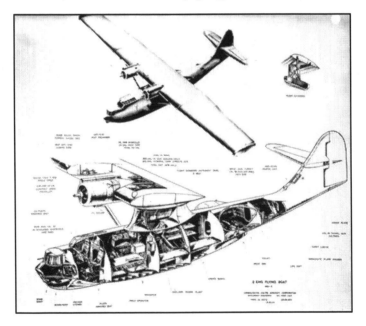

Figure 8.3. Cross section view of a PBY Catalina, showing an interior that resembles a submarine.[10]

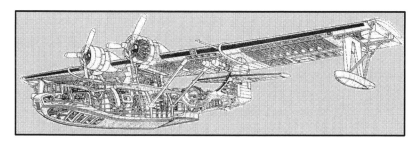

Figure 8.4. Cross section view of a PBY Catalina, showing its structural makeup.[11]

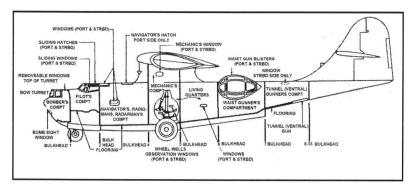

Figure 8.5. Cross section view of a PBY Catalina, showing its labeled parts.[12]

Due to the PBY Catalina's design and its relatively slow speed, it became an ideal aircraft to use in a variety of missions not suited to other aircraft, beyond just rescue missions. For example, Cats played a decisive role in providing surveillance of and intelligence from wide swaths of vast, open ocean. They also served in anti-submarine warfare, spotting or locating enemy submarines.

When Admiral Chester Nimitz received word of critical sightings of the Imperial Japanese Fleet, eventually leading to victory at the Battle of Midway in 1942, the reports came from a famous Navy PBY Catalina patrol, call sign "Strawberry 5."[13] Successes like that one caused the PBY Catalina to become a "grandfather" to new strategic uses of aviation, as in the case of later military aircraft like the U-2 and SR-71 Blackbird spy planes (surveillance) and the P-2 and later P-3 Orion aircraft (anti-submarine warfare), both used during the Cold War in the later twentieth century.

In addition to the PBY Catalina's use for surveillance missions, a second type of mission was to act as an attack gunship. The PBY Catalina's five .30 caliber machine guns (and at times also optional .50 caliber machine guns) were used to strafe enemies on beaches, on islands and in small boats, as well as to defend the aircraft from enemy attacks from the air or ground. This feature also allowed for PBY Catalinas on rescue mission flights to lay a protective ring of machine gun fire around downed pilots during combat conditions, allowing the Cat to swoop in to pick up the downed airmen. (That same technique is still used today by military rescue helicopters.)

A third mission use of the PBY Catalina was as a bomber, with it acting as an early incarnation of the later U.S. Air Force "stealth bomber." One variation of PBY Catalina used by the Navy had it painted jet black and fitted with five hundred pound bombs. These Navy "Black Cat Squadrons," as they were called, were virtually invisible to the Japanese military at night (the Japanese lacking radar), and could fly at low levels and low speeds, effectively bombing enemy positions with great precision.

The final way in which the PBY Catalina was used during combat was its main and central mission, as well as that of Bud: to rescue downed pilots and to evacuate those wounded in combat. Often these "defensive" missions were more dangerous than the offensive uses of the PBY Catalina, as pilots had to fly the rescue missions during active combat while avoiding enemy aircraft from above and ground fire from below. Choppy seas with unpredictable waves and wild weather also proved danger-ous to the aircraft's crew and to those they had scooped up during rescues. During rescue missions the PBY Catalina carried a medic (surgical tech) or a flight surgeon, along with emergency medical equipment, food, blankets and supplies.

Figure 8.6. Depiction of a PBY Catalina performing an air–sea rescue during World War II.[14]

Bud's squadron, equipped with the OA-10A(5A) version of PBY aircraft, would primarily conduct missions involving rescue and strafing, but not bombing. From what records have been preserved we know some of the particulars of Bud's aircraft, as well as the names of Bud's crew and his call sign. We also know that Bud's aircraft was not the same exact one during every mission. Instead, crews rotated among whatever PBY aircraft were available at their station at any given time.

Unlike the Army Air Force heavy bombers' tradition of a crew naming its aircraft, and often painting a picture of a female on its nose, the emergency rescue squadrons did not normally do so. But some did paint slogans and nicknames on aircraft, including the nickname "Snafu Snatchers" painted next to the image of a life raft ("snafu" referring to a plane accident and "snatchers" referring to the rescue crew members, like Bud, who plucked the plane's survivors from the ocean). Operationally, most Second Emergency Rescue Squadron aircraft also sported the phrase "Air–Sea Rescue" and an aircraft number on their fuselages or tails.

The following photos are of the type of Second Emergency Rescue Squadron PBY Catalina (OA-10A) aircraft flown by Bud and his crew during World War II, under Bud's command. Bud's crew on the aircraft was typically the same for each mission. First Lieutenant Frank Philby "Bud" Hayes was pilot and commander (with flight nickname "Ape"), and his co-pilot was First Lieutenant Richard E. Costine. Their navigator was Second Lieutenant Clayton L. "Greg" Gregersen, their engineer was Sergeant Robert N. Hubbard, their radar man was Sergeant Leonard Miller, their radioman was Sergeant Harlan M. Hagen and their surgical tech was Sergeant Meek.[15] And their aircraft, manufactured in Canada by Canadian Vickers Ltd.,[16] was assigned Army Air Force Service Number 44-34071 (CV-582) and flew missions under a call sign of either "Playmate 61"[17] or "Playmate 62." But before Bud was to command any missions in the PBY Catalina during World War II, he first had to learn to master it.

Figure 8.7. A U.S. Army Air Force Second Emergency Rescue Squadron PBY Catalina with the nickname "Snafu Snatchers" painted on its side, 1944.

Figure 8.8. A PBY Catalina sporting the phrase "Air–Sea Rescue," on tarmac during World War II.[18]

CHAPTER 9

U.S. Navy Training
and a Second Set of Wings

Naval Air Training Center—Pensacola, Florida

THE U.S. NAVY convinced the Joint Chiefs of Staff that the particular land–water characteristics of the PBY Catalina "flying boat" made it imperative for the Navy to be involved in training the Army Air Force's emergency rescue squadrons. The Army acceded to this demand, and the Joint Chiefs of Staff approved it and created the "PBY Project." Bud Hayes joined this unique joint-service training effort, learning to pilot the PBY Catalina in Pensacola, Florida beginning in mid-1944.

On May 14, 1944, Bud wrote home from the Naval Air Training Center in Pensacola, Florida for the first time. He had just been transferred from his navigation training at Selman Army Air Field in Louisiana, where his final work had been intense, as was the transfer itself. Bud apologized to his parents for the unusually long delay between his letters home. His training was so busy, he wrote, that he "turned down an invitation to the beach so [he] could write."[1]

As it turned out, women were flocking to the handsome pilots at the Pensacola naval base. Bud, no longer in isolated locations like the Douglas, Arizona desert or rural Louisiana, now enjoyed an active social life. Bud wrote, "I have a beautiful dinner date. Hope she isn't very hungry." But back at the base his PBY training continued:

> We have been flying every day lately and will be finished
> here in approximately two weeks. It's still not definite if we
> will get a leave or not. Most of the fellows did get them when
> they got to Keesler Field. I've got my fingers crossed.[2]

The intense PBY instructional program at the Naval Air
Training Center took place over a period of ten weeks. It included
cross-country flying as well as training for proficiency in water
landings, maritime basics, instrument flight, gunnery skills and
night flying (even though the PBY Catalina was primarily a
daylight operation aircraft). Training was particularly concentrated
on rough water and on seamanship techniques.[3]

Flying and pretty girls were not enough to distract Bud from
missing his home in Idaho, which he still hoped to visit before
being deployed to the Pacific. He had purchased a pair of wings
for his mother as a Mother's Day gift. (He would later also
purchase wings for his stepfather, George Jensen.) He wanted to
present the wings in person and not tell any of the locals back
home that he would be visiting: "Whatever you do, don't tell
everybody I am coming home. I don't care to go down to the
Kiwanis Club, etc. and feed them a lot of bull."[4]

In another letter from Pensacola (undated, but most likely
from around May 30, 1944), Bud wrote home about his mastery
of navigation by star fixes, writing, "I'm really getting to be a
celestial navigator."[5] Meanwhile, life in Pensacola continued to
include social calls from local women and base nurses. A box of
candy Bud's parents sent to him was a hit among his friends, and
there was even a little time for fun: "You see six of us fellows
live next to each other and run around together, so we share
everything, except dates. The nurses threw a party night before
last and asked us to come over. What a party!"[6]

Bud found his regiment under the Navy at Pensacola far more
lax than his experiences at Army Air Force bases. At one point he
was off with a group of other flyboys on an unauthorized "esca-

pade," and he worried about getting into trouble:

> I don't know how we are going to make out in the little escapade we had this morning. We took a PB-2 solo and landed out in the open sea, about two hundred miles out which is strictly forbidden because of heavy waves, U-boats, etc. and we got caught by an instructor on a nav [navigation] hop. We may be fined but I doubt it. Boy, were those waves high.[7]

But amid the excitement taking place in Pensacola, Bud's desire to visit his home in Idaho did not appear to wane. Bud wrote home that the chance of him obtaining a ten-day pass, during which he could visit home, was now fifty/fifty. In the meantime, the Navy at Pensacola was feeding him well—far better than the Army had fed him. Bud, seeming to reference his earlier letters from Douglas in which he expressed a longing for Idaho beef, had now found "real food": "When I was a cadet I used to wonder where all the steak was going. Now I know, the Navy gets it!"[8]

On June 13, 1944, Bud, still at Pensacola, penciled a note to his parents at noon, during a break from the flight line. For the first time he expressed frustration with the training he was receiving. Specifically, he was having difficulty passing the "code check" and was worried about being sent to Keesler Army Air Field in Biloxi, Mississippi, the last stop before deployment, without receiving Navy wings:

> It doesn't really matter, I guess, but I would like to have them. I will be in Keesler Thursday [approximately June 19] and if everything goes OK, I'll be home around the 21st. I will wire you when arriving. I am anxious to get home so I had better get a leave when I get to Keesler.[9]

As with most things military during World War II, best-laid plans rarely occurred on time—hardly ever as scheduled or as expected. In a letter postmarked June 19, 1944 (though probably written earlier), Bud expressed frustration at the changing dates for when his squadron would be leaving for Keesler. He was also still waiting for his long-promised ten-day pass so that he could return home to visit his family in Filer, Idaho. Bud had now been away from his Idaho home for over a year with several promised leaves having evaporated at the last minute amid the rush of the war and his multiple training transfers.

Bud's frustrations were compounding around this time. In addition to having to wait on his promised leave, he was having difficulty mastering twelve words of key, but complex, military code. The Florida heat and poor turnaround time with getting his uniforms cleaned were also on his mind. Bud eventually became so desperate that he sent some clothes home to Idaho to be cleaned in anticipation of collecting them during his extended leave and visit home, which had finally been issued:

> It is miserably hot here, a lot worse than California. I shipped a small box of clothes home. I wish you would get them and have them cleaned. I may wear them when I am home. I sent them collect because I thought I would be there to get them, but I will give you the money when I get home. I'll wire you when arriving.[10]

What Bud and his colleagues could not have known at the time is that the delays in attaining leave were a result of the Army Air Force command's final decisions about when to deploy its first and second echelons of air–sea rescue units. While Bud was completing his training in Pensacola, at Keesler Army Air Field in Biloxi, Mississippi the first echelon of the Army Air Force's Second Emergency Rescue Squadron was being deployed to the war in the Pacific. It was the first such deployment of the Army Air Force's new dedicated air–sea rescue units, occurring in July 1944. The Army Air Force would deploy the second echelon (Bud's echelon) the following year.

Bud, always diligent and determined, worked hard and ultimately mastered the code check with which he had been having difficulty. Just like at every training base to date, his tenacity and his dedication paid off. On June 17, 1944, Second Lieutenant Frank Philby "Bud" Hayes, U.S. Army Air Force, completed his training and received his Naval Aviator Badge (wings). In doing so, Bud became one of the select few pilots of those times (less than 150) to officially wear wings from both the Air Force and the Navy simultaneously.

Figure 9.1. Depiction of a U.S. Naval
Aviator Badge (wings).[11]

Bud's dual wings, as seen in some photographs of him, had an appearance of prestige. However, members of the Second Emergency Rescue Squadron rarely displayed their Navy wings other than during occasions when they wore formal uniform. Operationally they only wore the Army Air Force wings. This was a remnant of the long-simmering bitter feelings between the U.S. Army Air Force and the U.S. Navy over the Navy's efforts to block the Army Air Force from having its own air–sea rescue units, potentially costing the lives of downed airmen in the Pacific while the War Department debated the issue.[12]

It was June 1944, and Bud, having completed his training in Pensacola, was now off to Keesler Army Air Field in Mississippi. A month later, while at Keesler, he saw the first echelon of the Army Air Force's Emergency Rescue Squadron head out to join the war in the Pacific. Bud knew that early lessons the men of that air–sea rescue echelon learned from their wartime experiences would eventually help to better prepare Army Air Force personnel still training in the U.S. He also by then knew that it was only a matter of time before he was to put that knowledge, as well as his skill at piloting the unique PBY Catalina "flying boat" air–sea rescue aircraft, to use in the war in the Pacific.

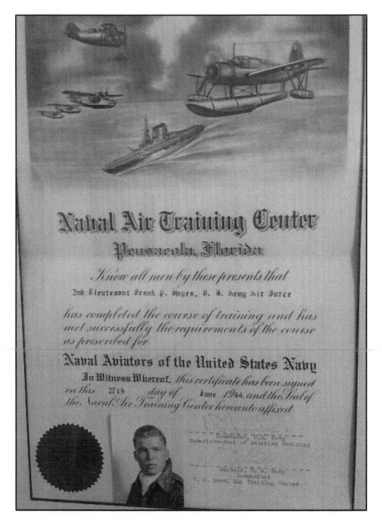

Figure 9.2. Certificate documenting Bud's completion of training in the PBY program under the U.S. Navy in Pensacola, Florida, June 1944.

CHAPTER 10

The Long Wait for War

Keesler Army Air Field—Biloxi, Mississippi

AS BUD WAS COMPLETING his PBY training and obtaining his Navy wings in Pensacola, Florida, events in the war were taking a decisive turn. June 6, 1944, was D-Day, on which the U.S. launched the largest air, sea and land invasion of Europe in history, with Normandy, France being the entry point. Over one hundred and fifty-five thousand troops hit the beaches at Normandy with U.S. Army Air Force and U.S. Navy support. This was the beginning of the Allied liberation of France. A great military surge from the west, with the goal of eradicating Hitler and his Nazi regime, had commenced. Meanwhile, from the east, the Red Army of the Soviet Union advanced, offering no reprieve to German Nazi units battling there. The Red Army pushed west, through the German army, eventually reaching Finland on June 9, 1944.

War in the Pacific also continued in intensity, and Allied missions there increasingly required the use of strategic air power. Naval and air bombardments of the Mariana Islands and Saipan were a prelude to the Battle of the Philippine Sea. During that battle the U.S. Navy achieved a major victory, downing over two hundred Japanese aircraft with the U.S. only losing twenty-nine planes in contrast. General MacArthur's forces continued to advance in New Guinea, taking Hollandia and clearing out remaining Japanese forces from that area in preparation for an Allied advance on the Philippines. As MacArthur's forces secured New Guinea, combat engineers rapidly prepared bases in the Pacific for the Army Air Force—some for the soon to be arriving Second Emergency Rescue Squadron.

Although American pilots were indisputably more proficient and effective than their Japanese counterparts, the war in the Pacific continued to result in many U.S. air and sea casualties. A need for increased air–sea rescue assets in the Pacific had manifested. As the U.S. Army Air Force established air bases on captured land, it desperately needed emergency rescue units to man them. By that time, in 1944, the Army Air Force only had three emergency rescue squadrons of its own—one deployed in the Mediterranean Sea in Europe, the other two in the Pacific. In the Pacific, the First Emergency Rescue Squadron was deployed in support of the Fifth Air Force, and the Second Emergency Rescue Squadron was deployed in support of the Thirteenth Air Force.

Back at home, operations at Keesler Army Air Field in Biloxi, Mississippi moved at a fast pace as the Army Air Force continually prepared new echelons of air–sea rescue units for deployment to the Pacific. By early March 1944, the Second Emergency Rescue Squadron stationed there was at a strength of 59 officers (mostly pilots) and 205 enlisted men.[1] Two days after Bud received his Navy wings in Pensacola in June 1944, he found himself among the men at Keesler Air Field, preparing for his inevitable deployment to the Pacific.

Biloxi lies in Harrison County, one of the southernmost points on the Mississippi Gulf Coast. For the third time (Louisiana, Florida and now Mississippi) Bud had landed in a subtropical climate. It was an area that was hot, humid, rainy and subject to severe thunderstorms and tropical storms. During World War II the Army Air Force built Keesler Field as a major basic training site, its presence stimulating a boom in the local economy.[2]

The Army Air Force was rapidly procuring PBY Catalina aircraft to match the speed with which it was now assembling rescue squadrons. Most of the aircraft were contracted by the U.S. Navy with the Consolidated Aircraft Company in San Diego. But due to the Navy's own needs, and likely also to interservice friction, PBY Catalina units from San Diego were not being made available to the Army Air Force. Instead, the Army Air Force's PBY Catalinas were manufactured under license from Vickers Aircraft Ltd. in Canada, specifically in Montreal, Quebec. The Canadian-manufactured "flying boats" were transported by ship to the Port of Savannah, in Georgia, where the Army Air Force's Hunter Field was nearby. Once the shipping crew had offloaded and reassembled the PBY Catalinas there, the emergency rescue squadrons would pick up the aircraft and conduct "shakedown" flights to test and ensure the operational condition of the aircraft.

During this period Bud and his Army Air Force colleagues were busy ferrying PBY Catalinas from the shipping point and conducting "shakedown" test flights. It was around this time that Bud met his eventual longtime navigator, who would become his best friend, Second Lieutenant Clayton "Greg" Gregersen, who wrote:

I never met "Bud" until we were crewed together at Keesler Field, Biloxi, Mississippi. This was about February or March of 1945. We trained in PBY's (sea planes) until May, then were sent to Hunter Field[3] near Savannah, Georgia to obtain a brand new airplane. Spent a few days "shaking down" the plane and will all get some leave just before being sent overseas.[4]

Bud also wrote of his experiences around this time, on June 29, 1944:

Arrived at Keesler Field this afternoon. From the word I get from the boys here it will take ten days to get my leave so you can judge when I will be home from that.

I got my Navy Wings yesterday and was so excited I forgot to salute the Admiral when I left. It keeps getting longer and longer before we get to combat.[5]

It had now been well over a year and a half since Bud left Filer, Idaho, and in letters to his parents, Fay Fern and George Jensen, he again expressed a desire to visit home before being deployed. Bud had experienced a Hollywood-like atmosphere when stationed in California and had met beautiful girls who wooed pilots in Pensacola. But at heart, Bud was still a farm boy from Filer, Idaho. He desired to return to Idaho's Magic Valley and immerse himself in its more serene way of life:

I didn't know how much I liked Pensacola until I left there. I guess it was the soft life that got me, the waves. I'd like to get back to the farm and do a little hard work for a change. I guess it will be more like July 14 before I'll see you.[6]

Bud turned twenty on July 3, 1944. Sometime around then, perhaps during the July 4 holiday, Bud finally received his long-anticipated two-week pass, allowing him to visit home in Filer, Idaho. He arrived at the Twin Falls Depot, where he found a Magic Valley that was busy with its fields, ranches and farms, all now raising food for both civilian and military needs. He also saw posters encouraging people to buy war bonds, experienced evening blackout regulations and had to use ration/allocation coupons for gasoline, tires and other needs. No doubt the local chatter at that time would have included talk about the five thousand to nine thousand Japanese who were by then living in the nearby relocation camp (Camp Minidoka, in Hunt, Idaho), and about nearby POW camps housing captured German and Italian soldiers (in Filer and Rupert). But those reminders of the ongoing war would take a back seat to Bud's joy at seeing his family and farm again.

Bud's family was thrilled to see him, and his sisters doted on him. During the visit Bud joyously held his new niece Mary Beth Peterson (his sister Mary's daughter) and his nephew Mike

Greene (his sister Nedra's son). Another niece, Carole Greene, was now eight years old and had grown since Bud last saw her. Although Bud's family members adored him and were proud of him, they were likely also concerned about his future. Where would Bud go from here? When would he return again? Would he ever return again? But for the time being such questions were kept at bay by good times with family and friends, and of course by good dinners of Idaho beef and potatoes (Bud's favorite).

Bud's time back home in Filer, Idaho was fleeting. The days passed quickly, and after tearful goodbyes with his parents, sisters, nieces, nephew and friends, Bud was off to Keesler again, this time to learn the Army Air Force's wartime plans for him. His family, though they wished for the best, knew all too well that it could be the last time they ever saw Bud.

Figure 10.1. Bud (age twenty) on leave at home in Filer, Idaho, July 1944. Left to right: Mary Frances, Bud, Nedra, Percy Greene and Bud's parents George and Fay Jensen.

Figure 10.2. Bud (age twenty) on leave at home in Filer, Idaho, July 1944. Here Bud stands with sister Mary (age twenty-two), his uniform displaying his two aviator badges (wings), one from the Army the other from the Navy.

Figure 10.3. Bud (age twenty) on leave at home in Filer, Idaho, July 1944. Bud stands in uniform with parents Fay Fern Jensen and George Jensen, to whom he wrote frequently throughout his time in service.

Stuttgart Army Air Field—Stuttgart, Arkansas

Bud's remaining time at Keesler was short. He sent his next letter home in August 1944, this time from Stuttgart, Arkansas. The U.S. Army Air Force had sent Bud to the Army Air Force's Advanced Flying School located there. Stuttgart is the county seat of Arkansas County, located forty-five miles southeast of Little Rock, Arkansas. Today it is a small town (with a 2013 population of 9,241), but it was even smaller in 1944, even with a military base located there.[7] The Army Air Force opened Stuttgart base in October 1942. Like other bases Bud had been assigned to, Stuttgart had been built quickly to support the critical mission of training pilots, mostly in twin-engine planes.

The Army Air Force's assignment of Bud to Stuttgart appears to have been part of somewhat of a holding pattern, with the Army Air Force not quite ready to assemble and assign the next echelon of Second Emergency Rescue Squadron PBY units. At Stuttgart Field, Bud received advanced training and additional information about "Navy fundamentals" necessary for piloting PBY aircraft like the Catalina. No doubt this was in direct response to updates coming from the initial emergency rescue squadron echelon that was already performing combat rescues in the Pacific. Bud, appearing restless, wrote home:

Here I am in the middle of Arkansas not knowing what to do next. We are here on temporary to fly AT-10s. We will get some good cross countries and I may even get to fly out to Idaho. We will go back to Keesler in October to finish with PBYs.[8]

Bud's frustration at this time mirrored the sentiments that U.S. Army General George S. Patton expressed to his troops of the U.S. Third Army that same year while awaiting combat, his forces having been held back from D-Day itself. Patton, keeping his troops motivated while they waited to join the fight, famously said:

Then there's one thing you men will be able to say when this war is over and you get back home. Thirty years from now when you're sitting by your fireside with your grandson on your knee and he asks, 'What did you do in the great World War Two?' you won't have to cough and say, "Well, your Granddaddy shoveled shit in Louisiana."[9]

Similarly, Bud did not intend to have to later say to family in Idaho that he spent the war flying circular training missions in Arkansas!

During Bud's time at Stuttgart Army Air Field he trained on the Beechcraft AT-10 aircraft, which was used to train pilots for multi-engine aircraft service. The aircraft's manufacturer, Beechcraft, saved on aluminum (which was scarce during the war) by building the aircraft primarily of wood. The AT-10 could carry two passengers and had a maximum speed just shy of two hundred miles per hour, with a range of 771 miles.[10]

Figure 10.4. A Beechcraft AT-10 airplane.

Bud's Idaho home and family remained on his mind amidst a suddenly-changing social environment. At Stuttgart many of his airmen friends, sensing their impending deployment to war, were getting married. For the most part the marriages tended to involve hometown sweethearts or rapidly-developed base-area romances. "All my buddies are getting married. I guess I'll be the only bachelor in the crowd," Bud wrote.

As with his previous Army Air Force bases, Bud found strict command at Stuttgart. It was a sharp return from the more relaxed environment he experienced while training under the Navy in Pensacola. There were Army martinets in place, who were often officers with no combat experience. Martinets appear in every army and in every military generation, and they are duly noted by servicemen like Bud:

We really have a "c.s." ["chicken shit"] colonel on this field. Second Lieutenants salute Second Lieutenants and if you don't you walk punishment tours: "Cadet stuff." This is an advanced Cadet base so I guess it's to be expected.[11]

Summer passed into fall 1944 with Bud and his unit still in Arkansas.

Overseas, events in World War II were progressing rapidly. In September 1944, the Allies recorded successes in capturing from the Germans Belgium, Luxembourg and much of France. The Soviet Union's Red Army acted like a buzz saw removing the Nazis from the Baltic States, Poland, Bulgaria and Romania. By October, the Soviet army had entered Czechoslovakia, Hungary and Yugoslavia (the Balkans) while the Allies liberated Greece. German forces were, step by step, being pushed back to Germany.

In the Pacific, U.S. forces captured the Caroline Islands, which soon thereafter became an important base for Allied operations. October 1944 saw other major U.S. advances against Japan in the Pacific as well, with the U.S. continuing to achieve victories through the significant use of air power. By October 20, U.S. forces arrived at Leyte, Philippines leading to General Douglas

MacArthur's famous landing on shore there during which he proclaimed, "I have returned." By month's end the Battle of Leyte Gulf was an Allied victory, with Japanese land and naval forces having been defeated, eventually to be pushed out of the Philippines altogether.

The year prior (1943), MacArthur's forces had achieved major victory over the Japanese in the Battle of the Bismarck Sea off Lae, New Guinea. That action highlighted the extraordinary value and tactics of U.S. Army Air Force air power, under command of General Kenney, who also used Royal Australian Air Forces during the battle. The Allies' use of air power remained a front and center need for MacArthur throughout the Pacific campaign, and he always had urgent need for air–sea rescue resources to support it.

By August 1944, in New Guinea, the Allies had expelled Japanese forces from the island of Morotai. Nevertheless, Japanese aircraft continued bombing the island, resulting in Allied loss of life there, as well as the loss of at least one aircraft. On October 10, 1944, two flights of the Army Air Force's Second Emergency Rescue Squadron were moved to Morotai Island, which was a strategic Army Air Force move to put rescue units closer to air strikes that were underway on Palau and the Philippines.[12] (Months later, Bud's aircraft and unit would be based there.)

In a letter from Bud in mid-October 1944, he made no mention of the Second Emergency Rescue Squadron units that were already deployed in the Pacific. He did, however, relate that he and others were lamenting that the war might end before they saw action. It remained unclear to Bud whether the Army Air Force had wartime plans for him, and what such plans might be.

It was certainly possible at that time that the Army Air Force might deploy Bud to the Pacific as an air–sea rescue pilot. But (as Chapter 8 of this book discussed), air–sea rescue was only one of many types of missions that the PBY Catalinas Bud was trained in could fly. Navy "Black Cat Squadrons," which had PBY Catalinas painted black, could perform nighttime search and attack missions. In the Pacific, missions flown by these squadrons proved spectacularly successful and seriously disrupted the flow of supplies and personnel to Japanese island bases.[13] But although Bud's military records state that he was certified "1022 Bomber pilot—2-Engine," there is no indication that the Army Air Force ever intended to deploy him for PBY bombing missions.[14] For the time being, while war raged in the Pacific, Bud was stuck in Arkansas wondering where, when and for what purpose the Army Air Force would deploy him. In Bud's own words:

> The way things look now we won't even start training at Keesler until Christmas, it doesn't look like we will ever get overseas. It looks like I'll be a shavetail for life. We can't get any promotions until we graduate from Keesler. I may go on a cross country to New York next week. I certainly hope so as I have [not] been there yet.[15]

Bud, having recently read an issue of a Filer, Idaho newspaper his parents sent to him from home, referenced an article indicating that stepfather George Jensen was buying another place. Bud asked his parents for details, and he also complimented a picture of his parents that his sister Nedra had sent. His parents had also recently sent new winter clothes, which Bud said he would have altered. By then he was sending home many of his summer clothes.[16]

Keesler Army Air Field—Biloxi, Mississippi

In November 1944, the Army Air Force transferred Bud from Stuttgart, in Arkansas, back to Keesler, in Mississippi. Bud wrote home again on November 10, 1944. He was spending a Saturday night in the barracks with buddies listing to the *Hit Parade* show on the radio. His frustration with the Army Air Force for having not deployed him yet was evident:

> We haven't even started training yet. We are still just signing

123

in twice a day and sleeping the rest. There isn't a darn thing to do unless you go to New Orleans and it costs about $15.00[17] every time you go. I just stick around here most of the time.

Just had intermissions to discuss the war. We decided that we wouldn't be in combat before July 1945 which would seem to indicate that the major offensive against Japan couldn't start until then. . . . There are still lots of rumors of when and where we are going, but nothing definite yet.[18]

Bud's hope to return home to Filer, Idaho for Christmas 1944 seemed unlikely to come to fruition as the Army Air Force had not provided him any leave. He asked his parents what people at home would want him to send as gifts. During the day his unit continued to be kept busy with flight school and flight operations:[19]

Here it is Christmas time and I am running around like a madman buying presents. Will send a box in the morning only I couldn't find a thing that I thought Carole would like and hope you could get her something and explain to her or let her think I sent it. I have a present for everyone else except Nedra but I better take care of that. I had a heck of a time getting any paper at all so I hope you will excuse the wrapping of the presents.[20]

As Christmas approached in 1944, Bud's unit was in its fifth week of intensive training and was still uncertain of its future. Bud wrote, "We really should be geniuses at something by the time we get through."[21]

Around this time Bud's writings also mention a letter he received from home informing him of stepfather George Jensen having been involved in a serious accident (most likely car accident) in which he was badly hurt. As with today's legal system, tort law was present and on mind. Bud wrote, "You ought to see a good lawyer and find out whether to sue them."[22] With his own money tight, Bud was grateful for a check his parents sent; "a real lifesaver," he said. In return he sent home George's favorite brand of snuff tobacco, writing, "I found a place where I can get Copenhagen some of the time, so if there is still a shortage let me know and I'll get some more."[23]

Figure 10.5. Second Lieutenant Bud Hayes at Keesler Army Air Field in Biloxi, Mississippi, 1944.

While Bud and his Army Air Force buddies prepared for Christmas while stuck at Keesler, ominous events were unfolding in the war overseas. Thomas Edison once remarked, "A light bulb burns brightest right before it goes out." In Europe, the German army was pushed to its limits from the west, by expanding Allied forces, and from the east, by an aggressive Red Army. Finding its back against the wall, the Germany army, similar to Edison's light bulb, prepared for one last desperate bright flash, ready to battle fiercely against Allied forces in December 1944.

With the Allies' guard down due to the Christmas holiday, on Christmas Eve 1944, the Nazis launched a long-planned strategic offensive involving two hundred thousand German soldiers, including elite armored and infantry forces. Taking advantage of weather that had already forced the grounding of Allied aircraft, the Germans launched their surprise attack through the Ardennes Forest in Luxembourg and Belgium. This commenced what would become known as the Battle of the Bulge.

Famously, during the offensive the Germans surrounded the U.S. 101st Airborne Division and other U.S. units at Bastogne, Belgium. The Germans, recognizing that the Americans were low on fuel, food and ammunition, sent a message to U.S. Brigadier General Anthony McAuliffe telling him to surrender his forces. General McAuliffe simply replied with one word: "Nuts." The response became a rallying cry to Allied troops who, under the lead of General Patton's Third Army, later liberated the units that had been cornered at Bastogne. By the end of January 1945, the Nazis, who had lost half their troops and seen their last-push offensive campaign collapse, retreated across the Rhine River back to their German homeland. The German army's light bulb was quickly fading, soon to go out completely.

At the same time, in the Pacific, the Empire of Japan made a similar final offensive push. Japan's highly-depleted air force sealed pilots into aircraft and used them as suicide attack bombs ("Kamikaze" pilots), intentionally flying aircraft into U.S. ships and other high-value targets. U.S. forces in the Pacific were en-

gaged in a long and bloody air, sea and land battle while attempting to capture the island of Iwo Jima. Offensives in the Philippines were gradually expelling the Japanese. In December 1945, the U.S. liberated Mindoro Island, followed shortly thereafter by its liberation of Northern Luzon, including the capital city Manila.
Soldiers and sailors back home in the U.S. certainly found news and casualty reports from the war in the Pacific disconcerting. In December 1944, though U.S. victories were being reported and German and Japanese forces appeared to be collapsing, the end of war in Europe and the Pacific still remained nowhere in sight. The new German and Japanese offensive pushes suggested that the war would go on for years to come.

War was raging during the Christmas holiday, but Bud was stuck in Biloxi, Mississippi with little to do, plenty of lousy food and the quandary of where he would find himself in the future. He wrote:

> We are only getting one day off for Christmas, but there is really no place to go but New Orleans and it's overcrowded so I guess it doesn't make much difference. . . . I received a bathrobe from Nedra. I must write and thank her for it. It's just the right thing I need.

> Just got back from mess and was it lousy lamb, lamb, lamb. That's the only thing we get to eat, boy I could really go for some Idaho beefsteak and potatoes. There are good chances that I'll get another leave before going overseas, if I do it will be in April or May.[24]

Bud concluded his letters for the year 1944 with his vision of returning home to his halcyon days in Idaho's Magic Valley, writing: "I'll be home one of these days and the more I think about it, I'm liable to become a farmer."[25] But that vision was not meant to be.

CHAPTER 11

Into the War at Last

N EW YEAR'S DAY 1945 arrived at Keesler Army Air Field in Biloxi, Mississippi with ongoing news of the German offensive and Allied counterattacks in Europe's Battle of the Bulge. The war in the Pacific also remained highly active, with both Allied and Japanese forces increasingly dependent on air power. Both the U.S. Army Air Force and the U.S. Navy were demanding the deployment of more air–sea rescue assets to the Pacific.

New on the war front at this time was America's Boeing B-29 Superfortress heavy bomber:

> In wartime, the B-29 was capable of flight at altitudes up to 31,850 feet (9,710 m), at speeds of up to 350 mph. This was its best defense, because Japanese fighters could barely reach that altitude, and few could catch the B-29 even if they did attain that altitude. Only the heaviest of anti-aircraft weapons could reach it, and since the Axis forces did not have proximity fuses, hitting or damaging the aircraft from the ground in combat proved difficult.[1]

This new technology, in the form of high-altitude bombers, made its debut in June 1944 during a bombing raid on Bangkok, Thailand. The B-29 was later used for intensive bombing missions on Tokyo and other targets in Japan and the Pacific theater. (Its most famous missions, dropping the atomic bombs, would occur many months later.) But this new aircraft technology brought with it to the Pacific new problems. The new aircraft were experiencing frequent mechanical failures and fuel emergencies (on top of pilot error, weather-related issues and losses from enemy fire). In the Pacific, unlike in Europe, more often than not these types of events led to crews having to ditch their aircraft in vast, open ocean waters. By 1945, demand for air–sea rescue units that could retrieve survivors from the water was at an all-time high.

Back at Keesler Army Air Field in early 1945, activity increased as preparations were finally underway for the next echelon of the Army Air Force's Second Emergency Rescue Squadron to deploy to join the war in the Pacific. If Bud knew what the Army Air Force's plans for him were at that time, he certainly did not reveal them in his letters home. Wartime censorship of such letters continued to be mandatory. It was perhaps also easier for Bud to address more mundane aspects of life at Keesler, so as not to alarm his family back in Idaho about his inevitable deployment to war:

> Have just been down to the flight surgeon to take another overseas physical, the only thing wrong with me is one cavity in the lower 16. Boy I really hate to go have it filled. . . . Haven't been doing any flying though, and I am really getting rusty.[2]

At the base, Bud's friends had introduced him to the game of golf and to the local golf courses, which he played on Sundays, when possible. He wrote, "They have nice courses here but the green fees are so high that you can't afford to play very often." He hoped to start flying again soon.[3]

Most of Bud's letters home from February to March 1945 did not survive to present day. In a later letter Bud mentioned that his mother Fay had traveled from Filer, Idaho to Biloxi, Mississippi to visit him on March 22, 1945. We know from family lore that Fay was a strongly-determined woman and a dedicated mother. Perhaps it was a mother's intuition, some sort of sixth sense, by which Fay knew that Bud would soon be deployed into combat. Or perhaps, whether he was soon off to war or not, she was simply not willing to let another full year pass before seeing her son again.[4]

One way or another, Bud's mother Fay was determined to visit him at Keesler, no matter what the cost, even amidst the hardships of wartime rationing. Travel from rural Idaho to Biloxi, Mississippi would have been long and costly at that time. But Fay managed it, all on her own. As Bud's family would later learn, any maternal premonitions Fay might have had about an impending deployment for Bud were accurate. This was Fay's last visit with her son Bud, and it was Bud's last in-person contact with any of his family members.

By March 1945, the increased tempo of war in the Pacific put immense pressure on the Army Air Force to move its additional air–sea rescue units into the war quickly. With the increasing use of air power in the Pacific, and aircraft going down amid heavy combat, lives were at stake and time was of the essence. The Army Air Force had to organize and deploy its PBY Project crews without any further delay.

Bud, still in Biloxi, wrote home with an urgency and tempo reflecting that of his surroundings. In his letter he indicated that there was barely even time to write it at all. The letter, from March 1945, also reflected that he had on his mind the perils of flying with equipment that was of variable reliability. And Bud did, of course, still have time to mention the poor Army food:

> We are flying like mad trying to get our time in. I went on a patrol over the gulf today and everything in the plane went crazy. All the radios went out, Voltage regulator wouldn't work, interphone went dead, in fact the only thing that ran was the engines. We go on quite a few cross country hops but hardly ever land at the town and come back to Keesler and land.
>
> I really hate this field worse every day, however we won't be

here Much longer. They are making us pay for mess cards by the month and the meals are lousy, so we usually eat somewhere else so we really pay double for a lot of meals.[5]

Bud was also keeping up with his reading of letters from his family. On his mind was the deteriorating marriage of Marvin Peterson to his sister Mary Frances (the two would later divorce): "I think it is terrible about Mary. She must be crazy, the best thing she could do with Marvin is knock him in the head."[6] He also worried about getting his income tax, which he calculated out to have him owing the government $5.00 ($66.00 today), in on time. World War II proved no shield from the Internal Revenue Service, even to those putting their lives on the line in service to the U.S.

For the first time Bud gave specific details about his upcoming deployment. The Army Air Force, having developed and heavily trained its air–sea rescue squadrons for use in the Pacific theater, was moving quickly to organize and staff additional echelons to meet rescue and tactical demands there. Bud was now fully commanding and managing a PBY Catalina crew of his own, and he initially found it difficult. He took the job seriously, but, as he observed, his own commitment was apparently not always matched by his more youthful crew members:

I'm not certain about getting leave since there is a real rush order on OA-10 (PBY) crews now. We are supposed to be finished the 24th of March. We will go to Savannah, GA for staging and then to Frisco [San Francisco, California] to P.O.E. [Port Of Embarkation].

I got so darned much responsibility with my crew that I'm dizzy. I catch hell because my engineer doesn't show up for class, and I don't even know that he is supposed to be there. I have a good navigator and my Co-Pilot is quite an artist. I have 7 men in my crew but some of them are sure kids. They think it's a big "game."[7]

Bud's long-awaited journey into the heart of the war in the Pacific finally arrived in early April 1945. Back in February 1945, the Army Air Force had begun rotating out men of the first echelon of the Second Emergency Rescue Squadron, returning them home to the United States after months in combat:

Ten (10) officers and twenty-one (21) enlisted men were returned to the United States under the provisions of WD Circular 373, 1944. "Return of Air Crew Personnel to the United States." All of these personnel had flown over 600 combat hours in this theater.[8]

Well-trained replacement units from Keesler, including Bud and the crew he was now commanding, had been readied for months. When the Army Air Force's orders for Bud and his PBY Catalina unit to move out to its embarkation point in San Francisco came in April 1945, there was a strictly-enforced complete blackout on letters and news from airmen. Bud's letters home stopped as he made his way to the Pacific, to war.

When the Army Air Force had deployed its first echelon of the Second Emergency Rescue Squadron by ship back in 1944, it took them far too long to get the Pacific, with many servicemen arriving there seasick and their equipment experiencing mechanical problems that delayed them in becoming operational. Lessons from that experience led the Army Air Force to instead have its units move directly to the Pacific theater via the very aircraft they would be using in war operations. This method of deployment had the advantage of giving pilots and crews extensive long-range flight experience in the PBY Catalina aircraft, allowing them to discover any possible heretofore unknown anomalies in aircraft or crew prior to entering the war zone. Each PBY Catalina crew flew its own aircraft and equipment west, making the trip as quickly as possible.

The flight distance from Keesler (in Biloxi, Mississippi) to Bud's point of embarkation (in San Francisco, California) is approximately two thousand miles. One of Bud's former crew members stated that the transit to San Francisco took an entire week.[9] Based on normal refueling stops, rest and required time for mechanical maintenance that each PBY Catalina would have required in transit, a trip like that typically would have taken a minimum of twelve hours of flight time alone. But with Army Air Force command wanting the aircraft and airmen to be in top shape by the time they arrived in San Francisco, much more transit time had been allotted in order to work out any potential problems.

Not long after Bud and the PBY Catalina "flying boat" crew he was piloting and commanding arrived in San Francisco (landing directly in San Francisco Bay), they were off to Hawaii. The long, waterborne takeoffs of strings of flying boats passing the Golden Gate Bridge must have been quite a sight to those watching from shore or from boats. The crews' flight route and plans were top secret at that time; but the journey to Hawaii would take them over twenty hours over open sea with no landmarks. Extensive coordination between the Army Air Force's units and the Navy, which provided standby fighter cover, was required.[10]

As extraordinary as the PBY Catalina's flying range was, even it could not make the jump from San Francisco, California to Hawaii nonstop. On the flight legs between these locations Bud and his colleagues experienced, for the first time, landing in the Pacific Ocean, where Navy seaplane tenders (ships) refueled the Cats. The refueling was done under cover of close protection from Navy fighters, preventing any possible Japanese attempt to discover and attack a squadron of the valuable flying boats.

The PBYs were well equipped with radio and radar equipment that allowed different PBY crews to coordinate their service pit stops. The Army Air Force and the Navy worked together to rendezvous the Cats with their refueling points, which were at one of four Currituck-class fourteen thousand ton seaplane tenders in the Pacific ocean. For example, the U.S.S. Currituck (AV-7)[11] was most likely used for this particular purpose before it too was eventually deployed to the Pacific, in the New Guinea and Morotai Island area.

The Navy Currituck seaplane tenders were full service "stations" for PBY Catalina (and later PBM Mariner) flying boats. The ships contained the full array of PBY spare parts, tools, fuel, oil, lubricants, tires and every other conceivable provision necessary for PBY Catalina service maintenance. No doubt the Second Emergency Rescue Squadron crews even got a full, hot Navy-cooked meal during service stops, reminiscent of the meals Bud so enjoyed during his training days with the Navy in Pensacola.

Hickam Field—Pearl Harbor, Hawaii

Once the Army Air Force's aircraft had been serviced the PBYs took off again for their destination in Hawaii. In Hawaii, the aircraft landed at Hickam Field, which by that time, in 1945, had been rebuilt and expanded after the 1941 Japanese attack on Pearl Harbor. At Hickam, mechanics gave each PBY Catalina a full 120-hour mechanical maintenance check, required before the Cats could proceed over ocean again.[12]

Bud's stay in Hawaii was short-lived, with little time to enjoy its beautiful beaches, its officers' clubs and ample social opportunities. In fact, Bud mentioned nothing at all of Hawaii in his letters, as his Second Emergency Rescue Squadron most likely never even left the Hickam Field base. Instead, the squadron made ready for war in the Pacific, and continued on what would amount to an over eighty-two hour route to Christmas Island, Tarawa, Guadalcanal and other spots that Allied forces had already liberated. Each tiny speck of an island made for refueling, needed maintenance, food, provisioning and rest.[13]

Hawaii's island of Oahu, and its city of Honolulu, had since the 1941 attack on Pearl Harbor become the nucleus of the Allied Pacific war effort. By 1945, almost every foot of the area was teaming with military activity. The famous American aviator Charles Lindberg, who moved there at the time to distance himself from the war in Europe and the embarrassment of his earlier support of isolationism and German appeasement (as this book discussed *supra*, in Chapter 3), observed: "There are airfields everywhere along the coast, it seems, and all day the air has been full of planes—bombers, fighters, transports—army, navy and marine."[14]

The Army Air Force did not allow Bud to write home during this period. For a son who usually wrote home about every two weeks, and certainly no less than once monthly, this period of silence must have been disconcerting, if not excruciating, to Bud's family back home in Filer, Idaho. What was happening with Bud? Where was he? Was he even still alive?

The family's questions were at least partially answered when a letter dated Tuesday, May 7, 1945, arrived at home:

> Haven't been able to write for some time, but I can write now. About all they will allow me to say is that I am in Hawaii now. If I don't answer any questions, it's because I haven't received any mail. It will take a long time for mail to reach me.[15]

On the very day Bud wrote that letter World War II ended in Europe with Germany's unconditional surrender. The Allies in Europe and the United States declared the next day, May 8, 1945, as V-E Day ("Victory in Europe" Day). As war raged on in the Pacific the question became whether Japan would follow suit in surrendering.

Adolph Hitler's army, and his grand plans for world dominance, had officially expired. By April and May 1945, Allied forces from the west and Soviet Union Red Army forces from the east were rapidly approaching Berlin, Germany and capturing Nazi forces that were in retreat. During those months 1.5 million German soldiers surrendered to the Allies.[16] The Allies had taken Italy from Mussolini, and Mussolini himself was shot by partisans in northern Italy. Those who dispatched him brought his body, and that of his mistress, to Milan's city square and hung them upside down for all to see.

From Adolph Hitler's underground Berlin bunker he watched Mussolini's fate unfold and he heard loud gun reports from Allied artillery and aircraft as they pounded closer and closer to him in Germany. With the Red Army fast approaching his doorstep, Hitler committed suicide on April 20, 1945. What was left of Hitler's Third Reich was delegated to German Admiral Karl Dönitz, who not long after surrendered to General Eisenhower in Reims, France and again in Berlin, Germany the next day.[17]

Bud's letters do not mention whether news of V-E Day and effusive celebrations of victory that permeated Europe, New York City's Times Square and elsewhere (likely even at home in Filer, Idaho) reached him in Hawaii. Bud's war, the one in the Pacific, remained as unrelentingly intense and focused as ever before. Europe, whether in war or victory, was far from Bud's mind. Japan, the direct instigator of war with America, still remained a dangerous and indefatigable threat that the U.S. and Allied forces had to defeat.

After years of intense stateside training, interspersed with benign check flights and long periods of waiting, the realities of war were now rapidly coming into focus for Bud and his PBY Catalina crew. Bud gave his family the heads-up that his heretofore reliable biweekly letters would now be a thing of the past. Bud was headed to war in the Pacific, where delivery of mail to and from military personnel was of no certainty.

Despite the now unpredictable nature of the mail, Bud still tried to write home from every place he went. The war he had seen in black and white Movietone newsreels at his stateside bases was about to become a real, live fury of color, action, sound, smell and touch: "I used to sit in the movies and see newsreels of theaters in the Pacific and it seemed a long ways off, but it seems pretty close now."[18]

Bud's future letters would identify places in the Pacific that the folks back in Idaho had never seen on a map, let alone heard of in school or trade. Perhaps Bud's mother Fay, being a schoolteacher, acquired every good world atlas available and a magnifying glass in order to see those tiny specks of land in the Pacific Ocean where her son now found himself. War in the Pacific would bring meaning to American author Mark Twain's famous observation that "God created war so that Americans would learn geography."[19]

Bud's first wartime mission came while he was still stationed in Hawaii in command of his PBY Catalina crew. The mission was for Bud's crew to search for a B-25 bomber that had gone down. Disappointingly, after a week of Bud's crew searching for the plane they could not find it.[20] Bud's next letter home, postmarked in late May 1945, was written on American Red Cross stationery from the base nurses' station in New Guinea. Bud was finally in the Pacific war-zone.

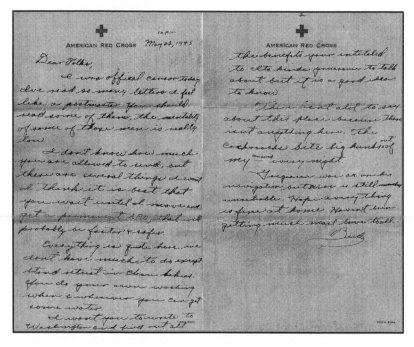

Figure 11.1. Lieutenant Bud Hayes's first letter home from New Guinea, May 22, 1945.

Army Air Force Field—New Guinea

New Guinea is located north of Australia and was part of the pre-World War II Netherlands (Dutch) East Indies colonial empire in Asia. While it appears small on an average-sized world globe, the island is nevertheless one of the largest in the Pacific. In fact, New Guinea is larger than the entire land area of the U.S. State of California.[21]

As a corridor and stepping stone to the Philippines and Japan, New Guinea was a key strategic area for the Empire of Japan. Japan invaded it in 1942 as part of Japan's larger plan to conquer Australia. Likewise, New Guinea became a key strategic locale for the Allied forces to attempt to halt Japan's progress. The Allies continued their advance there with the goal of liberating the Philippines and Formosa and ultimately of invading the islands of Japan itself.

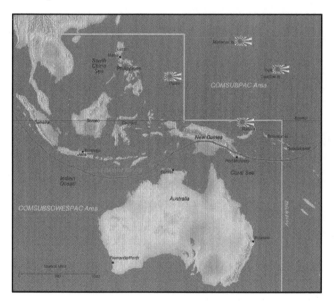

Figure 11.2. Map showing the location of New Guinea, to the north of Australia. New Guinea was Bud's point of entry to the war in the Pacific in 1945.

Beginning with the Battle of Coral Sea in May 1942, the Allied forces had in large part succeeded in halting Japan's advance and its plans for Australia. Allied forces (U.S. and Australia) under General Douglas MacArthur mounted air, sea, and ground operations to take New Guinea. Their assault on the Japanese forces there began with the successful capture of the eastern part of the island (Papua and northeast regions of New Guinea, including the city Port Moresby) in late 1942, continuing into 1943. The terrain and the unrelenting Japanese forces they faced made conquering the remainder of the island (the Dutch New Guinea region) difficult. U.S. and Australian forces pressed the Japanese forces for months during multiple successive actions. By late 1944, the Allies had succeeded in pushing the Japanese completely out of New Guinea.

By 1945, New Guinea served as a prime staging area for Allied war operations, particularly serving as a land base for the U.S. Army Air Force under General Kenney's newly-consolidated Thirteenth Air Force. These forces were necessary to support the next step, which was for the Allies to expel Japanese forces from the Philippines and Borneo. And the Army Air Force's extensive air operations there required the support of newly-arrived Army Air Force air–sea rescue squadrons, like Bud's. Between October 1944 and June 1945 these rescue squadrons, and PBY Catalina crews in particular, would perform around seven hundred successful air–sea rescues.[22]

Intense operations during the New Guinea campaign taught many lessons and techniques for improving the effectiveness of air–sea rescue missions, and those lessons and techniques had made their way back to Keesler Army Air Field in Mississippi where Bud had been training. Now it was Bud's turn. The Army Air Force had rotated him and the PBY Catalina crew he commanded into action in New Guinea, providing much-needed relief to the echelons that had already been stationed there for months. Thanks to those initial units, Bud's echelon of the Second Emergency Rescue Squadron was now better equipped with the air–sea rescue know-how that would allow it to provide key support to the Allied air campaign against Japan in Borneo and the Southern Philippine Islands.

The Allies' foray into and capture of New Guinea from the Japanese had occurred along both New Guinea's Southeast Coast and its Northeast Coast. In July 1944, hastily-constructed air bases were established off Hollandia, including on Middleburg Island to the southeast, about 2.5 miles off New Guinea's coast. Bud's PBY Catalina unit was, in spring 1945, stationed at Middleburg Island. But with the Allies' complete removal of Japanese forces from New Guinea having already occurred they soon deemed the Middleburg base inadequate for the continued campaign against Japan. The Allies ordered their forces to abandon the base by April 1945. Bud's unit moved to its new station on Morotai Island.[23]

Figure 11.3. Second Emergency Rescue Squadron base, with parked PBY Catalinas, on Middleburg Island, New Guinea, circa 1944–45.[24]

140

The Second Emergency Rescue Squadron's Morotai Island location placed it northwest of New Guinea and closer to areas of ongoing Southwest Pacific air operations over Borneo, the Philippines and Celebes (Dutch Indies islands). Air combat actions were taking place there and, hence, the rescue assets' now closer location made them more effective when dispatched for rescue missions. Morotai Island was much larger than Middleburg Island, allowing for multiple runways and longer runways, albeit in difficult conditions. The Army Corps of Engineers described:

Lying approximately 300 miles northwest of Caple Sansapor, Morotai is a mountainous island about 45 miles by 35 miles in size. The entire island except for a narrow coastal strip was covered with dense rain forests, interspersed with numerous rivers and streams. . . . The village of Gotalalamo, together with the Gila Peninsula was chosen as the site for an Allied base.[25]

Army engineers met the challenge of converting Morotai Island into a comprehensive airfield and supply and operations base that included three runways of five thousand, seven thousand and six thousand feet (the last one even expandable to seven thousand feet). There were substantial taxiways and fueling and maintenance facilities, as well as a major field hospital with a capacity of upwards of nineteen hundred beds.[26]

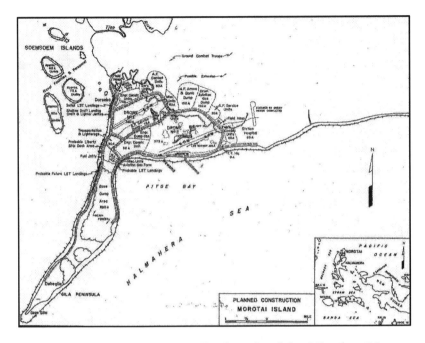

Figure 11.4. U. S. Army Engineering Map Number 24, depicting Bud's base of operations on Morotai Island, New Guinea, 1945.[27]

Bud's living conditions at the base on Morotai Island were a marked contrast from those at his stateside bases. Squadron crews such as Bud's lived in tents that offered minimal protection from the natural elements. Bud's training stints in Louisiana and Mississippi, where he complained of the oppressive heat and humidity, paled in comparison to the climate in the jungle environment of New Guinea. As Bud wrote in his letters home, the stifling hot, humid, rainy weather there was, "lousy weather for flying."[28] The rains turned the ground and roads into "a mass of thick gummy mud, and those in the flatland a very soft mulch of black humus."[29]

Figure 11.5. An example of Second Emergency Rescue Squadron living quarters on Morotai Island, New Guinea, 1945.[30]

American troops stationed in the Pacific also faced challenges in the form of tropical diseases, insects and parasites, at times as deadly as the Japanese enemy. Fresh water was scarce, having to be manually produced using mechanical fresh water condensers (of variable reliability), as were military rations, with whatever food was available being barely edible. And yet the airman persevered, focusing on whatever they could do to save American lives and bring the war to conclusion.

During the war the Army Air Force kept reports of missions and crews in various states of detail. Operations officers in the Second Emergency Rescue Squadron rotated in their documentation duties. Some wrote lengthy, detailed, descriptive narratives of each mission. Others simply logged the mission flight plan and hours for the record. Such inconsistencies were simply part of the natural fog of war.

Seventy years after the war, Robert H. Reed, who had served as General of the U.S. Air Force and Chief of Staff for the Supreme Allied Powers Europe (NATO), commented on the state of mission report record keeping during World War II:

> I'm reminded of the famous WWII combat mission report; "sub sighted—sank same." Though the drama associated with the many combat missions [of the Second Emergency Rescue Squadron] were unfortunately lost to war and squadron records, nevertheless, the drama between sighted and sank must have been excruciating and exciting. In Lieutenant Hayes's case, many of his exploits are reduced to "survivors sighted—rescued same."[31]

Alas, most mission records for Bud's Second Emergency Rescue Squadron remain incomplete. One of the squadron's original commanders, Captain Gerard F. Wientjes, did save some records, which are preserved by his nephew, Chief Warrant Officer James Teegarden. Teegarden maintains the largest archival collection on the Second Emergency Rescue Squadron, available at http://pbyrescue.com. Other records about the Second Emergency Rescue Squadron's missions have remained in the U.S. Air Force historical files or are dispersed across families and descendants of Second Emergency Rescue Squadron members. Where the rest of the Second Emergency Rescue Squadron mission report records are, only providence truly knows.[32]

What we do know, from stories passed down, is that most U.S. Army Air Force records toward the end of the war were on a ship bound for the United States. That ship was lost at sea, with Second Emergency Rescue Squadron records somewhat ironically ending up at the bottom of the Pacific Ocean.[33] What examples we can provide of the heroic Second Emergency Rescue Squadron rescue missions during World War II come from surviving records of the Borneo campaign, from June to August 1945. The missions documented in these records exemplify the hundreds of rescue missions that the Second Emergency Rescue Squadron performed during the war in the Pacific—some performed under the command of Bud himself. One can multiply these remaining documented missions to attain a good sense of the work, effort and stresses that Lieutenant Bud Hayes and his colleagues and their crews took on in their PBY aircraft throughout their time stationed in the Pacific.[34]

Bud's echelon of the Second Emergency Rescue Squadron stationed in the Pacific initially consisted of twelve PBY Catalinas and approximately seventeen other Army Air Force aircraft. On July 14, 1945, the Army Air Force divided the squadron into flight units (A–C) and assigned them to four areas along the New Guinea coast. (The Army Air Force would later, in early September, reconsolidate the units all to Morotai Island in order to provide better rescue coverage to Allied air operations taking place against the Japanese in Borneo and nearby islands.)[35]

U.S. Army Air Force General Kenney's growing, thousands-strong fleet of aircraft in the Pacific theater by then included B-24, B-25 and B-29 bombers, as well as P-38 and P-47 fighter aircraft (many based out of Morotai itself). These forces required rescue units like Bud's to be stationed nearby, not only for the practical matter of saving downed airmen, but also for morale, so that pilots and crew members would have confidence that if the enemy shot down their aircraft help would be on its way in little time. With the vast increase in air power, the war was taking a positive turn in the Allies' favor at the time Bud's Second Emergency Rescue Squadron moved to Morotai around April 1945. So much so that eight hundred of the new long-range B-29 bombers of the Twentieth Air Force for the first time began directly attacking Japan's mainland.[36]

Author Roscoe Creed, in his book *PBY: The Catalina Flying Boat* (chapter "The Air Force's Navy") wrote of the challenges faced by men like Bud and the PBY Catalina rescue men under his command: "The 2nd's services were in great demand from the start. Most flights were long and combat hours mounted by leaps and bounds. The planes were gone all day, so ground crews worked all night."[37]

If an aircraft was downed, surviving crew members would use a survival radio know as a "Gibson Girl" to call the Second Emergency Rescue Squadron for rescue, using the well-known distress signal "S-O-S." Once the rescue squadron was airborne it would attempt to spot the surviving crew members who would then be using sea-marker dyes, reflective mirrors and colored smoke, usually while floating in the ocean on rafts or debris.[38]

The "Gibson Girl" radio (so named because of its female-like hourglass shape) was a five hundred kilohertz hand-cranked rescue radio transmitter. At 4.8 watts it had a range of two hundred miles before a signal, like the "S-O-S" signal, would drop. The U.S. Army Air Force ordered aircraft operating over water to be equipped with the radio, which included a folded-up metal box kite and a balloon with a small hydrogen generator used to fly a wire antenna.[39]

Figure 11.6. A U.S. Army Air Force "Gibson Girl" emergency rescue radio from World War II, 1945.[40]

Given the PBY Catalina's speed, from the time it received an "S-O-S" distress signal from a downed aircraft, assuming it could pinpoint the aircraft's location, the PBY could arrive there to perform a rescue within two hours. However, distances in the Pacific were large, and pinpointing a signal from a downed aircraft was often problematic. Radio transmitter failures could quickly frustrate a search and rescue mission. Nevertheless, the Gibson Girl device, which is a simple one by today's standards, was a major factor allowing the Second Emergency Rescue Squadron to perform several hundred successful rescue missions and save several hundred downed airmen.

The Second Emergency Rescue Squadron's missions were never routine, and they were always dangerous. Take, for example, the rescue performed by a PBY crew under command of pilot Lieutenant Frank Rauschkolb (of Freewater, Oregon) on March 4, 1945. The rescue crew successfully saved three downed B-25 bombers and seventeen crewmen, all in one pickup and all in the face of enemy fire off the Zamboanga Peninsula, Mindanao, Philippines.[41] That PBY crew made an eleven-hour journey to return the rescued airmen to safety, which was a record for a rescue mission at that time.[42]

CAPT. WILL HELMANTOLER (right) of Wood River, co-pilot of Snafu Snatchers, Catalina flying boat that staged a record rescue of 17 airmen off Zamboanga.

Wood River Man Co - Pilot on Record Rescue of 17 Airmen

Figure 11.7. Newspaper photo of Lieutenant Frank Rauschkolb (left) and Captain Will Helmantoler (right) alongside a PBY Catalina bearing the "Snafu Snatchers" nickname after their crew's record-setting March 4, 1945, rescue mission.

As if the Second Emergency Rescue Squadron's rescue missions weren't challenging enough as they were, Japanese fighter pilots did not hesitate to use downed Allied aircraft as bait or decoys to attract Allied rescue aircraft and support aircraft that they could then attack. The risks of such missions are exemplified by one that then Flight Officer John F. "Jack" Leonard (who was later Bud's co-pilot during his final mission) participated in on May 19, 1945.[43] As Jack's PBY Catalina dropped to rescue the crew of a downed B-25 bomber, thousands of Japanese military men, who had been lying in wait on a nearby shore for that precise scenario, opened fire. Although Jack's Cat was badly damaged he somehow managed to pick up the entire downed bomber crew and safely return with them to his base.[44]

According to Bud's letters home, New Guinea was going to be a temporary stop for him and his crew. As Bud was now physically closer to the battles of war he tried as often as possible to turn himself mentally to thoughts of his Idaho home. He was already making plans for his return after war's end (and was of course still griping about the Army's food):

> I decided to go to school when I get back, but don't know where to go to. Wonder if you would get a copy of the GI bill of rights and find out just what the deal is.

> P.S. George, if they fed you any food in the old days like they feed us now, I don't see how you got so big. I can't eat this damn stuff.[45]

As it turned out, by May 24, 1945, Bud's Army Air Force life in New Guinea was as "hurry up and wait" as it had been back in the states. But as the last sentence of a letter from Bud indicates, he was always aware of the potential danger that surrounded him:

> I was official censor today. I've read so many letters, I feel like a postmaster. You should read some of them, the mentality of some of those men is really low.

> Everything is quiet here. We don't have much to do except stand retreat in clean khaki uniforms. You do your own washing whenever you can get some water. . . . There isn't much to say about the place. The cockroaches bite big hunks out of my exposed [skin] every night.

I want you to write Washington and find out all the benefits you're entitled to. It's kinda gruesome to talk about but it is a good idea.[46]

On a Sunday one week later, while still in New Guinea, Bud penciled a letter home about the monotony of having nothing to do during a lull in action, writing that he was, "still laying around in this hole." Army Air Force censors restricted him from providing any details about the base, and Bud, now further from home than he had ever been, expressed anxiety about not receiving letters, reminding his parents, "Remember to use Airmail" so that their letters had a better chance of getting through to him. He was still thinking ahead to the end of the war and possible post-war life and career moves. He had become intrigued by conversations with his Army friends about career opportunities in engineering, and he appeared to be considering the possibility of a college education rather than returning home to work on a farm. He even went so far as to ask his parents to find out what the entrance qualifications were for the Colorado School of Mines.[47]

On May 30, 1945, Bud, lying in bed, wrote home about the poor weather and the continued lack of mail from home. He hoped that the mail service would improve once he returned to an area with a more permanent Army Post Office address. His frustration with his conditions abounded.

The most excitement Bud had of late was a different kind of "snafu," the Army Air Force losing his military records, which delayed his forthcoming promotion to first lieutenant (which would eventually come later, in the Philippines). Bud wrote at the time:

Haven't as yet received a letter from you here, but I hope soon. I got Nedra and Carole's letter yesterday.

Nothing has happened except I lost my records, every darn one of them. I don't know what I did with them, but they just disappeared. I can't get promoted until they find them. Our tour here shouldn't last over one year.

They say these Japs are pretty damn good shots. Just finished standing retreat. What a mess they [new soldiers] don't even know how to hold one [rifle].[48]

Then, in a postscript at the bottom of the letter dated the next day (May 31, 1945), Bud wrote that he had received orders to quickly move out, and he told his parents, "Just found out I won't be able to write you for a few days."[49]

On June 11, 1945, Bud was still in New Guinea, but he wrote that his unit might soon be shipped to Borneo. This was roughly midway through the Allied battle to liberate Borneo, and the Thirteenth Air Force and the Second Emergency Rescue Squadron were called on to play a major role in that battle.[50] Over the next month Bud finally saw the action he had been anticipating. He and his crew would play an intense but heroic role saving downed airmen as the U.S. Army Air Force accelerated its bombing missions against the Japanese on Borneo and other islands of the Indonesian chain.

Borneo is the largest island in Asia and the third largest island in the world. It is slightly larger than the U.S. state of Texas (and roughly three and a half times larger than Bud's home state of Idaho). It is located in the Indonesian chain of islands, north of Java and east of Sumatra. Pre-war Borneo was a part of the Netherlands (Dutch) Indies Asian colonies.[51]

The island of Borneo was a critical source of materials fueling the Japanese economy and war machine during World War II, being a major source of timber, oil, natural gas, coal, gold and rubber. Hence, Dutch participation in the 1941 embargo against Japan (as this book discussed *supra*, in Chapter 3) deeply and negatively affected Japan's economy. The Empire of Japan invaded Borneo in 1941, around the time of the December attack on Pearl Harbor. Borneo's resources were critically necessary for Japan to continue advancing its military.

From May 1 to June 21, 1945, Australian troops under command of Lieutenant General Leslie Morshead, supported by the

U.S. Navy's Seventh Fleet, mounted attacks against Japanese positions on Borneo. Known as Operation Oboe, it soon also called for the support of the U.S. Army Air Force Thirteenth Air Force's bombers and fighters.[52] A major objective of the campaign was to capture or destroy the large oil refineries that Japan had seized from the Royal Dutch Shell Oil Company at Balikpapan, as the refineries were a major fuel source for Japan's forces. Once again, the campaign's success required the support of air–sea rescue units of the Second Emergency Rescue Squadron, including Bud's, as the Japanese downed U.S. and Australian aircraft over the ocean.

Second Emergency Rescue Squadron air–sea rescue missions were now frequent. And yet Bud's letters home during this period did not speak of any specific combat action. Whether out of censorship or out of Bud's concern of worrying his parents, Bud never disclosed operational details in his communications home. But as it turns out, Bud was in the thick of combat during the Borneo Campaign, rescuing B-24 bomber crews and Army Air Force fighter aircraft (usually P-38s and P-47s).

Most of Bud's missions in Borneo involved rescuing American pilots whom the Japanese had shot down or who were otherwise forced to ditch their planes in the ocean (as might occur due to fuel or mechanical problems). The missions were performed in the face of incoming enemy fire. At other times, Bud's aircraft and crew played the role of "gunship," strafing enemy positions below. This too involved taking on intense enemy fire. There was constant danger at every turn.

What precise details we know of Bud's missions in Borneo come to us thanks to James Teegarden's archive of Second Emergency Rescue Squadron records (at http://pbyrescue.com), as well as from records from the U.S. Air Force Historical Office. The first of those documented missions occurred on July 13, 1945. Bud and the crew that he commanded and piloted in his PBY Catalina took off from Morotai at 0800 hours, proceeded around the east side of the Halmahera Islands and by 1055 hours reached an "orbit point" around the island of Ambon. There Bud's crew performed a standard battle mission, with their aircraft acting as both an offensive gunship and a potential defensive rescue craft, standing by to look for survivors in case of a downed aircraft. At the end of the mission they landed safely back on Morotai Island at 1430 hours.[53]

Meanwhile, other Allied action also continued in the areas around Borneo and the Celebes Islands. PBY crews were now constantly running search and rescue missions, intelligence gathering missions and missions transferring scouts to remote islands. As always, amidst the heat of battle Bud took time to write home about the poor food: "We buy bananas and coconuts from the natives because the chow is lousy. They serve powdered eggs sometimes."[54]

One must keep in mind that Bud, while growing up, had become accustomed to Idaho beef, ham, potatoes, eggs and vegetables fresh from the farm. Even the best-cooked military cuisine would seem bland and tasteless by comparison. The meat the Army served, in contrast to Bud's beloved Idaho beef, was often referred to as "mystery meat," with its origins and labeling often ambiguous or flat out unknown. Bud's tendency to mention food in his letters, though partly a result of ongoing censorship that necessitated discussion of more mundane aspects of wartime life, is also an indication that home was constantly on his mind.

But Bud was not alone in his complaints about the food being served to servicemen in the Pacific during World War II. Countless others echoed his sentiments about the poor quality of the food. The fact is, providing adequate necessities in an overseas combat zone was a particular challenge for the Army Quartermaster Corps in the Pacific. The hot, humid conditions there caused fresh food to spoil quickly, as did, at the outset, the length of time it took to transport the food to remote areas of operation.

For the Army to deliver fresh meats, fruits and vegetables to its servicemen proved to be a near impossibility. Instead, the Army had little choice but to feed its men and women from canned, packaged or otherwise preserved food that did not require refrigeration. This included such "delights" as powdered eggs and the infamous canned pork product "Spam." Pre-packaged foods like this could be more easily prepared in field mess kitchens, where they were known as "B-rations" (or "K-rations" when used during missions like those of the PBYs). Even then, however, packaged foods were not impervious to damage or spoilage, with cans often rusting, paper packages deteriorating from wet conditions and heat causing spoilage. On top of it all, there existed ever-present varmints, rats and insects ready to steal any food, whether good food or bad.

Military personnel supplemented their diets as best they could from local sources, as Bud described in his letters.[55] For the time being, Bud could only dream of returning home to fresh Idaho beef and potatoes at war's end. But his morale did somewhat improve after runs to Australia brought him fresh food, including Australian "beef." Indeed, the Army Air Force, recognizing the importance of food to military morale, was allowing its servicemen to make more frequent trips to Australia for food, including for "fresh meat, eggs, vegetables, fruits and milk," allowing them to eat heartier breakfasts, lunches and dinners.[56]

But food was a sideshow from the main happenings of the time. A surviving record documents that on July 18, 1945, Bud and his crew led another mission, this time rescuing a B-25 bomber crew that was downed in enemy territory. Fortunately for us, an officer documented the mission in extreme detail. So as not to shortchange the story, the officer's mission report, which highlights the incredibly important role that Second Emergency Rescue Squadron units like Bud's played in the Pacific during World War II, is reprinted here verbatim:

Second Lieutenant Frank P. Hayes, pilot of "Playmate Six One," departed Morotai on the morning of 18 July 1945 with orders to search the Talaud Island Group and the vicinity of 04°46'N, 127°14'E, from which position an SOS signal had been intercepted by passing aircraft. As Lieutenant Hayes was approaching the position given, he noted mirror flashes emanating from the South shore of Merampit Island 04°49'N 125°08'E.

Investigation disclosed six white men on the beach, preparing to launch a dinghy. **Lieutenant Hayes** circled the survivors and landed 300 yards off shore. The six men reached the rescue craft in fifteen minutes and were taken aboard at 1135. After jettisoning 400 gallons of gasoline, take-off was accomplished and **Lieutenant Hayes** returned to base, arriving at 1350.

The survivors, 1Lt R.D. Stover, T/Sgt B.F. Lewis, M/Sgt B. Miller, S/Sgt G.C. Pussey, all members of the 14th T.T. Squadron, were transferred to the 155th Station Hospital for examination and recuperation.

Lieutenant Stover, pilot of the ill-fated B-25 #469, stated that with a skeleton crew and three passengers he departed Hollandia on the morning of 13 July, heading for Morotai. However, encountering heavy weather and with no navigator aboard, he became lost and overshot his destination. When he broke out of the overcast, he found himself over a group of islands and having insufficient fuel to risk any further search for Morotai, he elected to ditch his plane in the shallow water just off shore and near a native village. The ditching procedure was entirely successful, all the occupants of the plane escaping without injury. With the help of friendly natives, part of their survival equipment was removed from the plane and taken to the nearby village where the survivors remained the first night.

The natives informed them that Japanese patrols frequented the island daily and that to remain in one place for over a few hours was dangerous. The following morning they were taken into the jungle and concealed throughout the day. The natives maintained contact with them and supplied them with food and water. After nightfall, the survivors and equipment were transported by native canoe to an adjacent island where they set up their "Gibson Girl" and began transmitting distress signals, which they later discovered were ineffective due to operational error.

During the remainder of the second night, they were concealed in the chief's house, the chief standing guard while they slept. On the first day of their sojourn on the island, a native informer notified the Japs of their presence which necessitated their constant moving. They hid by day and traveled from one island to another by night with the Japs ever in hot pursuit. On the night of 17 July, they received a message written in a mixture of Malayan and English stating that the Japs knew of their whereabouts and were closing in for the kill. They immediately left the village and hid in the jungle throughout the remainder of the night, transmitting distress signals almost constantly which were picked up early on the morning of 18 July by a passing aircraft, the position plotted and transmitted to Rescue Headquarters. A rescue plane and a crash boat were dispatched immediately upon receipt of the message. Since the Japs were closing in, the survivors abandoned all their equipment with the exception of the dinghy and were preparing to make a dash for the open sea when the rescue plane arrived. Lieutenant Stover felt certain their rescue could be attributed to the excellent assistance of the local natives and the final effectiveness of the Gibson Girl. Lessons learned from this rescue are that the services of a navigator on long over-water flights are essential and that air crews be briefed in the proper operation of survival equipment.[57]

This mission appears to have even attracted the attention of news reporters embedded with the U.S. military in the Pacific. Reporters issued the story via cleared military press wire services, and it appeared in two Idaho newspapers on August 10, 1945: The *Times-News* and *The Twin Falls Telegraph*, both out of Twin Falls, Idaho. The story headlines were "Filer Pilot Saves 6 Airmen Shot Down off Jap-Held Isle" and "Frank Hayes Takes U.S. Airmen from Jap-Infested Island." In addition to the news stories describing the circumstances surrounding Bud's successful mission, they also stated the following:

Lieutenant Hayes' sea-rescue unit is credited with saving 500 air crewmen whose planes were downed far from their home airbases. Fliers of the 13th Air Force, which had battled the Japs from the Guadalcanal to China, report the Catalina planes "are the best insurance a man can have when he goes on a mission."

Though the news articles' headlines are, of course, not "politically correct" today, they are indicative of the style in which news was being reporting during World War II. The words used clearly reflected the readership's antipathy at the time toward Japan in light of the 1941 attack on Pearl Harbor. Both individual families and the public at home would have been pleased by such good news.

The few surviving reports of Bud's missions reflect his acute piloting, navigational and leadership skills, often displayed during risky combat missions over the ocean and often involving the rescue of downed American bomber crews. In addition to the records of Bud's missions that this book has already presented, additional records show that Bud and his crew were involved in a near-daily routine of searching the ground and the ocean from their PBY Catalina. Still other records show that Bud and his crew also continued to use their PBY Catalina as a gunship, providing cover fire for combat operations taking place below.

For example, records show that on July 20, 1945, Bud's mission was to "Cover strike on Cenasena Island," with take-off at 0555 hours. The records go on to show that the mission was coordinated with "squadrons of Leopards" (Royal Australian Air

Force combat aircraft). After Bud's PBY Catalina and crew successfully provided air cover, they returned to Morotai at 1650 after nearly eleven hours of nonstop flight.[58]

Similarly, on July 29, 1945, Bud and his crew's mission in their PBY Catalina was to "Cover strike at Sedati, orbit at Lembeh Island." This was both a gunship mission and a potential search and rescue mission, with the PBY standing by to "orbit" in case the enemy downed aircraft during the combat portion of the mission.[59] Missions for Bud and the crew he commanded continued throughout the month of July and into August. They searched for other downed B-24 bomber aircraft on a consistent, near-daily basis and had to quickly respond to "S-O-S" signals from downed aircraft and to sight life rafts in vast, open swaths of ocean. Surviving records show that such missions were usually only interrupted by groundings due to weather or rare lulls in combat (and thus lulls in calls for rescue). Due to the constant missions, to the physical demands of the PBY Catalina and to challenges posed by the tropical environment, PBY Catalina pilot and crew fatigue was an ongoing difficulty they could only overcome through tenacity and dedication.

During both World War I and World War II an aviator's goal was to become a "Flying Ace." To be an "Ace," one had to have five or more verified aerial victories.[60] For fighter pilots during World War II, each confirmed kill of a Japanese enemy aircraft they shot down in the Pacific was later signified with its own individual Japanese "rising sun" flag painted under the successful pilot's cockpit canopy. For bomber pilots the tradition was similar, only the paintings were instead of bombs they had dropped.

In contrast, the Army Air Force's air–sea rescue squadrons had no "Ace" designation. The squadrons' crews worked together on PBY Catalina runs as a cohesive team, not as individuals. And because the crews rotated aircraft, there was normally no way of signifying on the aircraft the number of individual lives a respective crew had saved. Instead, the number of lives the crews saved on their runs collectively was kept on a tote board outside an operations tent at base.[61] And individual life rafts painted on the side of each PBY aircraft served as a representation of how many successful rescues the aircraft itself had accomplished. Overall, the Second Emergency Rescue Squadron's crews' work was, unlike their fighter and bomber counterparts, somewhat unheralded, with no particularly special individual awards or recognitions other than the traditional Air Force Air Medal.

Figure 11.8. U.S. Army Air Force Major Ben Mathis, Captain Gerald F. Wientjes, Captain Lloyd Humphreys and Captain Clarence Solander stand next to a board depicting a PBY Catalina and the number of men the Second Emergency Rescue Squadron had rescued to date in New Guinea, circa 1944–45.[62]

Figure 11.9. The side of a World War II-era PBY Catalina airplane painted with individual life rafts representing the number of lives the aircraft had been involved in saving.

What PBY crew members lacked in official awards or insignia for their good deeds was made up for by the pure euphoria that crews like Bud's felt with each life they saved. Whereas victory and success for fighter and bomber pilots came, necessarily, in the form of taking lives, for PBY crews victory and success came in the form of saving lives. The flip side was, of course, that any life that PBY Catalina rescue crew members were not able to save they considered a defeat, as well as a source of great sorrow and disappointment. But with no time to mourn, PBY pilots and their crews, whether successful or defeated in their prior mission, would rise anew the next morning for their next mission. With lives to save, the lack of respected designations like "Ace" was of no consequence to emergency rescue squadrons doing their duty.

PBY Catalina crews' joy at saving lives was enough to distract them from less-than-ideal internal flying conditions aboard their PBY Catalina "flying boats," which hardly involved the comfortable seating found with modern-day airline travel and even on modern-day military aircraft. PBY Catalinas were cramped, with seemingly every inch of non-crew space inside the aircraft claimed for necessary equipment, electronics, weaponry, parts, medical supplies, provisions and other stored items. A small bunk area and a galley, much like you might find on an actual boat, were located aft, providing some respite from otherwise uncomfortable conditions. The noise during a PBY mission included the loud roar and vibration from dual Pratt & Whitney Wasp fourteen-cylinder piston engines, chatter over the radio, radar pings, clanking from the metal fuselage, rattling parts and storage items, the occasional pop of a rivet and, of course, the report of machine guns when fired.

The ride aboard a PBY during a mission was a bumpy one, perhaps reminding Bud of his days spent manning farm tractors on the hard and unpredictable soil of Idaho farms. The aircraft would jolt and swerve throughout flight. This, combined with the PBY Catalina's relatively low ceiling, would preclude it from flying during extreme weather conditions like thunderstorms, so as not to injure the crew within. Nevertheless, PBYs would still hit tropical heat updrafts, heavy winds, surprise thunder clouds and ubiquitous tropical rainstorms. They often also performed evasive maneuvers to avoid enemy fire. So the ride aboard a PBY Catalina would always have its inevitable rough spots.

Adding to a crew's discomfort aboard a PBY aircraft during a mission, the air in the cabin involved a mixture of fuel exhaust fumes, cigarette or cigar smoke and odors from oil, seawater, human sweat, cordite from fired weapons and even at times from an overflowing toilet. A crew could attempt to mitigate such smells by opening portals to the outside, letting in cleaner, yet more humid, tropical air. All of the adverse internal mission flight conditions were compounded for the crew by extreme tropical heat and a complete lack of any kind of air conditioning. On clear days the hot, equatorial sun would pound down on a PBY Catalina, essentially baking the crew inside. But this was Bud's workplace, and that of all "rescue men" like him, and so they made what best of it they could during their daily missions. Lives, and the success of Allied campaigns in Borneo and the Indonesia region, depended on it.

With Lieutenant Bud Hayes piloting and commanding them, Bud's crew was constantly standing watch during their missions, peering through binoculars to look for any life raft (appearing as a tiny speck), or for a flash from a mirror from downed airmen below, or for any enemy that might seek to do them harm. Bud's rescue mission on July 25, 1945, proved that even the most attentive rescue crews could sometimes come up empty-handed.

On that day, during action in the Celebes Islands (in the Indonesian chain of islands) a B-24 bomber ditched in the sea after either being hit by Japanese fire or experiencing a more natural aircraft malfunction. Bud and his crew took off and began what would be an over ten hour detailed search of the waters below, trying to find the downed bomber's crew, which had sent an initial distress call. But Bud and his crew never spotted the downed bomber or its airmen.[63] As was the case in such situations, it is possible that the bomber's crew had been killed or captured by the Japanese enemy, or that it was lost to the sea aboard a sinking aircraft or a failing life raft before Bud's crew could reach them.

During such missions Bud was not one to give up easily. He was ever-determined to save downed airmen, and he would push missions, aircraft and crew to their limits trying to do so. During his crew's over ten-hour flight that particular day, they closely observed every island and every floating object in the sea below them. The PBY Catalina flew slowly, at low altitudes, exposing the aircraft and its crew to potential fire from enemy ground positions. Bud and his crew meticulously covered the entire search area from which the downed B-24 bomber's distress call, and later radio clicks, had originated.

Alas, the rescue crew's best intentions frustrated in not finding the bomber, at the end of the day Bud would have known from his training and experience the exact point at which their fuel, equipment and daylight had reached their absolute limits, necessitating

162

a return to base. Bud, commanding the PBY mission, had a responsibility to return his eight crewmen back to base safely. Due to wartime censorship, Bud remained unable to relay details of missions like that one in his letters back home to his parents. Even if the Army had permitted him to do so, Bud and his crew were now flying their intense missions on a daily basis, leaving him too tired to write in much detail. But for Bud's efforts during such missions the head of the U.S. Army Air Force in the Pacific, General George Kenney, awarded him the Air Medal. The award was officially memorialized in General Order Number 1951, issued September 10, 1945, as well as in a letter General Kenney sent to Bud's mother describing the recognition.[64]

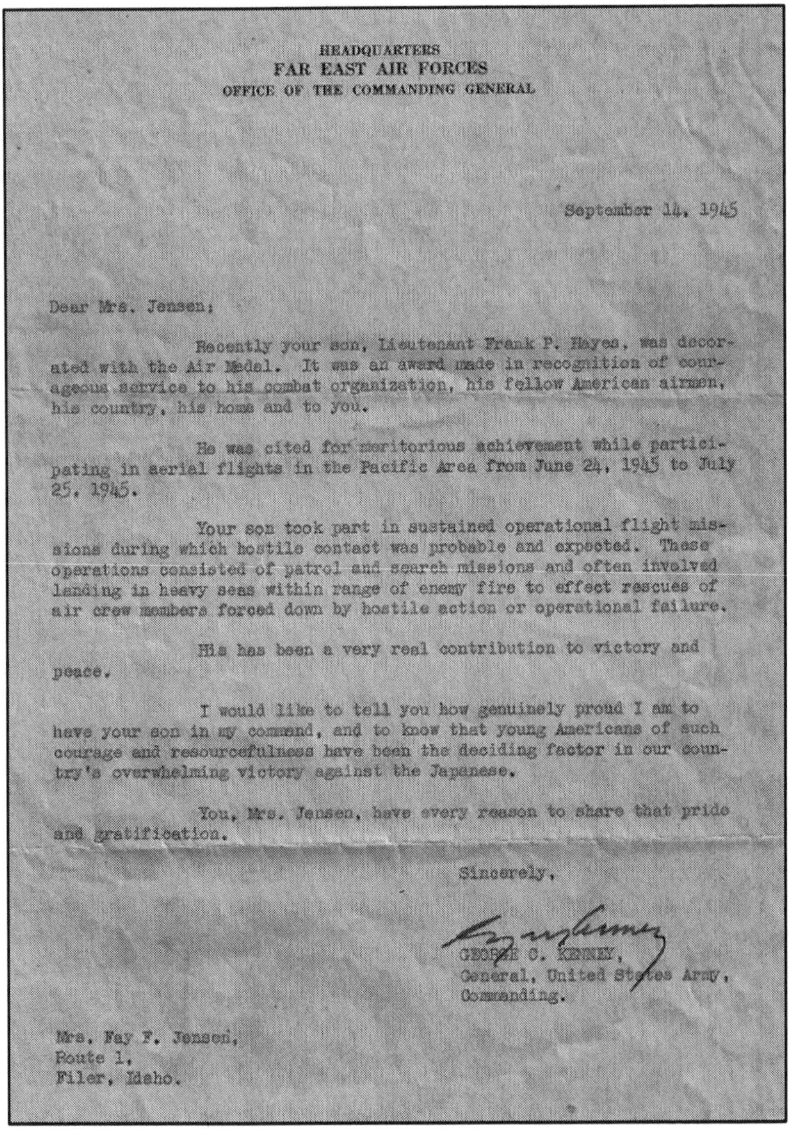

HEADQUARTERS
FAR EAST AIR FORCES
OFFICE OF THE COMMANDING GENERAL

September 14, 1945

Dear Mrs. Jensen:

Recently your son, Lieutenant Frank P. Hayes, was decorated with the Air Medal. It was an award made in recognition of courageous service to his combat organization, his fellow American airmen, his country, his home and to you.

He was cited for meritorious achievement while participating in aerial flights in the Pacific Area from June 24, 1945 to July 25, 1945.

Your son took part in sustained operational flight missions during which hostile contact was probable and expected. These operations consisted of patrol and search missions and often involved landing in heavy seas within range of enemy fire to effect rescues of air crew members forced down by hostile action or operational failure.

His has been a very real contribution to victory and peace.

I would like to tell you how genuinely proud I am to have your son in my command, and to know that young Americans of such courage and resourcefulness have been the deciding factor in our country's overwhelming victory against the Japanese.

You, Mrs. Jensen, have every reason to share that pride and gratification.

Sincerely,

GEORGE C. KENNEY,
General, United States Army,
Commanding.

Mrs. Fay F. Jensen,
Route 1,
Filer, Idaho.

Figure 11.10. Letter from U.S. Army Air Force General George C. Kenney to Bud's mother, Fay Jenson, announcing the awarding of the Air Medal to Bud for missions he flew in the Pacific between June 24, 1945, and July 25, 1945.

In the meantime, it was July 1945 when Bud next wrote to his parents. He was still based in New Guinea and, due to censorship, still tended to write about the more mundane happenings in his life at the base. In the letter, written "before the lights are turned out," he says he has to wake up at 3:00 a.m. the next morning to fly patrols. He was still frustrated about the lack of mail he was receiving from his parents, suspecting it was due to them not putting an "Air Mail" designation on their envelopes. But Bud had received letters from his niece, Carole (his sister Nedra's daughter, age nine), who was now writing to him once a week.[65]

In Bud's latest letter he also mentioned waiting in anticipation for a new pair of shoes to arrive from home, which he hoped to use on leave in Australia. As it would turn out later, he would receive neither the shoes nor the leave. Instead, the Army Air Force sent Bud and his PBY Catalina crew into action in the Borneo Campaign. There, Bud and his crew would find themselves pushed to their limits in multiple operations, including several heroic rescue missions for which they would receive commendations.

Further in Bud's 1945 letter, he expressed frustration with what he saw as poor performance from a PBY crew member. Bud had always been serious about his piloting and serious about the condition of his aircraft. And he was now equally serious about his officer and leadership responsibilities (traits that his school-teacher mother, Fay Fern, had no doubt instilled in him). By now Bud had seen casualties and, being responsible for the lives of eight men in a crew, he simply had no tolerance for incompetent crew members, writing, "They are still trying to ring Waas [most likely a co-pilot]] on me, but each time they do, I just tell them I won't fly if they send him with me."[66]

Bud's July 1945 letter also reveals that when he was not flying missions he and the rest of the squadron stationed on Morotai Island spent time battling the local animals and other natural elements. In Bud's own words:

We got up this morning and found that the rats had invaded us. They ruined everything we had that wasn't locked up. We had ice cream last night. I wasn't very good but it's mostly the idea I guess.

I really ought to clean up this tent, it's about as muddy as it is outside which is plenty. We don't even count a day if it doesn't rain.[67]

He went on to muse about how tough it would be when he got out of the Army and had to find work.

At the end of Bud's July 1945 letter he mentioned, for the first time, details from one of his combat (as opposed to rescue) missions. In this case Bud and his crew, flying their PBY Catalina as an offensive gunship, had confirmed hits on their enemy targets. Though Bud did not disclose the precise location of this action, he wrote: "We were on a strafing mission day before yesterday and got us a few small Jap boats. It's really duck soup when you catch them out alone."[68]

The next surviving record of Bud's missions was from August 1945, and it documents a particularly harrowing mission. Bud and his crew, then participating in the intense Borneo campaign, had once again been dispatched to find a downed B-24 bomber and rescue its crew. This time, however, their PBY Catalina encountered conditions directly threatening their own lives and requiring Bud to put his exceptional piloting and navigation skills into action to save his crew and those they had rescued. The mission, flown on August 2, 1945, is documented verbatim in the following action report (and is also presented in author Roscoe Creed's 1985 Naval Institute book titled *PBY: The Catalina Flying Boat*). Bud had his usual crew with him during the mission, including: co-pilot First Lieutenant Richard E. Costine, navigator Second Lieutenant Clayton L. "Greg" Gregersen, engineer Sergeant Robert N. Hubbard, radar man Sergeant Leonard Miller, radioman Sergeant Harlan M. Hagen and surgical tech Sergeant Meek. Details of the mission are as follows:

Lieutenant Frank P. Hayes, pilot of *"Playmate Six One,"* departed Morotai at 0455 in search of a missing B-24 crew that was reported down in the vicinity of 00°30'N, 126°00'E. Lieutenant Hayes arrived at the search area at 0725. After searching for approximately two hours without success, **Lieutenant Hayes** contacted *"Playmate Six Two"* and they started for home base together. At 1301 they were contacted by "Varmint" who had located several rafts true bearing from Cape Flesko. At 1515 **Lt Hayes** located the rafts 20 miles ESE of the location given. The rafts' actual position was 00°04'S, 124°41'E. A single one man raft and five one man rafts tied together. **Lieutenant Hayes** landed his rescue ship at 1540 in heavy swells and effected the rescue of one man from his raft. He then taxied 2 miles NNE, through heavy seas to the group of five one man rafts and picked up seven men. At 1630 he taxied North to find smoother water for take-off. At 1800 **Lieutenant Hayes** made four unsuccessful take-off attempts. His rescue ship was overloaded with water from taxiing, and the sea was just too rough. His crew was frantically bailing water, but large waves crashing over the ship made the effort futile. At 1850 he made one final attempt and finally the Catalina became airborne, the navigator's window broken by waves during the run. The radar, radios, and instruments were damaged by water and were of no use on the return to base. **Lieutenant Hayes** landed at Morotai at 2145.[69]

This mission exemplified Bud's determination and willpower under extraordinarily adverse conditions. A PBY Catalina normally operated during daylight hours, making it easier for crew members to spot downed airmen. But on this mission, the sun was rapidly setting at the time when Bud and his crew performed the rescue. And as if flying at night in a combat zone wasn't dangerous enough for Bud and his crew, their already naturally slow-moving PBY was further disadvantaged with no radio, with no radar and with other sea and battle damage. Operating over wide-open ocean during their mission they had been sitting ducks for the enemy, and they were at risk of potentially overflying their home base on a tiny island or being overtaken by the sea. It was the dead of night by the time Bud and his crew returned to their base on Morotai Island on the day of their harrowing mission. This meant they had to "fly blind" with only stars and manual mathematical calculations to guide them. Both Bud and his navigator's celestial navigation skills, and their intense training from places like Selman Army Air Field in Monroe, Louisiana, had been put into action, allowing them to safely reach Morotai. It was a successful mission to say the least for Bud and his crew, with them somehow managing to bring a damaged aircraft full of rescued survivors safely back to a small island in pitch darkness over a raging ocean and enemy territories.

Figure 11.11. An Allied rescue of a downed B-24 bomber crew in Netherlands East Indies, 1945.[70] The sight of downed pilots shown here is similar to what Bud and his crew would have seen during rescue missions.

Figure 11.12. Middleburg Island Air Field, New Guinea, 1944.[71] The size of the island demonstrates the challenges crews like Bud's would have faced spotting an island base under adverse circumstances like the ones they found themselves in during their mission on August 2, 1945.

Figure 11.13. A U.S. Army Air Force PBY Catalina parked on the runway on Morotai Island where Bud and his crew returned safely after a harrowing mission on August 2, 1945.[72]

By late August 1945, the Allies had brought their Borneo campaign to a successful completion. The Army Air Force next deployed the Second Emergency Rescue Squadron, including Bud, to the Philippines, where General MacArthur and the Allied forces were in a final push to clear Japanese forces from the Philippines for good. General Kenney and the Allies, having captured Luzon in the Philippines, wasted no time establishing Clark Air Base there in order to bring air operations in the Philippines to their full capacity. It would be the ideal base from which the Allies could attack Japan and win the war. The always-in-demand Second Emergency Rescue Squadron, including Bud, was moved there to support the combat efforts.

Meanwhile, General MacArthur had set up his Supreme Allied Command in Manila to prosecute the final phases of the war and ultimately to invade Japan's home islands. The tempo of war and its attendant Army Air Force rescue missions hastened. All could foresee that the end of war was nearing, but still did not know when or where the Allies would deal their decisive final blows. Bud's own squadron and crew carried on, hoping for the end of war, but not yet feeling it.

CHAPTER 12

On to Action in the Pacific Theater

THE ALLIES HAD DEFEATED Hitler and Germany, Italy's Mussolini was gone and the Allies now concentrated their efforts on liberating the Pacific from the grip (albeit a weakening one) of Prime Minister Hideki Tojo and his Imperial Empire of Japan. In July 1945, U.S. and Australian ground and air forces invaded Borneo. Simultaneously, U.S. General Douglas MacArthur conducted operations in the Philippines, and on July 5, 1945, he declared the Philippines liberated from Japan.

While all this was happening a secret military research center hidden in the desert of Southern New Mexico, near Los Alamos, was hard at work. There, the "Manhattan Project," headed by Major General Leslie Groves, of the U.S. Army Corps of Engineers, and J. Robert Oppenheimer, a noted physicist, was nearing its completion of the world's first atomic (nuclear) weapon—a radical new age weapon designed to end World War II.[1] On July 16, 1945, though blacked out from news coverage at the time, the first atomic bomb (nicknamed "Fat Man") was successfully test exploded at the remote Alamogordo Bombing and Gunnery Range.[2]

Whether the atomic bomb would indeed end the war was to be seen later. For the time being, General Douglas MacArthur and the Supreme Allied Command in Manila were focused on eliminating the Japanese from the remainder of their Asian conquests and on planning a direct invasion of Japan's home islands. Mac-

Arthur moved quickly to plan the Allies' next steps, thinking always of defeating Japan and ending the war. The U.S. Army Air Force by then had units stationed nearby at Clark Air Base on the island of Luzon in the Philippines.

Once General MacArthur had finalized his plans for an invasion of Japan (with the goal of winning the war), he was ready to set the plan into motion. The prospect of such a campaign was ominous, with the Allies remembering the losses they suffered in the ultimately successful prior Battle of Okinawa (from April 1 through June 23, 1945). The island of Okinawa, at the tip of Japan's string of islands, is 340 miles from the Japanese homeland. For eighty-two days during the Battle of Okinawa the Allies mounted the largest amphibious assault in history. The carnage was massive as not just Japanese soldiers fought the advancing Allies but so, too, did local civilians, who voluntarily threw themselves into the fight. In the end, American forces suffered sixty-five thousand casualties, including fourteen thousand dead.[3]

The death toll from the war in the Pacific ultimately surpassed that from the war in Europe. By the end of the New Guinea campaign in August 1945, Japanese forces had killed seventeen million to twenty-four million military personnel and civilians in Asia.[4] "Estimates are that for each month of 1945 that the war in the Pacific continued, upwards of two hundred and fifty thousand innocent people died."[5] As General MacArthur prepared to invade Japan, he reported to the Joint Chiefs of Staff and President Truman that although he was confident the invasion would ultimately be successful, he predicted it could involve anywhere from five hundred thousand to one million American casualties.[6]

In order for the Allies to accomplish their objectives during the invasion of Japan, MacArthur would need to have extensive air power on hand. He particularly needed the new B-29 heavy capacity bomber, as aided by fighter support from the U.S. Army Air Force. But as MacArthur continued to put his planned invasion of Japan into action, U.S. Navy aircraft carriers were for the most part deployed too far out of range to be of use during the planned campaign. So the question became, where would MacArthur get the aircraft units he needed in order to make the invasion of Japan a success?

MacArthur was by that time aware that the U.S. Army Air Force had been steadily moving aircraft units (of the Fifth and Thirteenth Air Forces) into Dutch New Guinea as a staging area for eventual combat actions. During the Borneo campaign these units had demonstrated their ability to achieve success and victory. However, many Army Air Force units, including those of Bud's Second Emergency Rescue Squadron, languished in New Guinea waiting to be ordered into new combat zones. As Bud's letters from around late summer 1945 confirm, after his crew's intense action in the Borneo campaign, they once again had relatively little to do. Even worse, airmen at his base had to endure unhealthy living conditions while awaiting new orders.

A military report on August 4, 1945, indicated that U.S. Army Air Force squadrons at that time had 2,306 "serviceable units," some of them spread out for thousands of miles, others concentrated in New Guinea.[7] With this number of fighters, bombers and transport aircraft, most of them flying and fighting over water, the Army Air Force's PBY rescue units would once again be essential and integral strategic players in rescuing downed fliers, running reconnaissance missions, strafing and other assigned duties during MacArthur's advance on Japan.

MacArthur, working with U.S. Army Air Force General George Kenney, told General Kenney to assemble his Army Air Force units, dividing them among the Fifth and Thirteenth Air Forces. The planes in these units were to be moved forward into action immediately, even though many of them were in bad operational condition and lacked spare parts.[8] Bud and the rest of the Second Emergency Rescue Squadron units in operation at that time were a high priority for moving to the front lines to support MacArthur's invasion of Japan. The Army Air Force transferred them from New Guinea to the newly-created Sorido Airstrip on the island of Luzon in the Philippines (later moved into Clark Air

Base).

Now at Luzon, and poised for MacArthur's advance on Japan, the Second Emergency Rescue Squadron was officially designated part of the 5230th Composite Rescue Group of the Thirteenth Air Force.[9] There, due to the squadron's role of rescuing downed airmen, it saw a revival of its nickname "Snafu Snatchers"[10] ("snafu," again, referring to plane accidents and "snatchers" referring to rescuers like Bud who plucked the accidents' survivors from the water). Fully organized under the Thirteenth Air Force, the Second Emergency Rescue Squadron, including Bud, was ready to put its unmatched air–sea rescue skills into operation in the Philippines in support of Allied aircraft's advance on Japan, saving lives there the way it had previously done in the New Guinea and Borneo campaigns.

Figure 12.1. A Second Emergency Rescue Squadron patch, depicting a PBY Catalina in front of Thirteenth Air Force insignia, that a Filipino painted at Clark Air Base in the Philippines, 1945.[11]

Figure 12.2. A depiction of a U.S. Army Air Force Second
Emergency Rescue Squadron PBY Catalina sporting the
"Snafu Snatchers" nickname next to an image of a
survivor in a life raft, 1945.[12]

The history of the U.S. Army Air Force's Thirteenth Air
Force is that it was created on December 14, 1942, for use in the
South and Southwest Pacific theater of war during World War II.
Its nickname, due to its location, was the "Jungle Air Force."[13]
Still in existence today, the Thirteenth Air Force played a major
role in the defeat of Japan in World War II, as discussed in the
following passage:

> Recent information reveals that WW II's key Pacific air force
> was the 13th Air Force. Probably unknown at the time, the
> aggressive 13th became the deciding factor in reducing the
> Pacific War's Japanese great military force to a non-entity in
> the South Pacific Theater. Defeat of the Japanese forces
> began with heavy bomber air support in the battle for the
> Solomons where the U.S. key offensive action of WW II
> began with the U.S. Marines landings on Guadalcanal in
> August of 1942.
>
> Next the 13th AF became the deciding factor in isolating and
> destroying Rabaul and Truk, Japan's most important bases
> and headquarters. Without these resources and reinforcements
> at Rabaul and Truk, every Japanese base, army and installa-

tion throughout the Pacific was left to survive on its own leading to the final defeat of that empire in 1945.[14]

Bud, stationed in the Philippines, next wrote home around August 14, 1945, announcing that his squadron had been moved, but writing only that it was now "somewhere in the Philippines." Bud and his crew's uniforms by then sported Thirteenth Air Force insignia.[15] He mused that the war might be over within five months.

On the island of Luzon, Bud and his crew had for a time lived in a hay field, "in the mud," but were transferred to regular barracks on the very day of Bud's letter. Bud was exasperated by the inflated cost of items in the Philippines and by the dishonest Filipinos he said he had encountered in his new location, writing:

They really have inflation here. It costs about ten dollars[16] to get your laundry done. When you try to get something in the restaurant, they hold you up, for example coffee costs 50 cents and no cream.[17] Slightly expensive.

To top it off some of these Filipino bastards stole my wallet and one other fellow's plus a 45 caliber pistol. We have the MPs working on it, but they won't find them. I lost my AIO [Air Instrument Operation] pass which I have to write to Washington DC about to explain my instrument card, address book and money. Two months ago these Phlips were working for the Japs and getting nothing for it. As soon as we got here they started charging outrageous prices for everything.[18]

Bud, returning in his letter to the subject of war operations, said that so far he and the PBY Catalina crew he commanded had rescued fourteen men and had flown over two hundred combat hours.[19] But again, due to wartime censorship, in Bud's letter he did not go into detail about any of those missions. Instead, it was only decades after the war ended that his surviving family members learned of the dangers and heroics involved in those missions. Bud's longtime navigator, Lieutenant Greg Gregersen, later sent a letter to Bud's mother Fay, in December 1945, in which he mentioned that Bud and their crew had by August 1945 flown nearly forty rescue missions.[20] By the end of the war that number was closer to fifty.

Figure 12.3. A pinup poster for the Second Emergency Rescue Squadron, showing the number of men the squadron had collectively rescued in the Pacific by war's end.[21]

At the end of August 1945, Bud's mother received a letter written by PBY Catalina squadron pilot, and Bud's then roommate, Lieutenant Keith W. Parks.[22] Lieutenant Parks informed her that Bud had sustained an injury—not from combat, but from recreational volleyball. Parks said he was writing the letter on Bud's behalf. During a volleyball game among airmen on base, Bud, "got his heart a little too much in the game and tipped the ball with his index finger, left hand" and fractured it while also chipping some bone. Parks wrote of Bud:

> He says he's going to get "drunk as a skunk" tomorrow night so you can rest assured that he is very much in condition. He won't be able to write for a week or two, so don't worry if you don't receive too many letters during that period.[23]

It is noteworthy that other than the injury to Bud's finger, his health remained strong wherever he was stationed in the Pacific. A significant number of American troops in the Pacific suffered (and many even died) from tropical diseases that were endemic to the jungle-filled islands on which servicemen were stationed. The most prevalent of these diseases were malaria (carried by mosquitoes), dysentery, dengue fever and other severe diseases from parasites in water and food. Yet amazingly, in none of Bud's letters did he ever mention (nor does his military record reflect) him having been sick. It is possible that his survival of diseases as a child and his zoonosis exposures at a young age on the family farm in Idaho allowed him to build up an extraordinary immunity that later sustained him in the jungle environments of the Pacific.[24] The finger injury would heal.

Just a few weeks before Bud's volleyball injury, important events took place that would set the wheels in motion to bring World War II to a swift and final end. President Franklin D. Roosevelt died in Hot Springs, Georgia on April 12, 1945. His Vice President, Harry S. Truman, assumed the office of President of the United States. Over the next months, Truman learned of Roosevelt's secret Manhattan Project and the potentially game-changing atomic weapon being developed, which was a secret that had been kept so close to the vest that as Vice President, Truman had known nothing of it. With this new knowledge Truman acted quickly and decisively, determined to end the war. By August 1945, the U.S. Army Air Force had, under General Curtis LeMay, already begun persistently firebombing Japan's homeland, mostly using B-29 bombers to do so. Nevertheless, the Empire of Japan continued to fight on. McArthur and military planners at the Joint Chiefs of Staff had previously told President Truman that a direct invasion of Japan's home islands (Operation Downfall) would likely result in at least five hundred thousand American casualties, not to mention perhaps millions of Japanese civilian casualties.[25] The U.S. forces' carnage-filled experience at Okinawa was still fresh on the minds of U.S. commanders. With the testing and perfection of the atomic bomb in July 1945, by August President Truman gave the order to end the war once and for all by dropping an atomic bomb on Japan. With the vast number of lives at stake if war continued, Truman saw this as "the least awful of the options available."[26]

On August 6, 1945, an atomic bomb known as "Little Boy" was loaded onto a specially-modified B-29 bomber named the Enola Gay, which was piloted by Colonel Paul Tibbets and his crew. They took off from Tinian Island in the Northern Marianas, approximately fifteen hundred miles south of Tokyo. Their flight to the target destination of Hiroshima would take the crew twelve hours.[27] From there, events proceeded as described in the following passage:

> On August 6 the U.S. dropped a uranium gun-type atomic bomb (Little Boy) on Hiroshima. American President Harry S. Truman called for Japan's surrender 16 hours later, warning them to "expect a rain of ruin from the air, the like of which has never been seen on this earth." Three days later, on August 9, the U.S. dropped a plutonium implosion-type bomb (Fat Man) on the city of Nagasaki. Within the first two to four

months of the bombings, the acute effects of the atomic bombings killed 90,000–146,000 people in Hiroshima and 39,000–80,000 in Nagasaki; roughly half of the deaths in each city occurred on the first day. During the following months, large numbers died from the effect of burns, radiation sickness, and other injuries, compounded by illness and malnutrition. In both cities, most of the dead were civilians, although Hiroshima had a sizable military garrison.[28]

Figure 12.4. Atomic bomb mushroom clouds over Hiroshima (left) and Nagasaki (right), August 1945.[29]

In addition to the pressure to surrender that the atomic bombs placed on Japan, on August 8, 1945, the Soviet Union declared war on Japan and, after ending Japan's occupation of Korea's Manchurian Peninsula, it invaded Japan from that position (to the northwest). By August 9, the Empire of Japan had finally had enough. Emperor Hirohito convened his war council and ordered that Japan surrender. The order was followed by an attempted coup, which failed. On September 2, 1945, Japan formally surrendered to General Douglas MacArthur and the Allies during proceedings in Tokyo Bay aboard the battleship U.S.S. Missouri (known as "Victory over Japan Day," or "V-J Day").[30]

Figure 12.5. The Empire of Japan surrenders to the Allies
aboard the U.S.S. Missouri, effectively ending
World War II, September 2, 1945.

Japan's surrender occurred on the very same day that Lieutenant Parks was writing to Fay Fern Jensen, informing her of her son Bud's broken finger. Also on that day, a member of Bud's Second Emergency Rescue Squadron, who had heard news of the surrender, recorded the following in his diary: "The war is over. No more sweating out raids in foxholes, no more missions where enemy fire is probable or expected."[31]

Nevertheless, despite Japan's surrender, poor communication from Japan (and the disbelief of many Japanese commanders) caused it to take several more months before "official" word of the surrender reached Japanese forces on remote outposts in the Philippines and elsewhere in the Pacific. Until they received that word, these forces held out in their positions on remote islands and in jungles. Meanwhile, for Allied forces stationed in the Pacific, news of war's end rolled into their bases. Airmen, soldiers, marines and sailors started to see the first signs of U.S. units

181

standing down, packing up, being deactivated and returning home to the states. Bud, however, was not among them. For Bud and his crew there was still work to do in the Pacific.

One of the few surviving Second Emergency Rescue Squadron recorded histories of its activities in the Pacific after Japan's surrender is from the month of September 1945. There had been a change of command over the emergency rescue squadrons from Major Gerard F. Wientjes (the uncle of Jim Teegarden, who is keeper of the extensive Second Emergency Rescue archive at http://pbyrescue.com) to Captain James L. Jarnagin. The Second Emergency Rescue Squadron still had fifteen PBY Catalina aircraft operating out of Clark Air Base on Luzon, Philippines. Over 126 Army Air Force missions were run in the surrounding area during the month of September 1945, with aircraft continuing to go down due to issues with weather, mechanicals or pilot error.[32]

By that time, the members of the Second Emergency Rescue Squadron who remained in the Pacific, like Bud, had moved from living in jungle conditions (which the Second Emergency Rescue Squadron had done from May 29, 1944, through September 17, 1945) to living in civilized military barracks. They were no longer living in the muddy conditions Bud had described in earlier letters. Instead, day-by-day Clark Air Base saw improvements in the condition of barracks, showers, mess halls and even the food, which was now fresher.[33] The Second Emergency Rescue Squadron report from September 1945 ended by certifying that the squadron was fully ready to carry on in the Pacific with its assigned mission.[34]

Bud, charged with being duty officer on base on September 12, 1945, wrote home. Mail delivery at the base was still slow and infrequent, but he had received some popcorn and commented that it was "just like home." His finger had healed a little crooked, and he worried that Army doctors might have to re-break it. Bud wondered when he might get to return to the states:

It's still the same old story, we haven't had a time set for us to come home. Most of the rumors are for a year and a half to two years. I don't see how they can I guess. There are 9 Cat [PBY] crews ahead of me in our squadron so I guess I'll be one of the last.[35]

As U.S. actions in the Pacific wound down, there were delays in Army Air Force members receiving promotions and deactivations. Army Air Force navigator, and then-second lieutenant, Bob "Spike" Ponders wrote of the frustration that he and others felt during this time:

I missed two promotions while overseas because of foul-ups in getting the paperwork done properly. My promotion from 2nd to 1st lieutenant was delayed a couple of months because of a mix-up on the paperwork. I had the time and grade, missions flown, and met all of the requirements but mistakes have been made on the paperwork and the recommendation had to be refiled. I met the requirements to be made captain but the war was over when my paperwork was turned in and the rules on procedures were changed and that paperwork was returned also. Since the war was over, the rules require more time in grade and since I was delayed and going from 2nd to 1st Lieutenant I was short of the new requirements for time in grade.

I was the next navigator in line to be relieved to return to the States when the war was over. When the war ended, they stopped sending new people over to relieve people already overseas, and instead started returning people to the States without replacing them—but set up certain rules to decide what order to use in returning people without regard to having replacements. I was sent to Clark Field outside Manila to await my turn to be returned to the States. The officials kept changing the methods of determining who would be returned to the States and about three times I got down to the point of being in the next group to come back to the States and then the system would be changed. I finally got disgusted with all the changes and having my hopes high and then being put back down the list that I signed up to stay another year overseas and then I knew when I would be coming home.[36]

But weighing more heavily on the remaining squadron members' minds was that they continued to be involved in difficult air–sea rescue missions, often over rough seas. The Army Air Force was still sending forces out to "mop-up" any remaining Japanese military holdouts in remote Pacific locations. And the emergency rescue squadrons were still running reconnaissance missions and missions to search for downed aircraft, one of which Bud wrote home about: "[Lieutenant] 'Pop' Guess made another tough rescue, 29 men in rough water. [Lieutenants] Parks and Guess are being promoted, I guess I never will be."[37]

On September 24, 1945, as the war continued to wind down and Bud remained stationed at Clark Air Base, he wrote home cynically about new officers arriving who had never seen combat and were desperate to have their war records show they were in "active duty" in a theater of war. Bud was by that time flying observation missions to, among other places, Hong Kong, Hainan (a Chinese island) and Formosa (now Taiwan). He and his PBY Catalina crew were also still actively engaged in ongoing rescue operations:

I directed another rescue the other day. I found a crew in the water about halfway to Okinawa, but the water was too rough to land so we called a surface ship and they picked them up (8). That makes my total [men rescued] 22.

God only knows when we will get home, all I know is that I'm fed up with this army. . . . I wish I was there [home] to help.[38]

This is the last of Bud's surviving letters. It was written on September 29, 1945, and sent to his sister Nedra in Twin Falls, Idaho. In the letter, Bud was again anticipating life after the Army

Air Force. Airmen and support personnel were rapidly returning home to the U.S. He was certain that with the war over he would soon receive orders returning him to his Idaho home.

Bud's final letter reflects the sentiment of most servicemen who were still stationed in the Pacific at that time. He had his fill of military life and combat. His past visions of glory and excitement and his previous enthusiasm to fly had dulled. His thoughts focused instead on returning home, on going to college and on possible careers—getting his life back together, perhaps even finding that long-sought relationship allowing him to settle down and start his own family.

For the time being, Bud enjoyed visits with the squadron chaplain, Patrick Coyle, who was a welcome friend and is mentioned in this portion of Bud's letter:

I haven't written for some time but things have been all messed up these last few weeks. We are in our tents now and ours is very nice.

One of the boys here and myself are trying to learn a little Spanish. We have an outline by Greenfield of Purdue U. (Hablo español bien?) I have decided to take it in college. I haven't decided where to go as yet, but I think I'll go with one of the fellas that is here with me.

I don't think I will be home for at least six more months but I suppose that it's just as well. Just so I get home before school starts next year.

Chaplain Coyle just stopped by the tent. He is a real army chaplain. He doesn't think a thing of dropping in for a beer and shooting the bull with the boys. All I can say is that here is a grand person all around.[39]

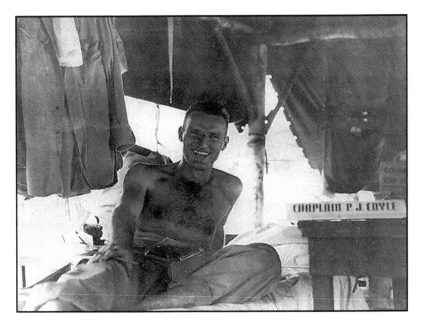

Figure 12.6. Bud's friend U.S. Army Air Force Second Emergency Rescue Squadron Chaplain Patrick J. Coyle, at Clark Air Base on Luzon, Philippines, 1945.[40]

Bud's final letter also mentioned that his anxiety over not receiving mail from home for months had finally been relieved. Military V-Mail had delivered an entire two and a half months of letters from home to him, increasing his desire to return home to Idaho. New PBY crews were by then rolling into Clark Air Base and slowly taking over flying duties: "We got some green crews in from the states and they have been doing most of the flying," Bud wrote.[41] This perhaps gave Bud renewed hope that he might soon return to his home and see his family in Filer, Idaho. Things were looking up.

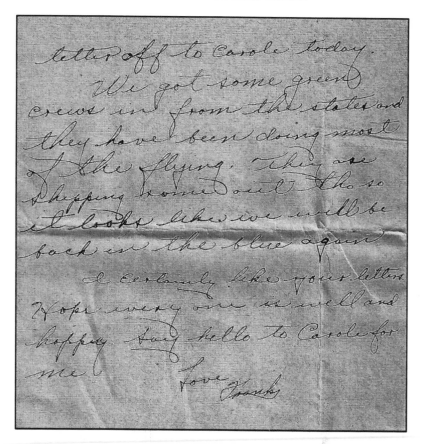

Figure 12.7. A portion of Lieutenant Frank Philby "Bud" Hayes's last known letter home to his family, September 29, 1945.

CHAPTER 13

Bud's Final Mission

L IEUTENANT FRANK PHILBY "BUD" HAYES'S final mission began in a PBY Catalina on October 7, 1945, and soon thereafter ended in tragedy. For one to fully understand what befell Bud and his crew during their fateful mission that began that day, it is important to present more about the particular difficulties involved in piloting PBY Catalinas. Although multiple elements contributed to the disastrous outcome of Bud's final mission, the inherent and unavoidable difficulties of controlling PBY Catalinas was certainly a factor.

Put plainly, the PBY Catalina (OA-10A) aircraft was not an easy airplane to fly. Catalinas (which, as this book mentioned several times *supra*, were sometimes called "flying boats") were developed in the late 1930s from the innovative vision of the Consolidated Aircraft Company's founder, Reuben Fleet, and were far ahead of their time in terms of perfected amphibious aircraft. The PBY Catalina was both a boat and an airplane, possessing the advantages and liabilities of each. Its unique design and its large wing fuel tank capacity allowed it to be one of the few military aircraft that could sustain flight for virtually a full day without refueling. Hence, PBY Catalina runs of ten or more hours were not uncommon.

For a pilot to successfully operate a Catalina required a combination of exceptional skill and pure brute strength. Taking off from or landing on land or calm waters (as might be found in lakes or bays) was of no great difficulty for a PBY Catalina and its crew. But negotiating rough seawaters, like Bud and the rest of the Army Air Force's Second Emergency Rescue Squadron did on a near-daily basis while stationed in the Pacific, was a far different story.

The PBY Catalina was sixty-five feet long and twenty feet in height, with a wingspan of about 104 feet, the wings being mounted over the fuselage about eight feet above the pontoon bottom hull/fuselage. The aircraft's size and configuration presented a challenge for pilots flying in open seas, as they had to confront resistance from moving water which slowed takeoff speeds making it harder for the pilot to attain lift. In addition, and far too often, choppy sea waves caused a PBY Catalina to be misbalanced during attempted takeoffs. The aircraft had no flaps and thus required long runs of two to three miles (depending on weight load) on water to generate sufficient lift for takeoff. The cockpit was relatively large in order to accommodate stocky pilots like Bud who were more physically capable of controlling the plane.

A PBY Catalina takeoff at sea required close coordination of pilot, co-pilot and, up in the wing spar, the flight engineer. The engineer managed engine power signals through a light-panel on the pilot's dashboard. Once the engines achieved the desired power levels, the pilot would operate the wing controls to "rock" the plane, keeping the wing floats out of the water and keeping the wings themselves as horizontally balanced as possible to maximize lift. At the same time, the pilot would be handling the throttle, the elevators and the rudder (with foot controls). And with left arm pulling forward the yoke (a control wheel), the pilot would then bring the Catalina's nose up at just the right moment, achieving lift. While the pilot was performing those duties, the co-pilot would wrap his arms around the aircraft's yoke and, against the heavy water resistance, would use it to assist the pilot in rocking the aircraft and eventually pulling it back and achieving lift.

That entire test of strength, coordination and team effort was a routine requirement in getting a PBY Catalina to successfully take off from the sea. From there, it was a long, slow, lumbering climb to attain altitude. It was common for a Catalina to take on extra weight in the form of seawater or survivors they had rescued, which often necessitated that the pilot calculate needs and jettison fuel or that the crew rapidly pump out water to lighten the aircraft for achieving lift and altitude. Overall, sea-based takeoffs in a PBY Catalina were always a challenge, even for the most experienced PBY pilots.[1]

Figure 13.1. A U.S. Army Air Force Second Emergency Rescue Squadron PBY Catalina during sea-based takeoff in the Pacific, 1945.[2]

Maintenance challenges were also a constant with the PBY Catalina, even in the best of times. PBY Catalinas operated on long flights in remote locations, which meant the aircraft at all times had to carry a supply of spare parts, portable work stands, a sea anchor and related repair equipment, as well as a certified aircraft mechanic and a flight engineer. The PBY Catalina, like other machines manufactured during World War II, was assem-

190

bled quickly, with any defects in workmanship corrected later on in the field. During the war a Cat would operate all day, and would then undergo maintenance at night and be back on the taxiway at base the next day. In the morning, Army Air Force air–sea rescue crews, which were not assigned permanently to one respective aircraft, would take the first Cat available on the tarmac for their respective missions.

As rugged as the PBY Catalina was, freeze-thaw, vibrations and other such factors gave it a propensity over time to pop rivets in the fuselage or the floating hull below (which were sometimes additionally or alternatively damaged with bullet holes from incoming ground fire).[3] Other elements, such as the natural accumulation of bilge water, added weight to Catalinas, which complicated or even impeded takeoffs. In a documentary about the PBY Catalina, World War II-era PBY mechanic Clarence Lee Coon mentions that mechanics like himself innovatively carried a large bag full of wooden golf tees, which worked perfectly for plugging rivet (or bullet) holes in the aircraft's floats.[4]

By the end of World War II, PBY aircraft were approaching or were at airframe limits of wear and tear. Proper aircraft maintenance was often running behind schedule, and parts were in short supply. The Cats were simply not on the Army Air Force's list of maintenance priorities at war's end. Mechanics did what they could to keep the aircraft flying, including cannibalizing parts from disabled Catalinas.

Meanwhile, the Army Air Force was busy transporting men and equipment back to the states and carrying out other transport missions, including to Japan and liberated areas of Asia. Bud's Second Emergency Rescue Squadron was making due with whatever Catalina repairs were possible. But on October 7, 1945, all of the factors surrounding PBY Catalina operation and the Cats' condition at the end of the war, along with the unpredictability of mother nature, would converge in a perfect storm leading to tragic results on Bud's final mission.

Into the remainder of September and October 1945, Allied

aircraft continued to fly missions scouting and investigating remote islands in the Pacific where some Japanese soldiers had not yet received word of Japan's surrender and the war's end.[5] The details of Bud's final mission come to us from an official Missing Air Crew Report and from post-action report letters written by Second Emergency Rescue Squadron Chaplain Patrick J. Coyle and by Bud's navigator the day of the mission, Lieutenant Clayton L. "Greg" Gregersen. Details of the mission also come from an investigative statement made by Captain Silverio L. Cadiao of the Philippine Army.[6]

In late September 1945, squadron commander Captain James L. Jarnagin delivered long-awaited news that the Army Air Force had approved Bud's promotion to first lieutenant. Bud (wearing his new insignia) and his new co-pilot were called in to Captain Jarnagin's office so he could brief them on a new mission they were assigned to carry out the next week. Bud's co-pilot throughout the war, Lieutenant Richard Costine, had already rotated back to the states. Flight Officer John "Jack" Leonard, age twenty-one, was Bud's new co-pilot.

John "Jack" Leonard and Bud were the same age. Likewise, they had both wanted to fly for as long as they could remember, and both joined the U.S. Army Air Force shortly after high school graduation. Jack hailed from Hackensack, New Jersey, a suburb about twelve miles from New York City. He came from a family with five boys and one girl. Two of his brothers were also serving in the Army during World War II. (His older brother, Bill, hit the Normandy beaches on D-Day, and his younger brother, Larry, later joined the Navy, becoming a decorated sailor in the Korean War.) Jack was an experienced co-pilot, having flown over forty-two combat missions while serving in the Second Emergency Rescue Squadron. He had been awarded the Air Medal and the Purple Heart. Jack had a reputation of being friendly to everyone, was skilled at drawing and other artwork and was handsome.[7]

Figure 13.2. Second Lieutenant John "Jack" Leonard, Bud's co-pilot by the end of September 1945, and on Bud's final mission beginning on October 7, 1945.[8]

Bud and Jack hailed from opposite ends of the U.S. continent, grew up in a small town versus a metropolitan suburb and came from a small family versus a large one (one Methodist, the other Catholic). But they shared a common bond in their love of flying and in their dedication, professionalism and patriotism. The two hit it off immediately.

At the time of Bud and Jack's new mission briefing in late September 1945, Jack Leonard was waiting for a promotion from flight officer to second lieutenant, which was in the final stages of approval but was delayed by slow-moving paperwork (and was only eventually awarded posthumously). During the briefing the two pilots reviewed maps, coordinates, mission details and operational details. This was to be a routine "pickup and deliver" operation, far from the risky combat and rescue missions Bud had flown during the preceding months. Orders were for Bud, Jack and their PBY Catalina crew to transport a reconnaissance party of Army Signal Corpsman (a "recon team") that was investigating a sighting of a downed aircraft on Mt. Madia (near Culasi, on the Philippine Island of Panay).[9]

The mission itself began the following week, on October 7, 1945. It was a Sunday morning. Bud was up early, allowing him to hit the mess hall for food fresh out of the oven. There he met Jack, and the two ate a hearty breakfast. The Philippine weather that day was already pushing over eighty degrees Fahrenheit, carrying with it the usual heavy humidity. An Air Force meteorology report advised that they could expect a high temperature in the nineties, 100 percent humidity, clear and sunny skies and moderate tropical breezes. There was nothing untoward on the weather horizon, other than the usual potential for a pop-up rainstorm. Overall, it appeared to be good weather in which to fly a PBY Catalina mission.

After breakfast, Bud and Jack, both religiously observant, headed for the chaplain's tent to attend the Sunday morning service offered by Bud's friend Father Patrick J. Coyle. Father Coyle, who was chaplain of the Second Emergency Rescue Squadron, had provided extraordinary spiritual support to the men of the squadron throughout their intense combat and rescue missions during the previous months. In the best tradition of the Army Chaplain Corps, he was trained to minister for multiple religious denominations. Coyle had a keen skill at bridging all religious sects and appealing to the almighty to protect the men of the Army Air Force.

Next up that morning, Bud and Jack assembled their crew. Apart from Jack, Bud's crew consisted of most of the same PBY Catalina crewmen who had flown with him throughout his service in the war. The aircraft that day was to be well staffed with highly skilled and highly experienced professionals. They included navigator Second Lieutenant Clayton L. "Greg" Gregersen, radioman

Sergeant Leonard Miller and flight engineer Sergeant Robert Hubbard.[10]

The reduced crew size was due to the end of combat conditions in the Pacific. With PBY Catalinas no longer carrying machine guns, ammunition and extra stockpiles of supplies and emergency equipment, gunners and medical techs were no longer included as crewmembers. On this particular mission that lighter load and the increased space allowed for the room and weight needed to carry the Army search team that Bud's crew would be transporting.

As was the practice at the time, Bud's crew grabbed the first PBY Catalina they came across on the tarmac at Clark Air Base that day. The Catalina they chose was Number 44-34052, an aircraft that had seen much action but had nevertheless been cleared as airworthy and ready for operation that day. This PBY, like all others in the U.S. Army Air Force fleet, had been manufactured by Canada's Vickers, Ltd. Bud, his co-pilot Jack and his flight engineer Sergeant Hubbard did their normal detailed pre-flight check, which revealed that everything seemed to be in order. Jack and Hubbard gave Bud a "thumbs up" signal. The crew was ready to commence its mission.

On-board the Catalina, Bud and Jack went through a takeoff checklist and proceeded with their fine-tuned art of firing up the Catalina's Wasp engines. Bud pressed the ignition while Jack feathered the primer switch and Hubbard monitored the mechanicals. Engine one's fourteen cylinders sputtered to life, then engine two's did likewise. Once the engines both reached eighteen hundred revolutions per minute, the pilots were clear for routine takeoff. Jack steered the plane along the Clark Air Base taxiway, then turned onto the main runway. The PBY Catalina, reaching a speed of eighty knots, was quickly aloft, and its crew was on its way out over the Pacific like so many times before.

Once Bud and his crew departed Clark Air Base on Luzon, they headed south to the southern tip of the island of Panay where Iloilo City was located, a distance of approximately 350 miles. At a normal cruising speed (117 miles per hour), that leg of the flight would take approximately three hours. There was no longer any need for the crew to push the Catalina's engines, nor any need to squint through binoculars at the ocean below scanning for life rafts or Japanese enemy combatants. Those concerns had faded into the past, along with the war itself.

Upon the PBY's landing on Panay, the crew picked up the Army recon team that was awaiting its flight. The recon team was from the 594th Joint Assault Signal Company, headed by First Lieutenant William Kell and assisted by Philippine Army Captain Silverio L. Cadiao, who served as guide and translator. Other members of the team were Staff Sergeant John T. Garvey, Private First Class Thomas J. McCary and Private First Class Wayne H. Peoples.[11]

Bud's longtime navigator, Lieutenant Clayton L. "Greg" Gregersen, was aboard Bud's PBY Catalina that day. He later sent a letter to Bud's mother Fay, which documents the events that unfolded after the crew landed on Panay. The events are described in the following excerpt from that letter (in which Gregersen refers to Bud by his pilot nickname of "Ape," which he was probably given due to his stocky build):

We were ordered to pick up an investigating party at Iloilo, Panay, Island, Philippines. The party was to be flown to a designated desolate beach on the west coast of Panay, put ashore there and picked up a few days later.

The nose window of the plane cracked out when we landed; thus we had to beach the plane, and radio for parts, repairs and mechanics. Help arrived two days later and our plane was repaired.

On [Wednesday] October 10, in the afternoon, the party arrived on the beach [at Culasi, toward the northwest point of Panay Island], ready to be flown back to Iloilo. We attempted to take off about six o'clock that evening.

The water was very treacherous at that time and place. The takeoff promised to be a difficult one. Just as Ape got flying speed, trying to pull the plane off the water, the swells changed direction and lengthened their troughs. We were thrown into a bad bouncing altitude and the third bounce was our last. The plane had been hurled over forward (nose down), and crashed hard into a huge swell. The plane simply disintegrated from the wheels forward. The entire plane sunk out of sight less than twenty-five minutes after we started the takeoff.

The crew chief and I got the life raft out and picked up the wounded men in the water. On taking a check I found that Ape, his co-pilot and one passenger were missing. A Filipino scout and I tried to dive and swim into the plane to recover the men. Before we could make any headway, the entire plane started sinking rapidly, and to save ourselves we had to swim clear.

The natives from the nearby village of Culasi cared for us and tended our hurts. Today, all but three of the survivors are on their feet and back on duty. Sergeant Hubbard and Sergeant Miller are still in the hospital at Mindoro. God himself spared those of us who are alive today. I also know God himself has taken care of Ape and his soul in the peace and quiet. We loved him, all of us.

The Navy dispatched divers and boats to attempt recovery of bodies and wreckage. I joined them on their trip. Unfortunately, the water was too muddy to dive in, on top of being 140 feet deep. We found nothing.[12]

The "swell" that Lieutenant Gregersen described was a "rogue wave," which is a known phenomenon in the Pacific. It is a random, larger-than-normal wave. Witnesses to the one that hit Bud's PBY Catalina that day said that the wave was well over

197

twenty feet high at the moment of impact on the aircraft. Such a wave would constitute literally tons of water pushing into the aircraft at high pressure.

As for the disintegration that Gregersen referred to in his letter, it is believed from the official Missing Air Crew Report documenting the incident that the swell made a direct hit to the PBY's nose (where the compartment housing the flight crew is located), causing the nose to break apart from the main fuselage and sink quickly. As it sank, water pressure would have sealed the bulkhead door behind the cockpit (which was by that point backside up under the water). The water pressure also would have sealed the cockpit ceiling hatch, which was sideways under water. It is possible that the force from the wave's impact might have also knocked out the cockpit's occupants.

This was not the first time that rogue waves were responsible for a PBY Catalina's demise in the Pacific. Such waves were a known hazard for Second Emergency Rescue Squadron operations. For example, First Lieutenant Bob "Spike" Ponder, a navigator in the Second Emergency Rescue Squadron during World War II, tells of a PBY Catalina crashing amid larger-than-usual waves during the New Guinea campaign earlier on in 1945:

> The waves were quite high at that time and the plane crashed while trying to take off, killing some and injuring more people. In getting the plane airborne from the water, ideal conditions would be to have a chop or small to medium size waves for takeoff. If the water is real calm, it is difficult to get the bottom of the plane to lift off the water. If the waves are too high they tend to throw the airplane into the air before it reaches enough airspeed and the plane belly-flops onto the next wave and breaks apart or the plane comes down nose first and dives into the next wave which can also cause the plane to break apart. In this case, the plane came down nose first.[13]

The website Archaehistoria also contains examples of PBYs succumbing to rough wave conditions, in those cases off the Florida coast. The PBY's components were separated by bulkheads, and in at least one of the crashes in Florida a bulkhead in the nose/cockpit area separated.[14] It was not so unlike what happened to Bud's Catalina in the Pacific.

If a rogue wave hit a PBY from behind or laterally, sometimes the aircraft would sink but would remain relatively intact. And that would in turn sometimes allow the crew to escape. But due to the location of PBY Catalina bulkheads, the aircraft was more susceptible to breaking apart under the extraordinary weight and pressure of a direct hit around its nose. Had Bud's PBY Catalina been at a different angle on the day of his final mission, the outcome from the rogue wave might have been quite different.

The Missing Air Crew Report from Bud's final mission states that all on-board the Catalina at the time of the accident were able to escape from the main fuselage, except for three men. The three men who did not escape were Lieutenant Bud Hayes (the pilot), Flight Officer Jack Leonard (the co-pilot) and Private First Class Wayne Peoples (of the Army recon team), all of whom went down with the aircraft. Private Peoples had apparently wanted to watch the takeoff from the cockpit, and the pilots allowed him to do so. As for the survivors, four of the men on the recon team were seriously injured and hospitalized. They included Lieutenant William Kell, Sergeant Thomas McCary and Sergeant John Carvey. Bud's crew members Sergeants Miller (radioman) and Hubbard (flight engineer) were also injured.[15]

In response to the crash, the Navy dispatched PT boats to assist in the rescue. They transported the injured survivors to the military hospital on the island of Mindoro where all ultimately fully recovered. The Navy also dispatched divers who, with the help of local fisherman, tried to recover the three men who went down with the PBY. However, the waters were too turbulent, impeding visibility and causing the recovery operations to be abandoned at that time. Reliable reports from local fisherman stated that the plane had settled on the coastal sea-shelf at a depth of approximately thirty yards (or ninety feet).[16] The aircraft was simply too deep for the Navy's dive technology at the time. The Missing Air Crew Report states, with some precision, that the remains of Bud's PBY Catalina are "at course 190°, 1,500 yards off the shore of the barrio of Culasi, Province of Antique, Panay, Philippines," in approximately one hundred feet of water.[17] The report further states that, "The circumstances of loss of the aircraft and crew were such as to preclude any possibility of recovery of the missing personnel at the time of the crash or subsequently."[18] That assessment was based on the technology and the recovery resources then-existing, in October 1945. There is no record of any further attempts to retrieve the aircraft and the bodies within. First Lieutenant Frank Philby "Bud" Hayes, Second Lieutenant John Leonard and Private Wayne Peoples, who all sank in the Pacific's waters in their PBY Catalina on October 10, 1945, have remained there for over seventy years.

Back in Bud's hometown of Filer, Idaho, his mother Fay received word of the loss of Bud by telephone from a local Army representative. Because the phone service at her farm was a party line, the sad news was not private; every neighbor heard the shocking news at the same time. The Army made an official in-person visit to the farm shortly thereafter. And formal notice of Bud's status was dispatched by letter that same day from headquarters at Clark Air Base. In the dispatch, Second Emergency Rescue Squadron Captain James L. Jarnagin offered his deepest sympathies and confirmed that the crash had been witnessed by natives of the barrio of Culasi on Panay, Philippines, who also assisted in the rescue of survivors.[19]

Post-crash letters that survive to this day, including the one from Captain Jarnagin, are replete with praise for Bud, revealing that his colleagues, his commanders and even the Army Air Corps generals at Allied Headquarters held him in high esteem. Throughout everything Bud had experienced since volunteering to serve in the war he never lost his warm, friendly, gregarious and helpful personality, which he had developed growing up as a farm boy in Filer, Idaho. But he was also a serious pilot and a serious commander whose expertise and experience was valued and admired up the chain of command. Captain Jarnagin wrote to Fay:

> I know it will be a consolation to you to know that your son was greatly admired and respected. He was a fine gentleman and officer in the true American tradition. Your grief and sorrow at this time is shared by every member of this organization. The respect your son has earned by his diligent work will long remain in our memories.[20]

Chaplain Patrick J. Coyle of the Second Emergency Rescue Squadron, who Bud spoke so highly of during his tour of duty, also wrote a heartfelt letter to Bud's mother. That letter, from Luzon, Philippines on October 29, 1945, stated, "Your son was well thought of in the squadron and I had the pleasure of knowing him well." Even Supreme Allied Commander General Douglas MacArthur himself dispatched a personal letter of condolence to Bud's family, on October 31, 1945. Though the letter was short and standard to form, it was nonetheless a significant act from a General who had lost thousands of men in the victory over Japan and was deeply involved in the military occupation of Japan at the time of the letter. Such letters were a mark of General MacArthur's admirable values.

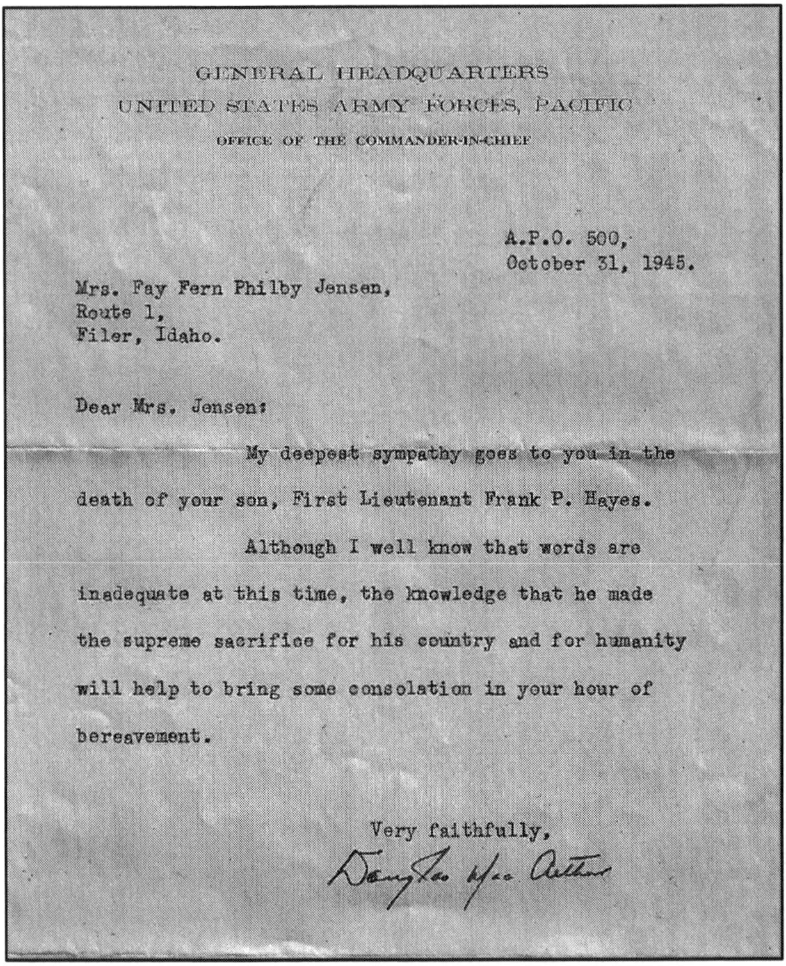

GENERAL HEADQUARTERS
UNITED STATES ARMY FORCES, PACIFIC
OFFICE OF THE COMMANDER-IN-CHIEF

                                        A.P.O. 500,
                                        October 31, 1945.
Mrs. Fay Fern Philby Jensen,
Route 1,
Filer, Idaho.

Dear Mrs. Jensen:

          My deepest sympathy goes to you in the

death of your son, First Lieutenant Frank P. Hayes.

          Although I well know that words are

inadequate at this time, the knowledge that he made

the supreme sacrifice for his country and for humanity

will help to bring some consolation in your hour of

bereavement.

                              Very faithfully,

                              Douglas MacArthur

Figure 13.3. Letter of condolence from Supreme Allied Commander General Douglas MacArthur to Bud's mother Fay Fern Jensen, October 31, 1945.

The reaction back in Filer, Idaho to the loss of Bud was undoubtedly one of extreme distress and disbelief. Bud's final letters led all to believe that he would be home shortly. Conversation had surely already been underway between the Jensen, Hayes and Greene branches of Bud's family, as well as among their neighbors and friends, about plans for welcoming Bud home; perhaps even about a welcoming parade in Filer or Twin Falls. They had likely also been wondering what college and job opportunities awaited Bud; or perhaps they hoped he might rejoin the family farming business. All we know for certain about the reaction back home comes from family member recollections. For example, Bud's niece, Carla Faye Grabert-Lowenstein, recalls being told that her grandmother (Bud's mother, Fay Fern) cried out, "They took my son!" in despair, and later in great anger at the Army Air Force.[21]

From around the time of the loss of Bud until Fay Fern's death in 1979, she never again spoke of Bud or the circumstances surrounding his tragic final mission. The records of Bud's service that the author used in writing this book had been packed in a box and secreted away in basements for over seventy years. And most photos that Bud mentioned having sent home from war with his letters have disappeared, perhaps having been disposed of by mother Fay, who likely found them too painful to look at again.

Bud's sister Mary Frances (Hayes) Grabert, who had been with Bud during his first flight so many years earlier in Admiral Byrd's airplane, also did not speak about the loss of Bud for nearly seventy years. That was partly the result of grief, but partly also because she simply did not know the full story behind his death. Nevertheless, Bud's photos and his pilot diplomas hang lovingly on the walls of Mary's Twin Falls, Idaho home. And now, thanks to the unearthing of the box containing Bud's letters and service records, she also has the story behind Bud's wartime training, service and tragic accident.

Although Bud's letters and records help to tell his extraordinary story, there are still unanswered questions about his accident. A somewhat preliminary question is, why did the U.S. Army Air Force not deactivate Bud and send him home immediately at war's end? Bud had worked tirelessly in service throughout 1945, being involved in many harrowing combat and rescue operations in which he, his crew and his aircraft came close to peril. At war's end, with no more combat operations, surely less-experienced pilots could have been rotated into the Pacific, sending more weathered pilots like Bud home. Bud's demise during a seemingly routine post-war mission appeared senseless to his family.

Another question surrounding Bud's death is, what precisely caused his PBY Catalina to so easily break apart when the fatal wave hit it? From various reports and from recollections of airmen who served around the end of the war, we can presume that post-war maintenance of PBYs was not as stringent as during the war, and wear on the airframe of the Catalina Bud flew during his fateful mission might have played a role in its ultimate disintegration. By the time of the accident, bombing and fighter action had ended. With PBY Catalinas no longer needed for combat missions, the aircraft and its squadrons had become a lesser priority for Army Air Force maintenance resources. It was a complaint often raised among men in the remaining post-war rescue squadron.

There is also the question of why the Army Air Force and the Navy never salvaged Bud's downed PBY and brought its three crew members' bodies back to their homes for proper honors and burial. The Missing Air Crew Report this chapter references only recently resurfaced (in March 2016). Furthermore, due to the backlog of military paperwork around the end of World War II, investigative documents for Bud's accident were unexpectedly waylaid, not officially processed until 1948 and 1949 (at least two years after his accident). Those documents also only recently resurfaced.

None of the records about Bud's accident indicate any plans to ever recover his downed PBY Catalina or the men inside. And that was a common outcome for aircraft that went down in the Pacific around the time of the war. The technology of that time simply did not allow for such deep-water recoveries, and there was no reason to believe that it ever would in the future. Of course by modern standards we now know that Bud and his aircraft are not in waters too deep for eventual recovery. But for now, seventy years on, they remain under the sea, fifteen hundred yards off the northwest tip of Panay Island.

Putting aside the questions about Bud's death, one thing we do know for certain is that he foresaw the possibility of it. Prior to his death, Bud, who always had family and home on his mind, had taken serious preparations to provide for his family should he pass away in service during the war. When he was at Keesler Army Air Field in Biloxi, Mississippi in spring 1945, and his deployment was inevitable, he obtained his benefit information and secured life insurance.

The insurance Bud obtained was a term life insurance policy in the face amount of ten thousand dollars,[22] issued by National Services Life Insurance on March 22, 1945 (effective retroactively to February 8, 1945).[23] The life insurance policy named Bud's mother, Fay Fern Jensen, as the primary beneficiary, and named contingent beneficiaries as follows: "Nedra Hayes Greene (Sister), Mary Frances (Hayes) Peterson (Sister)—$5,000 each."[24] Upon Bud's death, Fay chose monthly payments rather than a lump sum and began receiving insurance payments on October 10, 1945.[25] By the time of Fay's death in March 1979, she had received up to 413 payments totaling $20,815.20. Bud had helped provide for his family members throughout his childhood while working on the family farm and on neighboring farms and, thanks to his foresight in obtaining life insurance, he continued to help provide for them even in death.

In October 1946, one year after Bud's death, the U.S. Army Air Force sent a letter to his mother Fay listing the decorations and awards Bud had received throughout his service.[26] They included a September 16, 1943, Service Accolade (approved by the President of the United States) and a 1945 Cold War Recognition Certificate (approved by the Secretary of War). They further included the American Campaign Medal, the Asiatic-Pacific Campaign Medal and the World War II Victory Medal. And last, but not least, was listed Bud's U.S. Army Air Force Aviation

Badge (his wings) in addition to his Sharpshooter Badge (with Carbine and Pistol Bards).

Subsequently, on April 12, 1947, Fay also received a record (a notice) documenting Bud's Air Medal award. The record contained the following note: "It is an honor for me to forward this decoration," signed Robert P. Patterson, Secretary of War.[27] (U.S. Army Air Force General George C. Kenney had officially awarded the Air Medal to Lieutenant Frank Philby "Bud" Hayes on September 10, 1945.)[28] The record also included this description of the Air Medal award:

FOR: Meritorious achievement while participating in sustained operational flight missions in the Southwest Pacific Area, during which hostile contact was probable and expected. These operations consisted of patrol and search missions and often involved landing in heavy seas within range of enemy fire to effect rescues of air crew members forced down by hostile action or operational failure. The courage and devotion to duty displayed during these flights reflect great credit on the United States Army Air Forces.

Figure 13.4. The Air Medal that the U.S. Army Air Force awarded to Bud on September 14, 1945.

On August 17, 2016, Brigadier General Eric R. Calip (Defense and Armed Forces Attaché, Republic of the Philippines Embassy to the United States) issued posthumously to Bud's sister Mary Frances (Hayes) Grabert additional medals and citations, which First Lieutenant Frank Philby "Bud" Hayes had earned for his service during the liberation of the people of the Philippines, with the gratitude of their nation.[29] The awards included the Philippine Liberation Medal, the Military Civic Action Medal and the Republic of the Philippines Presidential Unit Citation badge.

Epilogue

THE SECOND WORLD WAR and the Allies' victory in it proved to be seminal events in world history, the impact of which continues to carry forth today. During the course of the war in Europe and the Pacific combined, 16.1 million Americans served in the military.[1] The U.S. Army and the U.S. Army Air Force suffered an estimated 318,274 service men and women killed or lost in action.[2] In addition, they lost 43,584 aircraft during the war, mostly from combat action.[3] The U.S. Navy suffered similar losses. Over the last two years of Navy aerial combat, Navy fighters shot down 5,300 Japanese aircraft; but for every nineteen aircraft the Japanese lost, the U.S. Navy lost one.[4]

The heavy toll from World War II was felt in every U.S. state. But for U.S. states that already had relatively small populations prior to the U.S. entry into the war (like Bud's home state of Idaho), the losses were particularly devastating. The 1940 Census showed that Idaho was among the smaller states population-wise, with around 522,000 people.[5] Bud's home of Twin Falls County recorded a 1940 population of 36,403.[6]

The War Department summarized World War II's population toll on the State of Idaho in the following report:

The State of Idaho contained .040 percent of the population of the United States and its possessions (excluding the Philippine Islands) in 1940 and contributed 0.38 percent of the total number who entered the Army. Of those men and women of Idaho who went to war, 3.98 percent failed to return. This figure represents 0.49 percent of the Army's total dead and missing.[7]

Idaho soldiers, airmen, sailors and marines lost in the war totaled 1,419. Eighty-six of them, including First Lieutenant Frank Philby "Bud" Hayes, were from Twin Falls County.[8]

In the seventy years since the end of World War II, thousands of books, papers and documentaries have been produced about the war, and many have documented heroic Air Force fighter and bomber units and individuals. However, relatively little has been written about the heroic rescue pilots and crews of the Second Emergency Rescue Squadron—the "Snafu Snatchers," who saved several hundred downed pilots and crews during the war. Many of their records are lost to history. Those records that survived are mostly only available to us from the families, descendants and past associates of those who served in the PBY Catalina "flying boats."

Some former PBY Catalina servicemen of the Second Emergency Rescue Squadron are still alive today. But now in their nineties, their memories of service during World War II have begun to fade. Other PBY Catalina servicemen passed on after the war, and still others are alive today but suffering from dementia. They are all part of a generation that served valiantly but rarely spoke about the war after returning home. Ken Samuelson, in his research on World War II and Korean War veterans, found, "Combat veterans rarely talk about war. It's more common that they don't at all, and if they do, it's to men who too have seen war or to psychiatrists for *narrative medicine* if the memories canker and break toxic."[9]

World War II veterans (altruistic people then and now) know time is fleeting. Many decades post-war some begin to speak with more detail about their service, often for the first time to their families and friends, often after being pressed by said families and friends to do so. Their respective stories reside in family records and lore, in state, federal, local and university archives, in veterans' oral history programs and in books like this one that seek to preserve memories and facts. Bud Hayes's story joins those of so many other World War II service men and women as a way to memorialize their hardships but also their victories during World War II—its important lessons, whether bad or good, not to be ignored.

There is an ancient Judeo-Christian saying that, "Whoever destroys a soul, it is considered as if he destroyed an entire world. And whoever saves a life, it is considered as if he saved an entire world."[10] It is an interesting facet that while the battles of World War II raged on destroying lives on all sides, the Second Emergency Rescue Squadron's primary mission was to save lives. Each life that men like Bud saved was similar to that vision of "saving the world."

One can, in fact, calculate the estimated generational impact that the Second Emergency Rescue Squadron might have actually had. By war's end, the Second Emergency Rescue Squadron had rescued a recorded 724 airmen during its operations in the Pacific Theater.[11] Bud Hayes and his crew alone recorded twenty-two saved lives.

Statistics on the population of the United States suggest that by 1950 the average family had 3.77 children, and the next generation 2.3 children.[12] Using those figures we can calculate the estimated number of descendants of the over seven hundred airmen the Second Emergency Rescue Squadron saved during World War II. Their direct descendants would have collectively totaled around 2,730 children. Those children would then, collectively, have produced a next generation of 6,280 children. And it is not out of the realm of reason to estimate that seventy years post-World War II over 9,000 descendants of those who were rescued are alive today, all owing their very existence to the heroic men of the Second Emergency Rescue Squadron. For Bud Hayes and his crew alone, the estimate is that they are responsible for having ensured the lives of over 270 descendants who are alive today.[13] The descendants have raised families, gone to work, started businesses, told their stories and helped America grow into the world power and the beacon of freedom that it is today. As for the rescued men themselves, few are alive today. By now they are aging parents, grandparents and great-grandparents who are well into their nineties. Successive generations are now passing these men's stories down, making sure that they and their heroics are not forgotten. As their memories begin to fade, and as they begin to pass away, it is imperative that we preserve the history of their bravery and sacrifices.

Following World War II, the United States endured the great challenges of the Cold War, but again prevailed, this time over the Soviet Union (which met its demise in 1986 as signified by the fall of the Berlin Wall). Idaho continued to play an important role in preserving freedom during that conflict and also does so today. Key in this ongoing role is Mountain Home Air Force Base, which is located 105 miles northwest of Bud's hometown of Filer. The base, established in November 1942 to train B-24 Liberator crews, is today a key center for the U.S. Air Force. It is home of the 366th Fighter Wing "Gunslingers" (who fly F-15Es and F-15SGs), and it is part of the Air Combat Command.[14]

Bud Hayes's story represents the transformative effect World War II had on millions of Americans, many of whom, like Bud, came from humble beginnings. The Hayes family had spent over a century farming, taking them everywhere from Ireland to Illinois to Nebraska and ultimately to Idaho. As in so many families, each generation of Bud's family followed the other in the family business or profession.

World War II put together in foxholes, on beaches, on ships and aboard aircraft individuals of diverse backgrounds, educations, religions, cultures and locations. Bud's letters, in which he early on wrote of returning to his family farm in Idaho, reflected in later months of the war the influence that his interactions with his varied colleagues had on him. He had begun to write about the

211

possibility of attending college, mentioning the Colorado School of Mines in particular. That was perhaps a result of his interactions with service buddies who hailed from lucrative mining engineering families. Later he wrote about the possibility of attending Purdue University, again reflecting his developing interest in engineering. Or perhaps that interest came from Bud's increasing level of skills sophistication with aircraft, the complex PBY Catalina in particular.

A window of opportunity for war veterans to attend college was one of the great innovations of World War II, as created by the "GI Bill":

Officially the Servicemen's Readjustment Act of 1944,[15] the G.I. Bill was created to help veterans of World War II. It established hospitals, made low-interest mortgages available and granted stipends covering tuition and expenses for veterans attending college or trade schools. From 1944 to 1949, nearly 9 million veterans received close to $4 billion from the bill's unemployment compensation program. The education and training provisions existed until 1956, while the Veterans' Administration offered insured loans until 1962. The Readjustment Benefits Act of 1966[16] extended these benefits to all veterans of the armed forces, including those who had served during peacetime.[17]

Over 2.2 million war veterans who heretofore would have returned to the family tradition of the farms, mines, shops or factories of their fathers and grandfathers instead returned and headed to colleges and universities. Others (5.6 million others) returned to specialized trade training as an alternative route of life on which they could achieve their American dreams. Spread before World War II veterans were opportunities to use their minds and talents to attain an education, and to use that education for innovation, entrepreneurship and advances in all fields. This led to a great post-war American economic and technological expansion, and even to man landing on the moon (in 1969). Five

World War II veterans went on to become President of the United States: Dwight Eisenhower (Army), John F. Kennedy (Navy), Richard Nixon (Navy), Gerald Ford (Navy) and George H.W. Bush (Navy).

But what about those thousands of "farm boys" from the American heartland like Bud Hayes who left their fields, ranches, farms and families to join the war effort with visions of returning there at war's end? Were they too afforded this American dream? Well, Bob Dole was a farm kid from Russell, Kansas who had fought in the U.S. Army's Tenth Mountain Division during the war. After being wounded in battle in Italy and being highly decorated, he returned to the United States and earned his law degree at the University of Arizona. He later became a distinguished U.S. Senator from Kansas, Senate Republican leader, head of the Republican Party and later a candidate for U.S. Vice President and for President.

Likewise, George McGovern grew up in the small farm town of Avon, South Dakota and joined the Army Air Force, eventually serving during the war as a B-24 Liberator pilot. After the war he returned to college at Dakota Wesleyan University. He later became a history professor, then U.S. Senator from South Dakota, leader of the Democratic Party and a candidate for U.S. President.

William Rehnquist also served during World War II after growing up in the American Midwest, in Shorewood, Wisconsin. He was the son of an equipment salesman, and he joined the Army Air Force in its meteorology (weather measurement) instruments program. After the war he returned to college, got his law degree from Stanford University and later became U.S. Solicitor General, associate justice of the U.S. Supreme Court and, later, Chief Justice of the U.S. Supreme Court.

World War II servicemen achieving success after the war were not just confined to government and politics. A farm boy growing up in Norfolk, Nebraska was named Johnny Carson. He joined the Navy during World War II, served in the war, then returned to the U.S. post-war and attended the University of

Nebraska. He went on to become a pioneer in television entertainment, hosting the long-running Tonight Show (on NBC). He won the Presidential Medal of Freedom and Kennedy Center Honors, among other awards and recognitions.

There was also Russell D. Johnson, who grew up in Ashley, Pennsylvania, a small coal-mining town in the state's northeast. He joined the U.S. Army Air Force during World War II and became a B-25 bomber navigator, flying forty-four missions in the Philippine campaign. In March 1945, Johnson (then Second Lieutenant) was on a bombing mission against Japanese forces around the city of Zamboanga on the island of Mindanao, Philippines. Japanese forces hit his B-25 bomber, and his crew ditched it in the sea, resulting in the death of his co-pilot and broken ankles for himself. Johnson and the surviving crew were rescued by a PBY Catalina of the Second Emergency Rescue Squadron. After the war Johnson used his G.I. Bill benefits to study and to then begin a career in acting. He appeared in movies and TV dramas in the 1950s, most notably as "The Professor" (Ray Hinckley) on CBS Television's iconic sitcom "Gilligan's Island." The series ran from 1964–67, and many still see it today in worldwide reruns.

The Hellers, poor Jewish immigrants in Brooklyn, New York (Coney Island), had a son named Joseph. He joined the Army Air Force during World War II and became a B-25 bombardier, flying over sixty missions in Europe during the war. When Joseph Heller returned home he went to college, ultimately graduating with a degree from Columbia University. He became a famous author, most known for the book *Catch-22*, which was about a World War II B-25 bombardier and was so famous that the book's title became a phrase that entered the modern American lexicon.

Alas, for Bud Hayes, his life was cut far too short, before he ever had the opportunity to realize his own American dream. But his and his squadron's service made infinite horizons possible for 724 other men, and for their descendants. These rescued men's names might not be up in lights, in headlines or on postage stamps, but they collectively became the face of post-war America, and its Greatest Generation. Yes, as the biblical saying went, each life saved is an entire world saved.

Consolidated Aircraft Company, the pioneering designer and builder of the PBY Catalina and the B-24 Liberator heavy bomber, produced thousands of aircraft around the clock during the war. From 1936–45 it built 3,305 PBYs (2,661 in U.S. plants). The last Catalina rolled down the factory line in 1945, the company never again to make a flying boat. In the company's planning for war's end, its aging owner and founder, Reuben H. Fleet, finalized a merger (in November 1943) with Vultee Aircraft to form Consolidated Vultee Aircraft (better known as Convair).

In March 1953, General Dynamics, a diversified military equipment manufacturer, purchased Convair. The company then produced the Convair B-36 strategic bomber, the F-102 and F-106 fighter jets, commercial airliners and the Convair 880 and 990. By 1965 the company found itself unable to compete as an aircraft manufacturer and it concentrated instead on aeronautical and rocket subcontracting work, including for NASA's early space program (named Project Mercury). In 1994, General Dynamics sold Convair to McDonnell Douglas Corporation, which shut down and dissolved the company two years later, in 1996.[18]

PBY Catalina aircraft continued to serve after the end of World War II. Even though growth and technological advances in the use of helicopters rapidly supplanted the Catalina's air–sea rescue uses, the U.S. Army Air Force continued to use Catalina units for that service until 1947, with its last PBY decommissioned in 1953. The U.S. Navy did likewise all the way until 1957. The reconnaissance uses for PBY Catalinas were also eventually replaced, specifically by U-2 and SR-71 aircraft, which were eventually themselves replaced (by the year 2000) with the use of high-resolution satellites and unmanned drones. As for the PBY's gunship uses, those were very early forerunners of the

U.S. Air Force's AC-47 and AC-130 aircraft gunships that are in use today. Even the B-2 stealth bomber was foretold by the PBY Catalina, namely by the Navy's "Black Cat squadrons" (the PBYs that were painted black and operated at night to avoid enemy detection).

Many nations other than the U.S. also used PBYs after the war, retrofitting and modernizing them to meet Federal Air Regulation standards. The former aviation firm Steward-Davis of Orange County, California was one of many aviation firms that retrofitted PBYs with modern avionics, new turboprop engines and other improvements to form the new "super Catalinas" of the 1950s. One of the most famous non-war uses of PBYs was a weekly run by Qantas (Australia's national airline), which from 1943–45 (still during World War II) ran weekly passenger service using PBY 5As from Perth, Western Australia to Colombo, Sri Lanka, being known as "The Double Sunrise Service."[19] Alaska Airlines also used Catalinas, through the 1960s, for passenger and freight service to remote areas of Alaska. And Antilles Air Boats used Cats for passenger service in the Caribbean.

Today, many Catalina aircraft still see service in aerial fire-fighting, in remote air services and during air museum fly-ins. Others have become static displays at air museums. Some veterans who flew and manned Catalinas in the U.S., Canada and the United Kingdom have formed Catalina societies to preserve the Cats, both physically and in memory.[20] But the number of veterans participating in these societies grows smaller each year as they grow old and pass away. As for interservice rivalries (of the type exhibited between the U.S. Army Air Force and the U.S. Navy in the build up to the PBY Project), those live on today in what is now the U.S. Department of Defense.

Modern-day air–sea rescue is primarily handled by the U.S. Coast Guard, U.S. Navy, U.S. Air Force and even the U.S. Army. Their chosen aircraft for use in rescues is now helicopters. Air–sea rescue continues to be an important mission of both military and civilian services. The old "Gibson Girl" radio used during

World War II-era rescues has now been replaced by radios like the handheld CSEL radio, which retains a slight "body curve" that harkens back to its predecessor's "Gibson Girl" nickname.

Figure Epilogue 1. A modern CSEL survival device, successor to the World War II-era "Gibson Girl" transmitter.[21]

The base on Morotai Island, which had been so much the center of the Second Emergency Rescue Squadron's wartime activity, ceased to be necessary after World War II. The U.S. closed the base on January 7, 1946.[22] Like so many bases in

217

Europe and the Pacific, it was abandoned; but today one may still see vestiges of its former runways, now overgrown with brush. The squadron's other major base, Clark Air Base on the island of Luzon in the Philippines, was a major base of U.S. operations throughout the post-World War II Cold War era, and particularly during the Korean and Vietnam Wars. In 1991, under pressure from the Philippine Government, the United States removed its forces from Clark Air Base and turned it over to the Philippine Government. It then became Clark International Airport. By 2012, the Philippine Government, facing threats from China, invited the U.S. back to Clark, turning it into a U.S. Air Force base once more.[23]

Post-Vietnam War (from the late 1970s on), the U.S. experienced inflation, as well as growing costs from political demand for social programs and entitlements, which began to crowd out military spending. A "peacetime" U.S. military found its budgets increasingly constrained. Congress made massive reductions in the number of U.S. military bases. And it scrutinized the use of America's newest military weapons, with some, such as the F-35 Lightning fighter jet, being mandated shared among the Air Force, Navy and Marines (thus known as the Joint Strike Force Program).[24] Organizational changes in the military might gradually, but not totally, eliminate interservice turf battles among the different military services. That legacy remains yet to be fully purged from the military's traditions.

The lone U.S. Military memorialization of First Lieutenant Frank Philby "Bud" Hayes and his service with the U.S. Army Air Force's Second Emergency Rescue Squadron is at the U.S. Military Cemetery at Fort Bonifacio, Manila, Philippines (or the "Manila American Cemetery"). There, a plaque along the "Tablets of the Missing and Killed in Action" is dedicated to those from World War II who, like Bud, were buried at sea or went missing in action.[25] Bud's name is etched in stone there, and appears by digital memorial at the American Battle Monuments Commission website.

Figure Epilogue 2. The "Tablets of the Missing and Killed in Action" at the Manila American Cemetery and Memorial, Manila, Philippines. Bud's name is etched in stone there.

Bud's hometown of Filer, in Twin Falls County, Idaho, did not forget its native son First Lieutenant Frank Philby "Bud" Hayes either. The town of Filer and American Legion Post No. 47 held a memorial service for Bud at the Filer Methodist Church on Sunday, January 20, 1946.[26] And the next year, on May 24, 1947, the Filer Methodist Church presented Bud's parents, Fay Fern and George Jensen, with a gold star in honor of Bud, which had been taken from the church's U.S. flag that flew during World War II.[27]

In addition, the student body of Filer High School raised funds for a memorial plaque listing the names of "all men who were students from Filer High School and gave the last full measure of their devotion in World War II." The plaque, containing Frank Hayes's name, was dedicated by the Filer posts of the American Legion and Veterans of Foreign Wars in a ceremony on

Memorial Day, May 30, 1947.[28] Sometime years later the stone went missing. Filer residents had a new stone crafted and installed at the Filer, Idaho Cemetery, which included Bud's name along with those of other sons of Filer who died in World War II and the Korean and Vietnam Wars.[29]

Figure Epilogue 3. Memorial stone at a cemetery in Frank Philby "Bud" Hayes's hometown of Filer, Idaho. Bud's name is listed in the third column under the World War II heading.

On Memorial Day May 28, 1950, Twin Falls County dedicated a monument at Sunset Memorial Park in the City of Twin Falls honoring all the Twin Falls men who died during World War II. Bud Hayes's name is also included on that memorial monument.[30]

Twin Falls Air Field, where Bud met Admiral Richard E. Byrd and took his first flight in 1936, was renamed after World War II to Joslin Field/Magic Valley Regional Airport in honor of the first U.S. Army Air Force airman from Twin Falls County to die in action during the war. Sergeant Raymond Joslin, who served as a B-17 radioman in the air during the Japanese attack on

Pearl Harbor on December 7, 1941, then went on to fly bombers during the Pacific war. Joslin died on September 29, 1942, when his B-17 was hit by enemy fire while bombing ships near Shortland Island and Tonlei Harbor in New Guinea.[31] Ray Joslin was also from Filer, graduating from Filer High School four years ahead of Bud. Bud's sister Mary Frances related that the men's families knew each other. Coincidentally, Raymond Joslin (for whom the Twin Falls airport is now named) was the first airman from Twin Falls County to die during World War II-related service, and Bud Hayes was the last.[32]

The pain from the loss of Bud never diminished for his mother Fay Fern Jensen. After Bud's death she packed away his records and letters and never spoke about him for the remainder of her life. At very brief moments she would only say, "They took my boy!"; but she would say nothing more than that.[33] Loved ones' questions to her about Bud received silence in return. From time to time Fay would take out Bud's medals, hold them out in distress at the loss of her son and swear, then just as quickly pack them back away.[34] Fay later divorced George Jensen, and she remained a schoolteacher in the Twin Falls County school system until retirement, subsequently teaching in an elementary school at the Duck Valley Indian Reservation in Owyhee, Nevada. She passed away in Twin Falls, Idaho in 1979 at age eighty-four.

Bud's older sister Nedra Hayes Greene and her husband Percy ran a family trout farm (Greene and Blue Lakes Trout Farm) along the Snake River in Twin Falls County, and they had two children. Nedra died in 1996 at age eighty-two. Her daughter (Bud's niece) Carole Greene Kasel, who had so faithfully written to Bud during the war, later married Air Force veteran Ronald Kasel. The two originally also ran a trout farm, then later diversified into farming and cattle ranching. Carole is now retired with grandchildren and lives in Twin Falls, Idaho.[35] Nedra's son (Bud's nephew) Michael Greene ran the family trout farm business until he retired. He and his wife Dot also have grandchildren and are also residents of Twin Falls, Idaho.

Mary Frances (Hayes) Grabert is Bud's last surviving sibling. At age ninety-five she is long retired from the family farm, but she remains in her Twin Falls, Idaho home. She is a proud mother, grandmother and great-grandmother. Her bedroom and family room walls include photos of Bud, igniting cherished memories of her brother, including their ride together in Admiral Byrd's airplane. One of Mary's two daughters, Megan Feller, is currently retired in Kent, Washington and has grandchildren. Her other daughter, Carla Faye Grabert-Lowenstein (the author's wife), is an attorney and a former California Senior Deputy District Attorney. She lives in Conway, South Carolina running her independent law firm and is a proud grandparent. It is thanks to the gracious permission of Bud's sister Mary that after seventy years Bud's story has now come to light, is memorialized in this book and remains for current and future generations of family, Idahoans and all Americans.

Figure Epilogue 4. Bud's sister Mary Frances (Hayes) Grabert during World War II (left) and in 2011 (right).

Bud, his co-pilot and a passenger from their fateful final mission remain in eternal repose off the Culasi, Panay, Philippines coast in relatively shallow waters. Marine technology that today exists and would allow recovery of an aircraft at the depth at which Bud's lies might one day be used in a recovery mission to bring him home to Idaho. And in February 2017, the U.S. Department of Defense's POW/MIA Accounting Agency, as a result of this book's research, added to its task lists a project to locate and attempt to retrieve Bud Hayes's PBY Catalina. Bud Hayes's Idaho home, in the aptly named Magic Valley, resonated throughout virtually every letter Bud wrote home from the time he entered the U.S. Army Air Force. Even after ultimate tragedy and sacrifice, he would wish to return to his native ground there. Perhaps someday he will return home where his service can be duly recognized and his deeds and spirit celebrated, and where he can finally rest in peace in Idaho soil.

At the end of World War II's Battle of Britain, Sir Winston Churchill, commenting on England's having been saved by the Royal Air Force, famously remarked, "Never was so much owed by so many to so few."[36] The same can well be said about the role that First Lieutenant Frank Philby "Bud" Hayes and the Second Emergency Rescue Squadron played during World War II. As for the role Bud himself played, as his longtime navigator Lieutenant Gregersen wrote in 1945, Bud was quite simply among the best of pilots and the best of men:

[Bud] has the reputation of being of the best pilots; and is the best-liked pilot in the entire outfit. Only three times had he flown in this theater when I was not along trying to navigate as he piloted. He was a good man for all of his twenty-one years.[37]

In the twilight of General Douglas MacArthur's years he gave perhaps one of the most famous American speeches of all time while accepting the Thayer Award at the U.S. Military Academy—West Point, May 12, 1962. In his "Duty, Honor, Country" speech he described his admiration for the millions of military men under his command during his career. General MacArthur collectively described these men as if he was speaking about each individual one to each one's family. Bud Hayes was certainly among the men about whom General MacArthur spoke that day, and MacArthur's words indeed sounded as if they were spoken directly to Bud and to his Idaho family. A portion of those words is excerpted here:

Their story is known to all of you. It is the story of men-at-arms. My estimate of him was formed on the battlefield many, many years ago, and has never changed. I regarded him then, as I regard him now, as one of the world's noblest figures, not only as one of the finest military characters, but also as one of the most stainless.

His name and fame are the birthright of every American citizen. In his youth and strength, his love and loyalty, he gave all that mortality can give. He needs no eulogy from me; or from any other man. He has written it in red on his enemy's breast.

But when I think of his patience under adversity, of his courage under fire, and of his modesty in victory, I am filled with an emotion of admiration I cannot put into words. He belongs to history as furnishing one of the greatest examples of successful patriotism. He belongs to posterity as the instructor of future generations in the principles of liberty and freedom. He belongs to the present, to us, by his virtues and by his achievements.[38]

As famed radio journalist and commentator Paul Harvey used to conclude his broadcasts during World War II and later on ABC Radio, and as might now be said of Bud's life: "And now you know the rest of the story."[39]

Figure Epilogue 5. Then-Second Lieutenant Frank Philby "Bud" Hayes in uniform, displaying U.S. Army Air Force and U.S. Navy aviation badges (wings), in Filer, Idaho, July 1944.

From the Publisher

Thank You from the Publisher

Van Rye Publishing, LLC ("VRP") sincerely thanks you for your interest in and purchase of this book.

If you enjoyed this book or found it useful, please consider taking a moment to support the author and get word out to other readers like you by leaving a rating or review of the book at its product page at your favorite online book retailer.

Thank you!

Resources from the Publisher

Van Rye Publishing, LLC ("VRP") offers the following resources to authors and to readers.

For authors who enjoyed this book or found it useful, please consider having VRP edit, format, or fully publish your own book manuscript. You can find out more, and contact the publisher directly, by visiting VRP's website at www.vanryepublishing.com.

For readers who enjoyed this book or found it useful, please consider signing up to have VRP notify you when books like this one are available at a limited-time discounted price, some as low as $0.99. You can sign up to receive such notifications by visiting the following web address: http://eepurl.com/cERow9.

Acknowledgments

THIS WORK COULD NOT have been completed without the help, assistance, encouragement and resources of many people. My daughter's father-in-law, Dr. Billy Koen, Professor Emeritus, Nuclear Engineering, University of Texas at Austin, always encouraged me to "write a book." I credit his devoted persistence in setting the stage for this researched work along with, most especially, my wife Carla Faye Grabert-Lowenstein (Bud's niece). High praise goes to my late father Murray H. Lowenstein, a Korean War veteran, who gave me the love of history, literature and writing, and imbued throughout life the importance of patriotism and respect for those who fought to keep our nation free. And thanks to my uncles, published authors Dr. Jerold M. Lowenstein (a World War II veteran) and Dr. Ralph L. Lowenstein (a Korean War veteran), as well as cousin Anne F. Ziff, for their encouragement.

At the outset, great credit goes to Mary Frances (Hayes) Grabert, of Twin Falls, Idaho, who after so many years graciously allowed the author to open the box in her Twin Falls, Idaho home basement that contained her brother's records. Doing so opened this portal to his life, to his spirit and to the Second Emergency Rescue Squadron that had been closed for over seventy years. We are also indebted to other family members who had documents, pictures and materials. These family members include Dot and Michael Greene and Carole (Greene) Kasel of Twin Falls, Idaho.

Research for this book gave long-awaited closure to the family of Bud's co-pilot, Second Lieutenant John "Jack" Leonard. We are grateful to his brother Larry Leonard and the Leonard family, who now live in North Carolina, for the valuable information provided in support of this work and for their continued support. Special and extraordinary thanks and praise go to Chief Warrant Officer James R. Teegarden, U.S. Army, Ft. Rucker, Alabama. Jim's dedication for over thirty years in preserving every conceivable fact, picture and record of the Second Emergency Rescue Squadron was invaluable—all accomplished while he engaged in a distinguished military career of his own in the U.S. Army.

Like the author, Jim Teegarden's interest in and inquiry about the Second Emergency Rescue Squadron came from family—specifically from his uncle (mother's side), Captain Gerard F. Wientjes, one of the founding commanders of the squadron during World War II. Many of his uncle's records and photos were left to him and are preserved on his website (http://pbyres cue.com) and in other archives. Jim also traveled to a number of reunions and accumulated stories and materials that surviving members of the Second Emergency Rescue Squadron donated. He graciously gave permission for this book to use any and all of the materials from his website, and he served as a technical advisor in the production of this book. We are immensely indebted to Jim's dedication and work. The author has likewise shared with Jim, for inclusion in his archives, rare documents uncovered during research about Lieutenant Bud Hayes.

Invaluable materials about missions and internal documents of the U.S. Army Air Force and the Second Emergency Rescue Squadron from World War II were graciously provided by Colonel (U.S. Air Force, Retired) J.A. "Bill" Saavedra of the U.S. Air Force Historical Support Office Headquarters, Washington, D.C. We are grateful for Colonel Saavedra's personal and professional interest in the subject and his invaluable assistance throughout the research and writing of this book. Assistance in finding information about Bud's military memorials was provided by the American Battle Monuments Commission's Chief of

External Affairs Timothy Nosal, by U.S. Army Past Conflict Repatriations Branch (Fort Knox, Kentucky) Case Manager Laurie A. Jones and by historian and project manager Dr. Greg Kupinsky of the Defense POW/MIA Accounting Agency.

We obtained Lieutenant Hayes's military records and the long-thought-lost Missing Air Crew Report thanks to the personal interest and dedicated efforts of the following public officials and their staffs: U.S. Senator Mike Crapo (Idaho) and his Twin Falls District Staff Director Samantha Marshall; U.S. Senator Tim Scott (South Carolina) and his Columbia District Staff Member Briana Bateman; and U.S. Congressman Tom Rice (7th Congressional District, South Carolina) and his District Staff Director Andrew Mims. The documents were provided to us by the U.S. Army Human Resources Command, Fort Knox, Kentucky, and included the Missing Air Crew Report as well as confirmation of medals and citations and replacement documents related thereto.

We thank the Embassy of the Republic of the Philippines for its assistance in issuing Lieutenant Hayes's medals and citations from the Philippine people. For those efforts we specifically thank Brigadier General Eric R. Calip (Defense and Armed Forces Attaché, Republic of the Philippines Embassy to the United States) and Alfredo S. Cabalsi (Veterans Service Officer).

The documentary (available at *YouTube*) about Clarence Lee Coon, a sergeant mechanic in the Second Emergency Rescue Squadron, provided invaluable first-hand accounts about the squadron and its missions, as well as about operation of the PBY Catalina (OA-10A) aircraft. Likewise, Barry Schiff's video (also available at *YouTube*) about the Consolidated PBY Catalina is an outstanding summary of the aircraft and provides demonstrations of the work it performs.

Validation in the form of news articles and critical historical dates from Twin Falls was provided thanks to the efforts of Twin Falls local historian Ron Yates (Terrific Marketing LLC—Twin Falls) and the Twin Falls, Idaho Public Library. The documents provided proved to be valuable additions to this book.

Other sources used in this book include: Roscoe Creed's seminal book *PBY: The Catalina Flying Boat* (1985); Walter Borneman's *MacArthur's War* (2016); the Albert F. Simson Historical Research Center at Maxwell Air Force Base, Alabama; Warbird Alley's (http://www.warbirdalley.com) descriptions of aircraft; The PBY Preservation Society; the http://snappygoat .com public domain website; and the many sources listed in this book's bibliography. For general dates and events, maps and related material, we used open source public sources and records available on the Internet, including from Google Maps. Other internet resources, official military documents and sites we used are duly noted in this book's Notes and Bibliography sections.

We appreciate early consultative review by Dr. Jill Swenson of Swenson Book Development. The book is indebted to the editing, formatting and other technical and publishing assistance that John Siedel, President, and his team at Van Rye Publishing, LLC (www.vanryepublishing.com) provided.

In developing this book's story and assessing reader reactions I am indebted to a number of professionals who read early versions and provided feedback, invaluable reactions and enthusiastic support for this work. Those providing technical advice and advice on accuracy were:

- **Robert H. Reed**, General (four-star), U.S. Air Force (Retired); Former Chief of Staff, Supreme Headquarters Allied Powers Europe (NATO);
- **James Whitehead, Jr.**, Major General, U.S. Air Force (Retired); Former Assistant Director, National Air National Guard Programs, The Pentagon; Former FAA Operations Manager, Los Angeles International Airport; and current Director, Minter Field Air Museum, California;
- **J.A. "Bill" Saavedra**, Colonel, U.S. Air Force (Retired); Volunteer Historian, U.S. Air Force Historical Support Division, U.S. Air Force Office of History, Washington, DC;

- **Walter "Scottie" Scott**, World War II veteran; Ensign, U.S. Navy (Retired); World War II PBY Catalina pilot and flight instructor, Naval Air Training Center, Pensacola, Florida;
- **Charles Thrash**, Colonel, U.S. Air Force (Retired); Former Commander, 354th Tactical Fighter Wing and A-10 pilot, Myrtle Beach Air Force Base, Myrtle Beach, South Carolina;
- **Thomas "Buddy" Styers**, Colonel, U.S. Air Force (Retired); Former Commander, 554th Combat Support Group, Nellis Air Force Base, Nevada;
- **Nathan E. "Nate" Cagle**, Commander, U.S. Navy (Retired); Former Mission Commander, Patrol Plane Tactical Coordinator and P-3 Orion pilot, Patrol Squadron 9, Patrol Squadron 66 and Patrol Squadron 91;
- **James R. Teegarden**, Chief Warrant Officer 4 and UH-60 Blackhawk instructor pilot, U.S. Army Aviation Center of Excellence, Fort Rucker, Alabama; and Director, http://pbyrescue.com;
- **James Gatley**, Sergeant, U.S. Army (Retired); Former 285th Air Recon Battle Group, Silver Bell, Arizona; 101st Airborne Division; Scheduler, Prescott Support Co. (air transport / cargo services).

Other early-reader reactions came from my colleagues at Coastal Carolina University, Wall College of Business. Those colleagues include: Dr. Michal Latta (Marketing); Dr. Mark Mitchell (Marketing); David Fink (Management); Lee Shinaberger (Management, and former Civil Air Patrol pilot); Dick Drass (Management, and Retired Captain, U.S. Army Rangers); and Larry Cribb (former U.S. Coast Guard).

Finally, perhaps the highest acknowledgment and thank you should go to the late Fay Fern Philby Jensen of Twin Falls, Idaho who, despite her grief and deep upset over the loss of her son Bud, preserved his letters and other documents. Those letters and documents became the foundation for this book and the research behind it, and they have allowed history to not forget the extraordinary and heroic work of First Lieutenant Frank Philby "Bud" Hayes and the rest of the Second Emergency Rescue Squadron, Thirteenth Air Force of World War II.

And to Bud Hayes, there can be no higher thank you and praise from a grateful nation for his answering the call of family, Idaho and country, and for his ultimate sacrifice. We all live in hope that you may one day come home.

Notes

Dedication

1. As quoted in Merle Miller, *Plain Speaking: An Oral Biography of Harry S. Truman* (New York: Berkley Publishing Corporation, 1974), 26.

Preface

1. Murray H. Lowenstein, *Passover Haggadah* (Richmond: 1991).
2. George Santayana, *Reason in Common Sense: The Life of Reason Volume 1* (United States: Dover Publications, 1980), 284.

CHAPTER 1. Bud Hayes's Homeland: Filer Idaho and the Magic Valley

1. Tetona Dunlap, "Anatomy of a Canyon: Dissecting the Panorama," *MagicValley.com*, May 3, 2015, http://magicvalley.com/anatomy-of-a-canyon-dissecting-the-panorama/article_9b31def3-3663-59eb-892c-cbfd399e4d45.html.
2. Jim Gentry, *In the Middle and on the Edge: The Twin Falls Region of Idaho* (Twin Falls: College of Southern Idaho, 2003), 29.
3. "Quick Facts, Idaho," *United States Census Bureau*, accessed 2015, http://www.census.gov/quickfacts/table/PST045216/16.
4. "Westward Expansion," *Digital Atlas of Idaho, Idaho State University*, accessed 2015, http://imnh.isu.edu/digitalatlas/geog/explore/expand.pdf.

5. Bud's sister Mary Frances Hayes later married Carl Grabert (1898–1991). Carl's father had immigrated from Shulin, Germany to farm land in Broken Bow, Nebraska. His family later moved by wagon to Twin Falls County, Idaho where they established and worked on a farm as well as in a local dairy. The Graberts' Twin Falls farm continued in operation until Carl became ill in the 1990s.

6. John Hailey, *The History of Idaho* (Boise: Syms-York Company, 1910), 349.

7. 28 Stat 422 (1894); 43 U.S.C. 641 *et seq.*

8. Gentry, *supra* note 2, 153.

9. Pub. L. 57–161 (1902).

10. Gentry, *supra* note 2, 163.

11. Ibid., 173.

12. Ibid., 185.

13. Carla Grabert-Lowenstein, interview by author, December 17, 2015. Family lore says that the Irish ancestors originally were Catholic. However, a rift between the family and a local Catholic church occurred when a child was born and died before being christened. Thereafter the family associated as Protestants. The probable family location of Donegal therefore further logically follows as there is no evidence that the family was Catholic (Northern Ireland and Ulster even today are centers for Protestants). In America, by the turn of the century, the family consisted of practicing Lutherans or Methodists and, thus, appears to have not experienced the discrimination felt by Catholic Irish immigrants in nineteenth century America.

14. "The Great Famine of 1847," *Donegal Town Website*, accessed 2015, http://www.donegaltown.ie/Donegal-Town-History/The-Great-Famine/.

15. "In the pre-Famine period the average Irish adult male consumed 14 lbs. of potatoes—one stone per day when potatoes were in good supply. Even allowing for the fact that potatoes were eaten at each of the three meals every day, it is difficult to comprehend today how a healthy adult male could stow away say, 70 potatoes per day, and a woman not much less—55 potatoes per day on average." (*See* "'Famine 150'—Famine Facts," *Teagasc, the Food and Development Authority*, Winter 1996, http://www.ballinagree.freeservers.com/ffacts.html.

16. Joel Mokyr, "Great Famine, Irish History," *Encyclopedia Britannica*, accessed 2015, http://www.britannica.com/event/Irish-

Potato-Famine.

17. *Putnam County, Illinois*, accessed 2015, http://www.co.putnam
.il.us/.

18. "Quick Facts, Putnam County, Illinois," *United States Census Bureau*, accessed 2014, http://www.census.gov/quickfacts/table/
PST045216/00.

19. Henry A. Ford, *Earliest Historical Facts of Marshall-Putnam Counties Also Bureau and Stark Counties* (1860), accessed 2015,
http://genealogytrails.com/ill/marshall/1860FordsHistory/chapt8.htm.

20. Birthplace found from Mary Hayes's 1922 Birth Certificate.
(Source: Bureau of Vital Statistics, State of Idaho, "File No. 102852,"
June 19, 1922.)

21. "Fremont, Elkhorn and Missouri Valley Railroad," *Wikipedia*,
accessed 2015, http://en.wikipedia.org/wiki/Fremont,_Elkhorn_and
_Missouri_Valley_Railroad. By 1903, the Fremont, Elkhorn and
Missouri Valley Railroad had been acquired by the Chicago Northwestern Railroad (CNW). Then, in the late twentieth century, the CNW was
acquired by the Union Pacific Railroad (based in Omaha), which today
is the primary rail carrier to Southern Idaho. *See also Nebraska Railroad Museum*, accessed 2015, http://www.fremontrailroad.com.

22. Dot Greene, e-mail message to author, December 31, 2015. The
message provides the Philby genealogy from the Philby family Bible.
See also "Deshler, Nebraska," *DeshlerChamber.org*, accessed 2015,
http://www.deshlerchamber.org/. At the time the Philby family lived in
Deshler it was known for its local broom factory.

23. "History of the Magic Valley," *AndersonCamp.com*, accessed
2015, http://www.andersoncamp.com/info-and-amenities/history-of-
the-magic-valley/.

24. Dot Greene, e-mail message to author, January 1, 2016; *also*
Carla Faye Grabert-Lowenstein, interview by author, December 27,
2015. Records show that BK's wife, Mary Catherine Philby, died in
Filer a few years later (in 1921), leaving Fay to raise a family of four,
including BK, Nedra, Owen and herself. Details about Nedra's father
and the circumstances of her birth in Nebraska are unknown. Her son,
Mike Greene, recalled that when he would ask his mother or grandmother about Nedra's father neither would ever respond. (Source:
Michael Greene, interview by author, June 2, 2016.)

25. United States Census Bureau, "U.S. Census, Idaho," 1920.

26. The area was later also used for raising sheep that had been brought there by Basque immigrants from Spain (by way of South America, and later California). This led to conflicts between the sheep farmers and the cattle ranchers as the sheep destroyed cattle-grazing lands. The antipathy from those conflicts might explain later letters from Bud where he expresses an aversion for the lamb that the U.S. Army Air Force was feeding him, and he longed for his family's home-raised Idaho beef.

27. "Twin Falls County, Idaho," *State of Idaho*, accessed 2015, http://www.idaho.gov/aboutidaho/county/twin-falls.

28. United States Census Bureau, "U.S. Census, Idaho," 1940.

29. Hailey, *supra* note 6, 374.

30. Ibid.

31. Mary Hayes Certificate of Live Birth, provided by Greene, *supra* note 24.

32. "Frank Harmon Hayes," *Ancestry.com*, accessed May 2016, http://www.ancestry.com. A search for "Frank Harmon Hayes" at Anecstry.com showed that after he left his family he resided in Siskiyou, California through World War II. He later died in Dillon, Montana (date unknown).

33. Greene, *supra* note 24.

34. Ibid.

35. Carla Faye Grabert-Lowenstein, interview by author, December 31, 2015.

CHAPTER 2. Bud Hayes's Early Years

1. Frank P. Hayes, "My Autobiography, Filer High School, Filer, Idaho," 1940, 1.

2. Mary Frances (Hayes) Grabert, interview by author, December 31, 2015.

3. Hayes, *supra* note 1.

4. Ibid.

5. Ibid., 2.

6. Dot Greene, e-mail message to author, December 31, 2015. Percy added the "e" to the Green name to distinguish his business from a firm in Denver, Colorado that had a similar name. Thereafter the fam-

ily surname was spelled "Greene."

7. As a result of mechanization, today round bales of hay are typically five feet by six feet in dimension and can weigh up to seventeen hundred pounds. (*See* Dennis Hancock, "What Does a Round Bale Weigh?," *Forages, Southern Farmer*, September 2012, http://magissues.farmprogress.com/stf/SF09Sep12/stf050.pdf.)

8. Hayes, *supra* note 1, 2.

9. Admiral Richard E. Byrd was a native of the author's home state of Virginia. Richmond, Virginia's airport was named for him ("Byrd Field"). Later the airport was renamed Richmond International Airport, which now has a terminal named for Byrd. Admiral Byrd's brother, Harry Byrd, Sr., became Governor of Virginia as well as a longstanding and prominent U.S. Senator. His grandson, Harry Byrd, Jr., later also became a longstanding and prominent U.S. Senator from Virginia.

10. There is some ambiguity about whether Byrd himself was present during this visit. Some sources suggest the pilot Bud and Mary met might have been Alton Walker's pilot, Robert L. Myrick. Nevertheless, both Bud's autobiography and the firsthand witness recollections of Bud's sister, Mary Hayes (Grabert), clearly and specifically recall that it was Admiral Byrd they met, and we cannot find reliable evidence to the contrary.

11. Hayes, *supra* note 1, 2.

12. The average temperature for November 1936 in Twin Falls, Idaho was fifty-five degrees Fahrenheit (*See* "Past Weather Data, Twin Falls, ID," *Weather Source*, accessed 2015, http://weather-warehouse.com/WeatherHistory/PastWeatherData_Hollister_TwinFalls_ID_November.html.)

13. Mary Frances (Hayes) Grabert, interview by author, December 20, 2015.

14. After the cross-country flights, Walker sold the Byrd Fairchild aircraft to a division of the company that manufactured it, Fairchild Aerial Survey of Los Angeles, California. It ultimately was donated to the Smithsonian National Air and Space Museum. At the time this book was written the plane was on loan to the Virginia Aviation Museum in Richmond, Virginia, located next to the Richmond airport that has a terminal named after Byrd.

15. Hayes, *supra* note 1, 2. Due to inflation, $1.00 in 1934 would be $17.78 in 2015. Thus, Bud and Mary's sale of the pigs in 2015 dollars

would equal $693.42. It was quite a good sale for its time! (For monetary conversions *see* "Inflation Calculator," *Dollar Times*, accessed 2015, http://www.dollartimes.com/calculators/inflation.htm.)

16. Hayes, *supra* note 1, 2.

17. Eden, Idaho was a small town, at the time having a population of less than three hundred. It is located west of Filer, in Jerome County, Idaho. Bud's mother Fay had taken a schoolteacher position there.

18. Hayes, *supra* note 1, 3.

19. Equal to $168.00 in 2015.

20. Hayes, *supra* note 1, 3.

CHAPTER 3. Clouds of War Descend on Idaho and Filer

1. Summaries in this chapter come from a variety of generally-available facts about World War II. Information about the origins of the war has been well researched for and presented in hundreds of books on the subject. Perhaps one of the best of these books is the following award winning book: William L. Shirer, *The Rise and Fall of The Third Reich: A History of Nazi Germany* (New York: Simon & Shuster, 1960). The summaries in this chapter are offered as context to the environment in Bud's hometown of Filer, Idaho during the early years of World War II (1937–41), leading up to the formal U.S. entry into the war following Japan's attack on Pearl Harbor on December 7, 1941, and the U.S. declaration of war on December 8, 1941.

2. Sir Winston Churchill, "Speech to Parliament, (British) House of Commons" after Munich Agreement (London, October 1938).

3. A. Scott Berg, *Lindbergh* (New York: G.P. Putnam & Sons, Inc., 1998), 417.

4. American Experience, *The Radio Priest (Reverend Charles E. Coughlin)*, TV Episode (December 13, 1988: Public Broadcasting System).

5. Jim Gentry, *In the Middle and on the Edge: The Twin Falls Region of Idaho* (Twin Falls: College of Southern Idaho, 2003), 177, 178.

6. The Philippines and Guam were not classic "colonial" possessions of the United States in the sense that the other areas were colonial

possessions of the European nations. Instead, the United States acquired both (along with Puerto Rico) as part of a 1899 treaty with Spain that ended the Spanish–American War. The United States intended to rid these small nations of their disrespectful imperial ruler Spain, and to encourage them to self-govern their people, which was a key objective of civilian governor and future U.S. President William Howard Taft. This self-government would not become a reality until 1946, after the end of World War II. (*See* Doris Kearns Goodwin, *The Bully Pulpit: Theodore Roosevelt, William Howard Taft, and the Golden Age of Journalism* [New York: Simon & Schuster, 2013], 260.)

7. W.A. Mattice, "The Weather of 1941 in the United States," *Weather Bureau, Washington, DC* (1942).

8. Mary Frances (Hayes) Grabert, interview by author, February 8, 2016.

9. Eric Larson, "Filer's Pearl Harbor Survivor was Among Idaho's Last," *The Times-News* (Twin Falls, ID), April 15, 2011. Leroy Kohntopp later became one of the leaders of the Pearl Harbor Survivors Association.

10. "Pearl Harbor BP 19," *Boston.com*, accessed 2015, http://inapcache.boston.com/universal/site_graphics/blogs/bigpicture/2011 pearlharbor/bp19.jpg. The U.S.S. Maryland was hit, but was in relatively shallow water and only sank about eight feet, which allowed many to escape. (*See* "Leroy Kohntopp, U.S. Navy, U.S.S. Maryland," *Pearl Harbor Survivors*, accessed 2015, http://pearlharborsurvivors.home stead.com/KohntoppLeroy.html.)

CHAPTER 4. Bud Joins the U.S. Army Air Force

1. Michael Haynes, "Counting Soviet Deaths in the Great Patriotic War: Comment," *Europe-Asia Studies* 55, no. 2 (2003): 300–309.

2. General Douglas MacArthur had spent much of his early life in the Philippines. His father, General Arthur MacArthur, was the U.S. Military Governor of the Philippines from 1899 until William Howard Taft was appointed civilian governor general on July 4, 1901. (*See* Doris Kearns Goodwin, *The Bully Pulpit: Theodore Roosevelt, William Howard Taft, and the Golden Age of Journalism* [New York: Simon & Schuster, 2013], 267.)

3. "Civilian Exclusion Order No. 1," 8 Fed. Reg. (1942), 982.

4. "Japanese-American Internment Camps in Idaho and the West, 1942-1945," *FARRIT*, accessed 2015, http://farrit.lili.org/node/94.

5. The relocation of Japanese Americans remains a blot in the annals of U.S. history and was based on longstanding suspicion of and racial prejudice against Asians on the West Coast. There was no similar relocation effort for German Americans or Italian Americans, who were heavily concentrated on the East Coast, even though groups like the German-American Bundt were outright sympathetic to Hitler. Notwithstanding the internment camps, many Japanese Americans volunteered for the U.S. Army during World War II and served with distinction in Europe (most notably in the 442nd Infantry Regiment, which was one of the most decorated during World War II.

Fred Korematsu was a loyal American citizen, but was of Japanese ancestry. When he was faced with Civilian Evacuation Order Number 34, ordering him and other Japanese American citizens to leave San Leandro, California, he refused to leave under the notion that the order was a violation of his 14th Amendment and Habeas Corpus constitutional rights. A court convicted him, and his family relocated to Tanforan Camp in Topez, Utah.

In what later became a notorious decision, the U.S. Supreme Court upheld Korematsu's conviction. (*See Korematsu v. U.S.*, 323 U.S. 211 [1944].) Much later, on April 19, 1984, upon petition for a *writ of coram* (which was vacated due to judicial error), the U.S. District Court, Northern District of California, vacated Korematsu's conviction. (*See* 584 F.Supp. 1406 [N.D. Cal. 1984].) In addition, in 1983 Congress issued resolutions of formal apology to the Japanese American community, though the U.S. Supreme Court has itself never formally vacated its *Korematsu* decision. Fred Korematsu went on to be awarded the Presidential Medal of Freedom in 1998. He died in 2005.

6. "Japanese-American Internment Camps," *supra* note 4.

7. Ralph A. Busco, "A History of the Italian and German Prisoner of War Camps in Utah and Idaho During World War II," *Utah State University, University Libraries* Paper 1647 (1967), http://digitalcommons.usu.edu/etd/1647; *see also* Laurie Welch, "History of Idaho's Largest WWII POW Camp Preserved near Paul," *The Times-News* (Twin Falls, ID), January 22, 2013.

8. The Doolittle Raid caused negligible material damage to Japan, but it succeeded in its goal of raising American morale and casting doubt within Japan about the ability of its military leaders to defend their home islands. It also contributed to Admiral Isoroku Yamamoto's later decision to attack Midway Island in the Central Pacific—an attack that ultimately turned into a decisive strategic defeat of the Imperial Japanese Navy by the U.S. Navy in the Battle of Midway. Doolittle, who initially believed that he might lose all of his aircraft leading to his being court-martialed, instead received the Medal of Honor and was promoted two steps up to Brigadier General. (*See* "The Doolittle Tokyo Raiders," *DoolittleRaider.com*, accessed 2015, http://www.doolittle raider.com.)

9. Known as the "Burke-Wadsworth Act," Pub.L. 76–783, 54 Stat. 885 (1940).

10. Mary Frances (Hayes) Grabert, interview by author, December 22, 2015.

11. Mary's Royal Aristocrat typewriter, by its serial number, was one of the last manufactured by The Royal Typewriter Company at the time. Royal, founded in 1904, was an innovator in typewriters. It was headquartered in New York City, with its manufacturing taking place in Hartford, Connecticut. During World War II, Royal converted all of its manufacturing to support the war effort by making machine guns, rifles, bullets, aircraft propellers and airplane engine parts. It was not until September 1945 that Royal converted back to the production of type-writers. (*See* "About Us, History," *The Royal Typewriter Company*, accessed 2015, http://www.royalsupplies.com/about-us/.)

12. James Bradley, *Flyboys: A True Story of Courage* (New York: Little Brown and Co., 2003), 79.

13. As far as the rate of mortality, Bomber Command had one the highest rates of death of any service during World War II, save for the German submarine force. A total of 59,423 Royal Air Force crew members were killed out of a force of roughly 125,000 men, which is a rate of 47.5 percent killed. If wounded are added into that count, then the total casualty rate goes up to 54.3 percent. In the period prior to D-Day, the fatality rate alone was close to 65 percent. (*See* John Ellis, *Brute Force: Allied Strategy and Tactics in the Second World War*, [New York: Viking Press, 1990], 221.)

14. "Eighth Air Force," *Combat Losses*, accessed 2015, http://www
.taphilo.com/history/8thaf/8aflosses.shtml.

15. U.S. Army Air Force, "Form I-380 Identification Data (First Lieutenant Frank P. Hayes)," September 23, 1948.

16. Ibid.

CHAPTER 5. U.S. Army Air Force Pilot Training

1. Frederick J. Shaw, *Locating Air Force Base Sites: History's Legacy* (CreateSpace Independent Publishing Platform, 2012); *see also* Thomas A. Manning, *History of Air Education and Training Command, 1942–2002* (Randolph Air Force Base, Texas: AETC, 2005).

2. Edwin P. Hoyt, *Yamamoto: The Man Who Planned Pearl Harbor* (New York: McGraw-Hill, 1990); *see also* Kennedy Hickman, "Admiral Isoroku Yamamoto," *ThoughtCo.*, accessed 2015, http://militaryhistory.about.com/od/naval/p/Yamamoto.htm.

3. Colonel W.A. Robertson (Commandant and Base Commander, Santa Ana Army Air Base, Santa Ana, CA), letter to Fay Fern Jensen, June 24, 1943.

4. Ibid.

5. Ibid.

6. "Hemet, California," *City of Hemet*, accessed 2015, http://www.cityofhemet.org/.

7. Frank P. Hayes, letter to parents Fay Fern and George Jensen, July 31, 1943.

8. "Vol. VI. Men and Planes," in *The Army Air Forces in World War II*, eds. Wesley Frank Craven and James Lea Cate (Washington: Office of Air Force History, 1983), 557–85, http://www.ibiblio.org/hyperwar/AAF/VI/AAF-VI-17.html.

9. "Ryan PT-20 / 21 / 22 Recruit," *Warbird Alley*, accessed 2015, http://www.warbirdalley.com/pt22.htm.

10. Hayes, *supra* note 7.

11. "PT-22 Front Cockpit," *Warbird Alley*, accessed 2015, http://www.warbirdalley.com.

12. Barry Schiff, "Ryan PT-22: Not Just Another Pretty Face," *AOPA.org*, June 1, 2008, http://www.aopa.org/news-and-media/all-news/2008/june/01/ryan-pt-22-not-just-another-pretty-face. The detailed description of Bud's takeoff and flying in the Ryan PT-22 in this

portion of the book was adapted from the detailed descriptions in Schiff's article.

13. Ibid.

14. Ibid.

15. Hayes, *supra* note 7.

16. Frank P. Hayes, letter to parents Fay Fern and George Jensen, August 16, 1943.

17. $130.29 in 1943 equates to $1,810.27 in 2015. Longines men's watches of similar nature in 2015 cost this same amount.

18. Hayes, *supra* note 16.

19. Frank P. Hayes, letter to parents Fay Fern and George Jensen, September 8, 1943.

20. $173.67 in 2015.

21. $26.12 in 2015.

CHAPTER 6. Advanced Pilot Training and Officer Commission

1. "Vultee BT-13 Valiant," *Snappy Goat*, accessed 2016, https://snappygoat.com.

2. "Vultee BT-13 Valiant," *Warbird Alley*, accessed 2015, http://www.warbirdalley.com/bt13.htm.

3. Frank P. Hayes, letter to parents Fay Fern and George Jensen, October 18, 1943.

4. $70 in 2015.

5. Merced Army Air Field, "Aviation Cadet Class 44-B, U.S. Army Air Force," in *Flight Lines* (1943), 17.

6. "Welcome to Douglas, Arizona," *City of Douglas*, accessed 2015, http://www.douglasaz.org/. In 2015 Douglas's population was approximately eighteen thousand people.

7. "Douglas Municipal Airport," *Airports-Worldwide.com*, accessed 2015, http://www.airports-worldwide.com/usa/georgia/douglas_municipal_georgia.php.

8. U.S. Army Advanced Flying School, Douglas, Arizona, *Class Book* (1943), 13.

9. $250 equates to $3,474 in 2015. The major's contact got Bud's uniforms for $200, which is $2,770 in 2015. It was a substantial savings.

10. Frank P. Hayes, letter to parents Fay Fern and George Jensen, December 9, 1943.

11. Ibid.

12. U.S. Army Air Force, "Form I-380 Identification Data (First Lieutenant Frank P. Hayes)," September 23, 1948.

13. Frank P. Hayes, letter to parents Fay Fern and George Jensen, December 16, 1943.

14. "Cessna T-50 / UC-78 Bobcat," *Warbird Alley*, accessed 2015, http://www.warbirdalley.com/uc78.htm.

15. Frank P. Hayes, letter to parents Fay Fern and George Jensen, December 20, 1943.

16. Frank P. Hayes, letter to parents Fay Fern and George Jensen, December 30, 1943.

17. Ibid.

18. W. David Lewis and Wesley Phillips Newton, *Delta: The History of an Airline* (Athens: University of Georgia Press, 1979), 12.

19. Ibid.

20. Frank P. Hayes, letter to parents Fay Fern and George Jensen, February 21, 1944.

21. Mike Radowski, "Selman Army Airfield," *USAF-NAV-History.com*, accessed 2015, http://usaf-nav-history.com/selman.html.

22. Ibid.

23. Ibid.

24. Hayes, *supra* note 20.

25. During World War II the average officer base pay was $203.50 per month, which is approximately $2,750 in 2015. (*See National World War II Museum*, accessed 2015, http://www.nationalww2museum.org.)

26. $2,085 in 2015.

27. Hayes, *supra* note 20.

28. Ibid.

29. It is an interesting fate of history that men of landlocked states in the United States rose to prominence in the Navy. None other than Admiral Chester W. Nimitz, World War II's Commander in Chief, U.S. Pacific (CINCPAC), came from the Central Texas town of Fredericksburg.

30. "31 Things People From Idaho Have To Explain To Out-Of-Towners (#26 The Stars Are Much Bigger, Brighter And More Beauti-

ful In Idaho)," *MOVOTO*, accessed 2015, http://www.movoto.com /guide/id/things-people-from-idaho-have-to-explain/.

31. "Old-Fashioned Navigation," *Microsoft*, September 30, 2008, http://www.microsoft.com/Products/Games/FSInsider/freeflight/Pag es/OldFashionedNavigation.aspx.

CHAPTER 7. Army versus Navy: The Great Air–Sea Rescue Debate and the PBY Aircraft Project

1. James Bradley, *Flyboys: A True Story of Courage* (New York: Little Brown and Co., 2003), 42, 43.

2. Thomas A. Hughes, "Yamamoto Isoroku," *Encyclopedia Britannica*, June 15, 2016, http://www.britannica.com/biography/Yam amoto-Isoroku.

3. Ibid.

4. Bradley, *supra* note 1, 46, 50–51.

5. "William 'Billy' Mitchell: An Air Power Visionary," *HistoryNet*, accessed 2015, http://www.historynet.com/william-billy-mitch ell-an-air-power-visionary.htm.

6. Walter R. Borneman, *MacArthur at War: World War II in the Pacific* (New York: Little Brown and Co., 2016), 287.

7. Ibid., 262.

8. Ibid., 301.

9. David Sears, *Pacific Air: How Fearless Flyboys, Peerless Aircraft, and Fast Flattops Conquered the Skies in the War with Japan* (Cambridge: Da Capo Press, 2011), 183.

10. Borneman, *supra* note 6, 277

11. Ibid.

12. Ibid., 267.

13. Ibid., 264. The Allied strategy remained a political quirk because of the close ties of the United States to Europe, even though the United States entry into World War II itself was precipitated by the 1941 Japanese attack on at Pearl Harbor, Hawaii.

14. Ibid., 335.

15. "Vol. VII. Medicine, Morale, and Air–Sea Rescue," in *The Army Air Forces in World War II*, eds. Wesley Frank Craven and James Lea Cate (Washington: Office of Air Force History, 1983), 477.

16. Ibid., 481.

17. Robert J. Serling, *From the Captain to the Colonel: An Informal History of Eastern Airlines* (New York: The Dial Press, 1980), 189.

18. Ibid., 196–98.

19. "History of Air Sea Rescue," *PBYRescue.com*, accessed 2015, http://pbyrescue.com/History/air-sea.htm.

20. Craven and Cate, *supra* note 15, 479.

21. Ibid., 499.

22. Ibid., 479.

23. P.M. Hut, "Allowing Turf Battles To Impact The Project Team—Project Management Mistake #13," in *The Project Management Hut*, September 24, 2008, http://www.pmhut.com/allowing-turf-battles-to-impact-the-project-team-project-management-mistake-13.

24. Ibid.

25. "History of Air Sea Rescue," *supra* note 19.

26. Borneman, *supra* note 6, 365–66.

27. Craven and Cate, *supra* note 15, 480–81.

28. U.S. Army Air Force, "Second Emergency Rescue Squadron, Squadron Order No. 37, 6 February 1944," February 6, 1944, http://pbyrescue.com.

29. "History of Air Sea Rescue," *supra* note 19.

30. "Second Emergency Rescue Squadron, Squadron History," *PBYRescue.com*, accessed 2015, http://pbyrescue.com.

31. U.S. Army Air Force, "Second Emergency Rescue Squadron, Operations Order No. 149, 27 June 1944," June 27, 1944, http://pbyrescue.com.

32. U.S. Army Air Force, "Second Emergency Rescue Squadron, General Order No. 239, 23 September 1944," September 23, 1944, http://pbyrescue.com.

33. Sears, *supra* note 9, 186, 187.

34. Roscoe Creed, *PBY: The Catalina Flying Boat* (Annapolis: Naval Institute Press, 1985), 225–26.

35. Craven and Cate, *supra* note 15, 481–82. And also four other Emergency Rescue Squadrons: the First Emergency Rescue Squadron (serving in the Mediterranean), the Fourth (stationed at Iwo Jima to serve the Twentieth Air Force), the Fifth (serving with the Eighth Air Force in England) and the Seventh (which operated in the China /Burma/India theater). The emergency rescue squadrons plucked fighter

and bomber crews from the endless waters of the South Pacific, from atolls and from island beaches and returned them safely to their units.

CHAPTER 8. The PBY Catalina "Flying Boat" Aircraft

1. "Consolidated PBY Catalina," *Warbird Alley*, accessed 2015, http://warbirdalley.com/cat.htm. (Source was used for all preceding paragraphs as well.)

2. Roscoe Creed, *PBY: The Catalina Flying Boat* (Annapolis: Naval Institute Press, 1985), 26, 27.

3. AOPALIVE, *PBY Catalina*, Video, directed by Jim Slattery (August 28, 2014; San Diego: Greatest Generation Naval Museum), http://www.vimeo.com/99919467. The video discusses operating a PBY Catalina.

4. Creed, *supra* note 2, 27, 28.

5. Ibid., 34.

6. Ibid.

7. "Specifications, The Consolidated PBY 5A," *The Catalina Preservation Society*, accessed 2015, http://pbycatalina.com/specifica tions/; *see also* Creed, *supra* note 2, 310–13.

8. U.S. Army Air Force stock image "PBY 08," *StinsonFlyer.com*, accessed 2015, http://www.stinsonflyer.com/consolac/pby-08.jpg.

9. Official Navy Photo from "Catalina in Detail," *National Naval Air Museum*, accessed 2015, http://www.navalaviationmuseum.org /history-up-close/aircraft-in-spotlight/catalina-detail/.

10. "Consolidated PBY Catalina," *Snappy Goat*, accessed 2016, https://snappygoat.com.

11. "PBY Cutaway 2," *PBYCatalina.com*, accessed 2015, http:// pbycatalina.com/wp-content/uploads/2013/05/pbycutaway2.gif.

12. "Diagram 2," *DavesWarbirds.com*, accessed 2015, http://www .daveswarbirds.com/blackcat/diagram2.gif.

13. Creed, *supra* note 2, 100–18.

14. "Catalina in Detail," *supra* note 9.

15. Office of the Operations Officer (APO #719), U.S. Army Air Force, "Second Emergency Rescue Squadron, Mission Report, 18 July 1945," July 18, 1945, http://pbyrescue.com/.

16. Various records indicate that most U.S. Army Air Force PBY Catalinas were manufactured by Canadian Vickers, Ltd. in Montreal, Quebec, Canada, under subcontract with Consolidated Aircraft Company. Vickers also supplied the Royal Canadian Air Force and the British Royal Air Force. And Consolidated Aircraft Company itself produced most of the PBY aircraft assigned to the U.S. Navy.

17. U.S. Army Air Force, "Mission Report," *supra* note 15.

18. *PBYRescue.com*, accessed 2015, http://pbyrescue.com/.

CHAPTER 9. U.S. Navy Training and a Second Set of Wings

1. Frank P. Hayes, letter to parents Fay Fern and George Jensen, May 19, 1944.

2. Ibid. Keesler Field (now Keesler Air Force Base) in Biloxi, Mississippi was to be Bud's next stop after his PBY training in Pensacola, Florida.

3. Roscoe Creed, *PBY: The Catalina Flying Boat* (Annapolis: Naval Institute Press, 1985), 225–26.

4. Hayes, *supra* note 1.

5. Frank P. Hayes, letter to parents Fay Fern and George Jensen, circa May 30, 1944.

6. Ibid.

7. Ibid. The military procured few PB-2s from Consolidated Aircraft during the war as they were more expensive to make. The PBY Catalina was less expensive and could be mass-produced relatively quickly.

8. Ibid.

9. Frank P. Hayes, letter to parents Fay Fern and George Jensen, June 13, 1944.

10. Frank P. Hayes, letter to parents Fay Fern and George Jensen, June 19, 1944.

11. "Catalina 03," *Salimbeti.com*, accessed 2015, http://www.salimbeti.com/aviation/images/buck%20danny/catalina03.jpg.

12. James Teegarden (Director, PBYRescue.com), interview by author, February 5, 2016.

CHAPTER 10. The Long Wait for War

1. U.S. Army Air Force, "Second Emergency Rescue Squadron, Order No. 8, 28 February 1944," February 28, 1944, http://pbyrescue.com.

2. "Biloxi," *City of Biloxi*, accessed 2015, http://www.biloxi.ms.us/.

3. Hunter Army Air Force Base in Savannah, Georgia in the early 1940s was a training base for U.S. Army Air Force anti-submarine warfare, and it was later turned over to the U.S. Navy. It is believed that Vickers Ltd. shipped PBY Catalinas to the Port of Savannah, and they were then transferred to Hunter Army Air Force Base for initial service and shakedown flights before finally being transferred to the Second Emergency Rescue Squadron at Keesler Army Air Field in Biloxi, Mississippi.

4. Greg Gregersen, letter to Mary Frances (Hayes) Grabert, February 14, 1998.

5. Frank P. Hayes, letter to parents Fay Fern and George Jensen, June 29, 1944.

6. Ibid.

7. "Stuttgart, Arkansas," *Stuttgart Chamber of Commerce*, accessed 2015, http://www.stuttgartarkansas.org/.

8. Frank P. Hayes, letter to parents Fay Fern and George Jensen, August 18, 1944.

9. General George S. Patton, "Speech to the U.S. Third Army" (England, June 5, 1944). The speech also became popular as the iconic opening scene in the movie *Patton* (1970: 20th Century Fox), which won Best Picture at the Academy Awards in 1970.

10. "Beech AT-10 Wichita," *National Museum of the U.S. Air Force*, accessed 2015, http://www.nationalmuseum.af.mil/Visit/MuseumExhibits/FactSheets/Display/tabid/509/Article/196296/beech-at-10-wichita.aspx.

11. Frank P. Hayes, letter to parents Fay Fern and George Jensen, *supra* note 8.

12. Roscoe Creed, *PBY: The Catalina Flying Boat* (Annapolis: Naval Institute Press, 1985), 233.

13. "Consolidated PBY Catalina," *Warbird Alley*, accessed 2015, http://warbirdalley.com/cat.htm.

14. U.S. Army Air Force, "Second Emergency Rescue Squadron, Pilots Roster," *PBYRescue.com*, accessed 2015, http://pbyrescue.com.

15. Frank P. Hayes, letter to parents Fay Fern and George Jensen, October 18, 1944. A "shavetail" was a newly-commissioned officer, particularly a Second Lieutenant.

16. Ibid., 2.

17. $203.00 in 2015.

18. Frank Hayes, letter to parents Fay Fern and George Jensen, November 10, 1944.

19. Ibid., 2.

20. Frank P. Hayes, letter to parents Fay Fern and George Jensen, December 13, 1944. The "Carole" referenced in this letter is Bud's niece, Carole Greene (born in 1936), who is the daughter of his oldest sister, Nedra, and her husband Percy. Later in life Carole married Air Force veteran Ron Kasel who went into the trout farming business and later the cattle ranching business. Today Carole and Ron Kasel live in Twin Falls, Idaho. Nedra later had a son named Michael Greene who went into the family trout farming business. Michael, now retired, also lives with his wife in Twin Falls, Idaho.

21. Frank P. Hayes, letter to parents Fay Fern and George Jensen, December 20, 1944.

22. Ibid.

23. Ibid.

24. Ibid. Sergeant James Gatley, who was one of this book's early reviewers and is an Army Airborne veteran of combat in Afghanistan, noted that Bud's complaints about the food during World War II are complaints that have not changed in the over seventy years that followed the war. Sergeant Gatley remarked, "I found it humorous that Bud complained of the same things in his letters home that the soldiers of today complain about: Lousy chow, commanders who are prima donnas and don't know which end is up, and REMFs mucking up the battlefield who have no place being there at all." (Source: James Gatley [Sergeant, U.S. Army, Retired], e-mail message to author, June 5, 2016.)

25. Hayes, *supra* note 21.

CHAPTER 11. Into the War at Last

1. "A Tribute to the Great Boeing B-29 Superfortress," *B-29-Superfortress.com*, accessed 2015, http://www.b29-superfortress.com/.

2. Frank Hayes, letter to parents Fay Fern and George Jensen, January 16, 1945.

3. Ibid. At the bottom of the letter Bud asks George if he needs more snuff as Bud's base had a supply available while back in the states it was scarce.

4. Keesler Field Headquarters, "Identification Card and Visitors Pass (Fay P. Jensen)," issued March 22, 1945. The pass lists Fay as being five foot three inches tall, 130 pounds, with red hair and brown eyes. It was signed by Captain James C. Duff, and it had an expiration date of March 26, 1945.

5. Frank P. Hayes, letter to parents Fay Fern and George Jensen, March 4, 1945.

6. Ibid., 2. Bud's sister Mary had married Marvin "Pete" Peterson around 1942. They had one daughter, Megan Peterson (Feller) (born in 1943), who now lives in Kent, Washington. Pete was abusive to Mary and they subsequently divorced. This left Mary to raise her daughter alone, during the war, on her clerk typing pay and with some assistance from family. In 1955, Mary met Carl Grabert, a widowed farmer. Carl's family had also moved from Nebraska (from Broken Bow). Mary and Carl had one daughter, Carla Faye Grabert (born in 1956), who is the author's wife. Carl Grabert passed away February 17, 1991, at age ninety-three.

7. Ibid.

8. "Second Emergency Rescue Squadron, Squadron History," *PBYRescue.com*, accessed 2015, http://pbyrescue.com.

9. J. Howard Baker, *Clarence Lee Coon—2nd Emergency Rescue Squadron*, Video (April 9, 2015), http://www.youtube.com/watch?v=oaMmWf7RlPM. Clarence Lee Coon, from Drew, Mississippi, was drafted in 1943 and was assigned to the U.S. Army Air Force, which trained him as a multi-engine aircraft mechanic—an important crew position for PBY Catalinas. When the Army Air Force PBY Project commenced, he was sent to the Naval Training Center in Pensacola, Florida at the same time Bud arrived there, and the two were in the same squadron (the Second Emergency Rescue Squadron). Within the

squadron Coon was assigned to Lieutenant Bryan Guess's PBY aircraft, call sign "Playmate 42." Guess was eventually one of Bud's roommates in New Guinea.

10. Ibid.

11. "Currituck class heavy seaplane tenders," *Hazegrey Naval History*, accessed 2015, http://www.hazegray.org/navhist/carriers/us_sea2 .htm#curt-cl.

12. Mark Jones, *WW2: Consolidated PBY Catalina Flying Boat*, Video (February 6, 2015), http://www.youtube.com/watch?v=UITXR _Pzh-c.

13. Albert Chavez, "Humanitarian Missions: Former Army Air Forces Pilot Recalls Duty in Philippines," *Warbirds*, December 2002, 31.

14. "Military Aviation on Oahu, 1944," *Hawaii Aviation, State of Hawaii*, accessed 2015, http://aviation.hawaii.gov/world-war-ii/mili tary-aviation-on-oahu-1944/ (quoting from Charles Lindberg, *Wartime Journals* [New York: Harcourt Brace Jovanovich, 1970].)

15. Frank P. Hayes, letter to parents Fay Fern and George Jensen, May 7, 1945.

16. David Sim, "VE Day 70th anniversary: A look at Germany's surrender in 1945 and the end of World War II," *International Business Times*, May 6, 2015, http://www.ibtimes.co.uk/ve-day-70th-anniver sary-look-germanys-surrender-1945ww2-graphic-images-14 99979.

17. Ibid.

18. Hayes, *supra* note 15. Bud's mailing address during this period was: Lt. F.P. Hayes, APO 19221-AW-7, c/o San Francisco, Calif.

19. Mark Twain, *The Innocents Abroad*, (New York: American Publishing Co., 1899).

20. Frank P. Hayes, letter to parents Fay Fern and George Jensen, postmarked May 24, 1945.

21. New Guinea is 303,476 square miles; California is 163,696 square miles. (Source: "Google Maps," *Google*, accessed 2015, http:// www.google.com/maps.)

22. Lieutenant Colonel Benjamin E. Lippincott, *From Fiji Through The Philippines With The Thirteenth Air Force* (San Angelo: Newsfoto Publishing Company, 1948), 169.

23. Morotai Island today is part of the North Maluku Islands of Indonesia. The island is seven hundred square miles and contains

mountains, wooded areas and swamps. Beginning in 1944, it became a key base of operations for the U.S. Army Air Force in the Borneo Campaign. (*See* "Morotai Island," *Encyclopedia Britannica*, February 9, 2016, http://www.britannica.com/place/Morotai-island-Indonesia.)

24. "Photo No. 639," *PBYRescue.com*, accessed 2015, http://pbyrescue.com.

25. Major General Hugh J. Casey, *Engineers of the Southwest Pacific 1941–1945: Vol. VI. Airfield & Base Development* (Washington: U.S. Government Printing Office, 1951), 270.

26. Ibid.

27. Ibid., 271.

28. Frank P. Hayes, *supra* note 20.

29. Casey, *supra* note 25, 278.

30. "Photo No. 551," *PBYRescue.com*, accessed 2015, http://pbyrescue.com.

31. Robert H. Reed (General, U.S. Air Force, Retired; Former Chief of Staff, Supreme Headquarters Allied Powers Europe [NATO]), e-mail message to author, July 14, 2016.

32. James Teegarden, interview by author, February 5, 2016.

33. James Teegarden, e-mail message to author, January 11, 2016.

34. Ibid.

35. Roscoe Creed, *PBY: The Catalina Flying Boat* (Annapolis: Naval Institute Press, 1985), 231.

36. Walter R. Borneman, *MacArthur at War: World War II in the Pacific* (New York: Little Brown and Co., 2016), 475.

37. Ibid.

38. "Vol. VII. Medicine, Morale, and Air–Sea Rescue," in *The Army Air Forces in World War II*, eds. Wesley Frank Craven and James Lea Cate (Washington: Office of Air Force History, 1983), 486.

39. "History of Air Sea Rescue," *PBYRescue.com*, accessed 2015, http://pbyrescue.com/History/air-sea.htm.

40. Arnold Reinhold, "Gibson Girl, Own Work, CC BY-SA 3.0," *Wikimedia.org*, April 19, 2009, http://commons.wikimedia.org/w/index.php?curid=6605294.

41. The town of Zamboanga was an important port and industrial city occupied by Japanese forces. American and Philippine forces liberated the town and Mindanao from Japanese occupation over March 10–12, 1945.

42. "Wood River Man Co-Pilot on Record Rescue of 17 Airmen," *Alton Evening Telegraph* (Alton, IL), March 4, 1945.

43. Flight Officer John "Jack" Leonard served in forty-two missions and was awarded the Air Medal and the Battle Star (Source: Captain Theodore F. Kelly [Adjutant, Air Corps], "Non-Battle Casualty Report," October 15, 1945.) On land, the Japanese Imperial army also trained its soldiers to target and kill combat medics as a way to generate fear among U.S. soldiers and marines that no one would be there for them if they became wounded. (*See*: Bill O'Reilly and Martin Dugard, *Killing the Rising Sun: How America Vanquished World War II Japan* [New York: Henry Holt and Co., 2016], 104.)

44. During the war Jack Leonard was co-pilot for the flight team headed by Lieutenant Robert Davis, along with navigator First Lieutenant Laurence Craig. After the war he substituted for various co-pilots who rotated back to the states, were reassigned or were grounded for various reasons. (Source: Geoff Craig, e-mail message to author, May 5, 2016.)

45. Hayes, *supra* note 20. Bud's stepfather, George Jensen, had served in the Army during World War I.

46. Ibid.

47. Frank Hayes, letter to parents Fay Fern and George Jensen, May 27, 1945.

48. Frank Hayes, letter to parents Fay Fern and George Jensen, May 30, 1945

49. Ibid. Bud usually wrote home every couple weeks. His change to writing almost daily letters during this period is probably an indication of the anxiousness and longing for home that he was feeling amid the heat of combat missions.

50. Frank P. Hayes, letter to parents Fay Fern and George Jensen, June 11, 1945.

51. Borneo is 287,001 square miles; Texas is 268,597 square miles; and Bud's home state of Idaho is 83,642 square miles. (Source: "Google Maps," *Google*, accessed 2015, http://www.google.com /maps.)

52. "Borneo Campaign," *World War II Database*, accessed 2015, http://ww2db.com/battle_spec.php?battle_id=166.

53. Office of the Operations Officer (APO #719), U.S. Army Air Force, "Second Emergency Rescue Squadron, Mission Report, 13 July

1945," July 13, 1945, http://pbyrescue.com/.

54. Hayes, *supra* note 50.

55. Steven E. Anders, "Quartermaster Supply in the Pacific During WWII," *Army Quartermaster Professional Bulletin*, Spring 1990, http://www.qmfound.com/qmcpacific.htm.

56. Squadron History, *supra* note 8.

57. Office of the Operations Officer (APO #719), U.S. Army Air Force, "Second Emergency Rescue Squadron, Mission Report, 18 July 1945," July 18, 1945, http://pbyrescue.com/.

58. Office of the Operations Officer (APO #719), U.S. Army Air Force, "Second Emergency Rescue Squadron, Mission Report, 20 July 1945," July 20, 1945, http://pbyrescue.com/.

59. Office of the Operations Officer (APO #719), U.S. Army Air Force, "Second Emergency Rescue Squadron, Mission Report, 29 July 1945," July 29, 1945, http://pbyrescue.com/.

60. Kennedy Hickman, "Ace," *About Education*, accessed 2015, http://militaryhistory.about.com/od/glossaryofmilitaryterms/g/ace.htm.

61. "Photo No. 1324," *PBYRescue.com*, accessed 2015, http://pbyrescue.com.

62. AKA Captain Miller: WWII Living Historian, "Photos" (various), *Facebook.com*, accessed 2015, http://www.facebook.com/akaCaptainMiller/photos/pcb.242819425917012/242816709250617/?type=3.

63. Office of the Operations Officer (APO #719), U.S. Army Air Force, "Second Emergency Rescue Squadron, Mission Report, 25 July 1945," July 25, 1945. Secret-declassified, courtesy of the U.S. Air Force Historical Department.

64. George C. Kenney (General, United States Army, Commanding), letter to Fay Fern Jensen, September 14, 1945. Bud's Air Medal was awarded in "General Order No. 1951, 10 Sept. 1945," and his Battle Star—Southern Philippine Campaign was awarded in "General Order No. 69, 23 July 1945."

General Kenney (1889–1951) was General Douglas MacArthur's chief air strategist in the Pacific theater. He commanded the Fifth, Seventh and Thirteenth Air Forces, the last of which contained Bud's Second Emergency Squadron. In 1946, General Kenney became the first commander of the Air Force's Strategic Air Command, of which Mountain Home Air Force Base (located in Bud's home state of Idaho) is today a major member.

During World War II, administrative backlogs, bureaucracy and complexity often followed the military when it came to its paperwork, especially toward the end of the war. Bud's actual Air Medal was not physically received by him during his lifetime, but was instead posthumously presented to his mother, Fay Fern Jensen, on April 12, 1946.

65. Frank Hayes, letter to parents Fay Fern and George Jensen, July 24, 1945.

66. Ibid.

67. Hayes, *supra* note 65.

68. Ibid., 2.

69. Office of the Operations Officer (APO #719), U.S. Army Air Force, "Second Emergency Rescue Squadron, Mission Report, 02 August 1945," August 2, 1945, http://pbyrescue.com/; *see also* Creed, *supra* note 35, 236.

70. *PBYRescue.com*, accessed 2015, http://pbyrescue.com.

71. Ibid.

72. Ibid.

CHAPTER 12. On to Action in the Pacific Theater

1. The author's paternal uncle, Dr. Jerold M. Lowenstein (born in 1926), was in the U.S. Navy V-12 Program from 1943–46, while working on an accelerated degree in physics at both the Massachusetts Institute of Technology and Columbia University. Once he graduated he was assigned as an ensign to the U.S.S. Albemarle, which was a laboratory ship that delivered two atomic bombs for testing by naval vessels at the Bikini Atoll in the South Pacific. He then spent two years at Los Alamos as a nuclear physicist. After next receiving an M.D. degree at Columbia University, he trained in internal and nuclear medicine at Stanford University, founded the nuclear medicine department at California Pacific Medical Center and did research at the University of California, San Francisco.

2. "Manhattan Project," *U.S. Department of Energy, Office of Management*, accessed 2015, http://energy.gov/management/office-management/operational-management/history/manhattan-project.

3. Wilson D. Miscamble, "Obama, Truman and Hiroshima," *Wall Street Journal* (New York, NY), May 12, 2016, A15. Dr. Miscamble is

a history professor at the University of Notre Dame and is author of *The Most Controversial Decision: Truman, the Atomic Bombs, and the Defeat of Japan* (Cambridge: Cambridge University Press, 2011).

4. Miscamble, "Obama, Truman and Hiroshima," *supra* note 3.

5. Ibid.

6. Ibid.

7. Robert E. Bilstein, *Airlift and Airborne Operations in World War II* (Washington: Government Printing Office, 1998), 288.

8. Ibid., 289.

9. J.A. "Bill" Saavedra (Colonel, U.S. Air Force, Retired; Volunteer Historian, U.S. Air Force Historical Support Division, U.S. Air Force Office of History, Washington, DC), letter to author, January 12, 2016.

10. George Galdorisi and Thomas Phillips, *Leave No Man Behind: The Saga of Combat Search and Rescue* (St. Paul: Zenith Press, 2009), 543.

11. AKA Captain Miller: WWII Living Historian, "Photos" (various), *Facebook.com*, accessed 2015, http://www.facebook.com/aka CaptainMiller/photos/pcb.242819425917012/242816709250617/? type=3.

12. *PBYRescue.com*, accessed 2015, http://pbyrescue.com.

13. "13th Air Force," *Army Air Corps Library and Museum*, accessed 2015, http://www.armyaircorpsmuseum.org/wwii_13th_Air _Force.cfm.

14. "The 13th Air Force Veterans Association, Its Beginnings," *13th Air Force Veterans*, accessed 2015, http://www.13afvets.org/about .html.

15. Frank P. Hayes, letter to parents Fay Fern and George Jensen, August 14, 1945.

16. $132.00 in 2015.

17. $6.60 in 2015.

18. Hayes, *supra* note 15. Bud's reaction was typical of the times. There was longstanding antipathy (and abuse) that U.S. Army personnel directed toward Filipinos going back to the military governorship of General Arthur MacArthur (General Douglas MacArthur's father) from 1899–1901. These circumstances even led to an insurrection from Philippine natives. Governor General William Howard Taft's later efforts at a more respectful approach, and his attempt to establish Fili-

pino civilian self-rule, were steps in the right direction but nevertheless could not change Army soldiers' and officers' view of Filipinos as "inferior." (*See* Doris Kearns Goodwin, *The Bully Pulpit: Theodore Roosevelt, William Howard Taft, and the Golden Age of Journalism* [New York: Simon & Schuster, 2013], 269–70.)

19. Hayes, *supra* note 15.

20. Greg Gregersen, letter to Fay Fern Jensen, December 3, 1945.

21. *PBYRescue.com*, accessed 2015, http://pbyrescue.com.

22. Second Lieutenant Keith W. Parks was another PBY Catalina pilot in the Second Emergency Rescue Squadron. He roomed with Bud while the squadron was stationed in the Philippines.

23. Keith W. Parks (on behalf of Frank P. Hayes), letter to Fay Fern and George Jensen, August 31, 1945.

24. Bud's military records show no sick calls beyond the finger incident throughout his entire time in service. His records do show routine checks by the flight surgeon, as was required, but with no abnormalities discovered. Bud's only adverse health matter prior to his deployment were two dental fillings in his teeth on August 23, 1944.

25. R. Clements (Brigadier General, U.S. Air Force, Retired), "An Invasion Not Found in the History Books," *KilroyWashere.org*, September 16, 2006, http://www.kilroywashere.org/006-Pages/Invasion.html.

26. Miscamble, "Obama, Truman and Hiroshima," *supra* note 3.

27. "Tinian Island," *Atomic Heritage Foundation*, accessed May 1, 2016, http://www.atomicheritage.org/location/tinian-island.

28. The Manhattan Engineer District, "The Atomic Bombings of Hiroshima and Nagasaki," *AtomicArchieve.com*, June 29, 1946, http://www.atomicarchive.com/Docs/MED/index.shtml.

29. Ibid.

30. Tojo, Japan's Prime Minister during World War II, would not have a quick suicide like Hitler did in Germany. Instead, on September 11, 1945, General Douglas MacArthur ordered Tojo arrested and had his home surrounded by U.S. Military Police, at which point Tojo shot himself with a pistol but did not die. Tojo was taken to a hospital where he recovered. The International Military Tribunal for the Far East then tried him for war crimes, and it convicted him on November 12, 1948. Tojo was executed by hanging on December 23, 1948. (*See* "Tojo Hideki, Prime Minister of Japan," *Encyclopedia Britannica*, accessed

2015, http://www.britannica.com/biography/Tojo-Hideki.)

31. Roscoe Creed, *PBY: The Catalina Flying Boat* (Annapolis: Naval Institute Press, 1985), 236.

32. Office of the Operations Officer (APO #719), U.S. Army Air Force, "Second Emergency Rescue Squadron, Squadron History September 1945, Outline Facts," September 1945.

33. First Lieutenant Donald R. Moberg and Staff Sergeant Robert E. Roult, Office of the Operations Officer (APO #719), U.S. Army Air Force, "Second Emergency Rescue Squadron, Squadron History 1 September 1945 to 30 September 1945, Inclusive," September 1945.

34. Ibid., 3.

35. Frank P. Hayes, letter to parents Fay Fern and George Jensen, September 12, 1945.

36. "Second Emergency Rescue Squadron, Bob Ponder Story," *PBYRescue.com*, April 11, 2016, http://pbyrescue.com.

37. Frank P. Hayes, *supra* note 35.

38. Frank P. Hayes, letter to parents Fay Fern and George Jensen, September 24, 1945.

39. Frank P. Hayes, letter to sister Nedra (Hayes) Greene, September 29, 1945.

40. "Photo No. 141," *PBYRescue.com*, accessed 2015, http://pbyrescue.com.

41. Frank P. Hayes, *supra* note 39.

CHAPTER 13. Bud's Final Mission

1. J. Howard Baker, *Clarence Lee Coon—2nd Emergency Rescue Squadron*, Video (April 9, 2015), http://www.youtube.com/watch?v=oaMmWf7RlPM.Lee Coons.

2. "Photo No. 471," *PBYRescue.com*, accessed 2015, http://pbyrescue.com.

3. Rivets were an engineering challenge for the PBY Catalina's manufacturer, Consolidated Aircraft Company. The company attempted to mitigate the problem by making specially-hardened rivets, freezing the rivets prior to installation with the expectation that as they returned to their regular temperature they would expand and be extra secure in place. The PBY Catalina, however, was subject to extreme airframe stresses, not only from its regular takeoffs and landings (on both sea

and land), but also from heavy battering from seas during rescue operations. In the Pacific, the Cats endured both the immense jungle heat and also freezing temperatures aloft. The freeze and thaw, the metal fatigue, the corrosion from salt water and the operational stresses and loads that the Cats endured was simply too much for the manufacturer to account for in the aircraft's design. (Source: Discovery Channel, *Great Planes—Catalina PBY*, TV Episode [November 15, 2012], http://www.youtube.com/watch?v=rOVN11-WxHc.)

4. Ibid.

5. On Peleliu, Caroline Islands, soldiers from the Japanese Imperial Army's Fourteenth Division, who had been defeated in November 1944, remained active in large numbers, not fully captured by the Allies until August 22, 1947. (*See* Bill O'Reilly and Martin Dugard, *Killing the Rising Sun: How America Vanquished World War II Japan* [New York: Henry Holt and Co., 2016], n. 33.)

6. A search by the National Archives' Missing Air Crew Report Section, which maintains these military records from World War II, found a gap during the period of Bud's plane accident. The U.S. Air Force Historical Support Office also could not locate records of the crash, but had the author contact the U.S. Army Human Resource Command at Fort Knox which, amazingly, found Bud's service record dated March 23, 2016. By pure chance, an Army clerk had, in 1949, placed the only surviving copy of the Missing Air Crew Report documenting Bud's crash, along with an accident investigation summary, into Bud's personnel file. The author has since provided copies of the Missing Air Crew Report for the record to the National Archives, to the U.S. Air Force Historical Support Office and to the Defense MIA/POW Accounting Agency.

7. Larry Leonard, interview by author, May 14, 2016.

8. "John 'Jack' Leonard," photo courtesy of Larry Leonard and family.

9. American Graves Registration Service, Philcon Zone, "Case History For Remains Considered Non-Recoverable," April 25, 1949.

10. U.S. Army Air Force, "Second Emergency Rescue Squadron, Missing Air Crew Report, 10 October 1945," April 23, 1949. For unknown reasons, navigator Lieutenant Clayton L. "Greg" Gregersen's name mistakenly does not appear in the Missing Air Crew Report though he was present during the plane accident and chronicled the

events that surrounded it in detail.

11. Ibid.

12. Greg Gregersen, letter to Fay Fern Jensen, October 22, 1945.

13. "Second Emergency Rescue Squadron, Bob Ponder Story," *PBYRescue.com*, April 11, 2016, http://pbyrescue.com.

14. "Site FLOR8. Aircraft—'The House under the Sea': PBY-5 Catalina BuNo. 08136, Plane Side No. 44-P-8," *Archaehistoria*, accessed 2015, http://www.archaehistoria.org/solomon-islands-arch aeology/21-wwii-archaeological-sites-of-the-florida-islands/51-site-flor8-aircraft-the-house-under-the-sea-pby-5-catalina-buno-08136-plane-side-no-44-p-83.

15. Silverio L. Cadiao (Captain, Philippine Army, Retired), investigation statement, August 6, 1948.

16. Ibid.

17. U.S. Army Air Force "Missing Air Crew Report," *supra* note 10.

18. Ibid.

19. James L. Jarnagin (Captain, Second Emergency Rescue Squadron, Commanding [Philippines]), letter to Fay Fern Jensen, October 10, 1945 (postmarked October 28, 1945).

20. Ibid.

21. Carla Faye Grabert-Lowenstein (Bud's niece), interview by author, December 23, 2015.

22. $132,000 in 2015.

23. U.S. Army Air Force, "Form #72 Personal Affairs Statement (First Lieutenant Frank P. Hayes)," March 22, 1945. The form shows that Bud took the dependent's option, authorizing a Class F allotment for dependents of $100 a month from the Valley National Bank in Douglas, Arizona.

24. H.L. McCoy (Director of Insurance, Veterans Administration, New York, NY), letter to Fay Fern Jensen, December 28, 1945. Fay also received notice from the Veterans Administration, on December 11, 1945, that due to Bud's death in the line of duty she might be entitled to payment of a pension. But it turned out that the Jensens' income was too high to qualify for a pension, and the pension claim form was never completed or filed. Means testing of government benefits was already at work in post-war America.

25. National Service Life Insurance, "Notice of Settlement," March 25, 1946.

26. Charles D. Carle (Colonel, War Department, The Adjutant General's Office, Commanding), letter to Fay Fern Jensen, October 30, 1946.

27. U.S. Air Force, letter of notice to Fay Fern Jensen, April 12, 1947.

28. George C. Kenney (General, U.S. Army Air Force, Commanding), "General Order No. 1951," September 10, 1945.

29. Eric R. Calip (Defense and Armed Forces Attaché, Republic of the Philippines Embassy to the United States), letter to Mary Frances (Hayes) Grabert care of author, August 17, 2016.

EPILOGUE

1. *World War II Foundation*, accessed 2015, http://www.wwii foundation.org.

2. *The National World War II Museum, New Orleans*, accessed 2015, http://www.nationalww2museum.org.

3. *World War II Foundation*, *supra* note 1.

4. David Sears, *Pacific Air: How Fearless Flyboys, Peerless Aircraft, and Fast Flattops Conquered the Skies in the War with Japan* (Cambridge: Da Capo Press, 2011), 339.

5. United States Census Bureau, "U.S. Census," 1940.

6. Ibid.

7. U.S. War Department, "State of Idaho—World War II Honor List of Dead and Missing," June 1946, i.

8. Ibid., ii.

9. Matthew Stoss, "War Stories," *GW Magazine*, Summer 2016, 67.

10. Mishnah Sanhedrin, "4:9; Yerushalmi Talmud," in *Tractate Sanhedrin*, 37a.

11. Roscoe Creed, *PBY: The Catalina Flying Boat* (Annapolis: Naval Institute Press, 1985), 236.

12. United States Census Bureau, "Population Demographics."

13. 82 first generation + 189 second generation = 271 total.

14. "Mountain Home Air Force Base, History," *Mountain Home Air Force Base, U.S. Air Force*, accessed 2015, http://www.mountain

home.af.mil/library/factsheets/factsheet.asp?id=4316; additional information provided to author by Charles Thrash (Colonel, U.S. Air Force, Retired).

15. Pub.L. 78–346, 58 Stat.284m (June 22, 1944).

16. Pub.L. 89–358, 80 Stat.12 (March 3, 1966).

17. "G.I. Bill," *History.com*, accessed 2015, http://www.history.com/topics/world-war-ii/gi-bill.

18. Katrina Pescador, Mark Aldrich and San Diego Air and Space Museum, *Consolidated Aircraft Corporation (Images of America: California)* (Mt. Pleasant: Arcadia Publishing, 2008).

19. "The Catalinas," *Qantas Airlines*, accessed 2015, http://www.qantas.com/travel/airlines/history-catalinas/global/en. The single Indian Ocean hop of 5,652 kilometers (3,512 miles) was the longest nonstop regular passenger flight ever attempted in the world. Celestial navigation had to be used during the flight in order to maintain radio silence when flying over waters patrolled by enemy aircraft. The weight of fuel during the flight limited the Catalina's load to only three passengers and 69 kilograms (152 pounds) of diplomatic and armed forces mail. The flight took twenty-eight to thirty-two hours depending on winds. Qantas retired its PBY Catalinas in November 1958.

20. Emanuel Gustin, "Aircraft and Air Forces: Consolidated PBY Catalina," *Uboat.net*, accessed 2015, http://uboat.net/allies/aircraft/catalina.htm387.

21. Official Navy Photo from "Combat Survivor Evader Locator (CSEL) System," *Naval Air Systems Command*, accessed 2016, http://www.navair.navy.mil/index.cfm?fuseaction=home.displayPlatform&key=DBADA820-7AB2-4938-8C6F-141844C7AFA9.

22. Major General Hugh J. Casey, *Engineers of the Southwest Pacific 1941–1945: Vol. VI. Airfield & Base Development* (Washington: U.S. Government Printing Office, 1951), 263.

23. Carlo Munoz, "The Philippines re-opens military bases to US forces," *The Hill*, July 6, 2012.

24. "F-35 Lightning II Program," *JSR.Mil*, accessed 2015, http://www.jsr.mil/program/.

25. Manila American Cemetery and Memorial, Manila, Philippines, "Tablets of the Missing, Frank P. Hayes," January 5, 2016, http://www.wwiimemorial.com/Registry/plaque_tabletsmissing.aspx?honoredID=756912. The electronic database entry for the plaque erroneous-

ly lists Frank P. Hayes as from "Iowa" rather than from Idaho, and also erroneously lists him as "Second Lieutenant" rather than First Lieutenant. Thanks to a petition by the author, on January 22, 2016, the American Battle Monuments Commission corrected the electronic database entry, and it later advised that Bud's family is entitled to a commutative memorial marker. (Source: Martha R. Sell [Director, Public Programs, American Battle Monuments Commission], letter to author, February 4, 2016.)

26. "Filer Memorial Service for Lieutenant Frank P. Hayes," *Twin Falls Telegram* (Twin Falls, ID), January 18, 1946, 10.

27. Filer Methodist Church, Filer, Idaho, "Victory Star Wallet, World War II," May 25, 1947.

28. A. Elliott McDermid (Superintendent, Filer Rural High School), invitation letter to Bud's family, May 26, 1947.

29. Ron Yates (Twin Falls area historian), e-mail message to author, June 29, 2016.

30. "Memorial Day Dedication Planned," *The Times-News* (Twin Falls, ID), May 28, 1950, 397; *also* Ron Yates (Twin Falls area historian), e-mail message to author, April 2, 2016.

31. Yates e-mail message, *supra* note 30.

32. Ron Yates (Twin Falls area historian), e-mail to author, June 5, 2016.

33. Carla Faye Grabert-Lowenstein (Bud's niece), interview by author, December 2015.

34. Wynter Woodbury (Bud's grand-niece), e-mail message to author, May 21, 2016.

35. Carole's husband, Ron Kasel, was a B-29 flight engineer during the post-Korean War era up until 1956. What was originally their trout farm today continues on as a cattle ranch. (Source: Ron and Carole Kasel, interview by author, June 2, 2016.)

36. Sir Winston Churchill, "Speech to Parliament (British) House of Commons" (London, August 20, 1940).

37. Greg Gregersen, letter to Fay Fern Jensen, October 22, 1945.

38. General Douglas MacArthur, "Thayer Award Speech, 'Duty, Honor, Country,' to the U.S. Military Academy, West Point," (West Point, May 12, 1962), http://www.au.af.mil/AU/AWC/AWCGATE/au-24/au24-352mac.htm.

39. Paul Aurandt, *Paul Harvey's the Rest of the Story* (New York: Bantam Books, 1984).

Bibliography

"31 Things People From Idaho Have To Explain To Out-Of-Towners (#26 The Stars Are Much Bigger, Brighter And More Beautiful In Idaho)." *MOVOTO*. Accessed 2015. http://www.movoto.com/guide/id/things-people-from-idaho-have-to-explain/.

"35th Flying Training Wing (U.S. Army Air Forces)." *Pediaview.com*. Accessed 2015. http://pediaview.com/openpedia /35th_Flying_Training_Wing_(World_War_II).

"A Tribute to the Great Boeing B-29 Superfortress." *B-29-Superfortress.com*. Accessed 2015. http://www.b29-superfor tress.com/.

"About Us, History." *The Royal Typewriter Company*. Accessed 2015. http://www.royalsupplies.com/about-us/.

Air Force Historical Agency, Maxwell Air Force Base. "35th Flying Training Wing, Lineage and History."

"Aircraft Specifications" (various). *Warbird Alley*. Accessed 2015. http://www.warbirdalley.com.

"Ambon Island." *Encyclopedia Britannica*. Accessed 2015. http://www.britannica.com/place/Ambon-island-Indonesia

American Battle Monuments Commission, U.S. Military Cemetery, Manila, Philippines. "Tablets to the Missing."

———. "Frank P. Hayes." Accessed 2015. http://www.abmc.gov /node/518007#.V1v0FvkrKhd.

American Experience, *The Radio Priest (Reverend Charles E. Coughlin)*, TV Episode (December 13, 1988: Public Broadcasting System).

American Graves Registration Service, Pacific Zone. "Additional Information Required to Complete Investigations of Missing

Personnel Cases, Lieutenant Frank Hayes." August 19, 1948.

American Graves Registration Service, PHILCON Zone. "Case History for Remains Considered Non-Recoverable-REPORT." April 25, 1949.

Anders, Steven E. "Quartermaster Supply in the Pacific During WWII." *Army Quartermaster Professional Bulletin,* Spring 1990, http://www.qmfound.com/qmcpacific.htm.

Antaranews.com. Accessed 2015. http://antaranews.com.

AOPALIVE. *PBY Catalina.* Video. Directed by Jim Slattery. August 28, 2014; San Diego: Greatest Generation Naval Museum. http://www.vimeo.com/99919467.

Army Air Corp Library and Museum. Accessed 2015. http://www.armyaircorpsmuseum.org.

Aurandt, Paul. *Paul Harvey's the Rest of the Story.* New York: Bantam Books, 1984.

"Aviation Photos" (various). *Airliners.net.* Accessed 2015. http://www.airliners.net.

"Aviation Photos" (various). *Salimbet.com.* Accessed 2015. http://www.salimbeti.com.

Baker, J. Howard. *Clarence Lee Coon—2nd Emergency Rescue Squadron.* Video. April 9, 2015. Online video at http://www.youtube.com/watch?v=oaMmWf7RlPM.Lee Coons.

"Beech AT-10 Wichita." *National Museum of the U.S. Air Force.* Accessed 2015. http://www.nationalmuseum.af.mil/Visit /MuseumExhibits/FactSheets/Display/tabid/509/Article/196 296/beech-at-10-wichita.aspx.

Berg, A. Scott. *Lindbergh.* New York: G.P. Putnam & Sons, Inc., 1998.

"Biloxi." *City of Biloxi.* Accessed 2015. http://www.biloxi.ms .us/.

Bilstein, Robert E. *Airlift and Airborne Operations in World War II.* Washington: Government Printing Office, 1998.

Borneman, Walter R. *MacArthur at War: World War II in the Pacific.* New York: Little Brown and Co., 2016.

"Borneo Campaign." *World War II Database*. Accessed 2015. http://ww2db.com/battle_spec.php?battle_id=166.

Bradley, James. *Flyboys: A True Story of Courage*. New York: Little Brown and Co., 2003.

Bureau of Vital Statistics, State of Idaho.

"Burke-Wadsworth Act." Pub.L. 76–783, 54 Stat. 885 (1940).

Busco, Ralph A. "A History of the Italian and German Prisoner of War Camps in Utah and Idaho During World War II." *Utah State University, University Libraries*. Paper 1647 (1967). http://digitalcommons.usu.edu/etd/1647.

Cabalsi, Alfredo S. (Veterans Service Officer, Republic of the Philippines Embassy to the United States). E-mail message to author. August 16, 2016.

Cadio, Silverio L. (Captain, Philippine Army, Retired). Investigation statement. August 6, 1948.

Cagle, Nathan (Commander, U.S. Navy, Retired). Interviews by author. 2015–16.

Carle, Charles D. (Colonel, War Department, The Adjutant General's Office, Commanding). Letter to Fay Fern Jensen. October 30, 1946.

Casey, Major General Hugh J. *Engineers of the Southwest Pacific 1941–1945: Vol. VI. Airfield & Base Development*. Washington: U.S. Government Printing Office, 1951.

"Catalina in Detail." *National Naval Air Museum*. Accessed 2015. http://www.navalaviationmuseum.org/history-up-close/aircraft-in-spotlight/catalina-detail/.

Chavez, Albert. "Humanitarian Missions: Former Army Air Forces Pilot Recalls Duty in Philippines." *Warbirds*. December 2002.

City of Filer, Idaho. Accessed 2015. http://www.cityoffiler.com.

City of Monroe, Louisiana. Accessed 2015. http://www.monroela.us/.

"Civilian Exclusion Order No. 1." 8 Fed. Reg., 982 (1942).

Clark, General Wesley, K. "Never Leave A Soldier Behind." *Military.com*. December 15, 2003. http://www.military.com.

Clements, R. (Brigadier General, U.S. Air Force, Retired). "An Invasion Not Found in the History Books." *KilroyWashere.org*. September 16, 2006. http://www.kilroywashere.org/006-Pages/Invasion.html.

Coyle, Patrick J. (Chaplain, Second Emergency Rescue Squadron). Letter to Fay Fern Jensen. October 20, 1945.

Craig, Geoff (son of Second Emergency Medical Service navigator First Lieutenant Laurence Craig). E-mail message to author. May 5, 2016.

Craven, Wesley Frank and Cate, James Lea (eds.). *The Army Air Forces In World War II (Vols. VI and VII)*. Washington: Office of Air Force History, 1983.

Creed, Roscoe. *PBY: The Catalina Flying Boat*. Annapolis: Naval Institute Press, 1985.

"Currituck class heavy seaplane tenders." *Hazegrey Naval History*. Accessed 2015. http://www.hazegray.org/navhist/carriers/us_sea2.htm#curt-cl.

Department of the Army, Quartermaster Division, American Graves Registration Service (Pacific Zone). "Additional Information Required to Complete Investigation of Missing Personnel Cases." August 19, 1948.

"Deshler, Nebraska." *DeshlerChamber.org*. Accessed 2015. http://www.deshlerchamber.org/.

Discovery Channel. *Great Planes—Catalina PBY*. TV Episode (November 15, 2012). http://www.youtube.com/watch?v=rOVN11-WxHc.

"Douglas Municipal Airport." *Airports-Worldwide.com*. Accessed 2015. http://www.airports-worldwide.com/usa/georgia/douglas_municipal_georgia.php.

Dunlap, Tetona. "Anatomy of a Canyon: Dissecting the Panorama." *MagicValley.com*. May 3, 2015. http://magicvalley.com/anatomy-of-a-canyon-dissecting-the-panorama/article_9b31def3-3663-59eb-892c-cbfd399e4d45.html.

"Eighth Air Force." *Combat Losses*. Accessed 2015. http://www.taphilo.com/history/8thaf/8aflosses.shtml.

Ellis, John. *Brute Force: Allied Strategy and Tactics in the Second World War*. New York: Viking Press, 1990.

"'Famine 150'—Famine Facts." *Teagasc, the Food and Development Authority*. Winter 1996. http://www.ballinagree.free servers.com/ffacts.html.

"Filer, Idaho." *CityData*. Accessed 2015. http://www.citydata .com.

"Filer Memorial Service for Lieutenant Frank P. Hayes." *Twin Falls Telegram* (Twin Falls, ID), January 18, 1946, 10.

Filer Methodist Church, Filer, Idaho. "Victory Star Wallet, World War II." May 25, 1947.

"Filer Pilot Saves 6 Airmen Shot Down off Jap-Held Isle." *The Times-News* (Twin Falls, ID), August 10, 1945.

"Fliers Used As Jap Decoy Rescued From Watery Trap." *The Bergen Evening Record* (Bergen, NJ), Saturday, May 15, 1945.

Ford, Henry A. *Earliest Historical Facts of Marshall-Putnam Counties Also Bureau and Stark Counties* (1860). Accessed 2015. http://genealogytrails.com/ill/marshall/1860FordsHis tory/chapt8.htm.

Ford, Wallace S. (Lieutenant Colonel, U.S. Air Corps, Commanding), Headquarters 5230th Composite Rescue Group (APO #719), U.S. Army Air Force. "Report on Organizational History, 20 October 1944–31 December 1944." 1944.

"Frank Hayes Takes U.S. Airmen from Jap-Infested Island." *The Twin Falls Daily News* (Twin Falls, ID), November 3, 1936.

"Fremont, Elkhorn and Missouri Valley Railroad." *Wikipedia*. Accessed 2015. http://en.wikipedia.org/wiki/Fremont,_Elk horn_and_Missouri_Valley_Railroad.

Galdorisi, George and Phillips, Thomas. *Leave No Man Behind: The Saga of Combat Search and Rescue*. St. Paul: Zenith Press, 2009.

Gentry, Jim. *In the Middle and on the Edge: The Twin Falls Region of Idaho*. Twin Falls: College of Southern Idaho, 2003.

"G.I. Bill." *History.com*. Accessed 2015. http://www.history.com /topics/world-war-ii/gi-bill.

Goodwin, Doris Kearns. *The Bully Pulpit: Theodore Roosevelt, William Howard Taft, and the Golden Age of Journalism.* New York: Simon & Schuster, 2013.

"Google Maps." *Google*. Accessed 2015. http://www.google.com /maps.

Grabert, Mary Frances (Hayes) (Bud's sister). Interviews by author. 2015–16.

Grabert-Lowenstein, Carla Faye (Bud's niece). Interviews by author. 2015–16.

Greene, Michael and Dot (Bud's nephew and nephew's wife). Interviews by author. 2015–16.

Gregersen, Clayton L. "Greg." Letter to Fay Fern Jensen, October 22, 1945.

———. Letter to Mary Frances (Hayes) Grabert, February 14, 1998.

Gustin, Emanuel. "Aircraft and Air Forces: Consolidated PBY Catalina." *Uboat.net*. Accessed 2015. http://uboat.net/allies /aircraft/catalina.htm387.

Hailey, John. *The History of Idaho*. Boise: Syms-York Company, 1910.

"Halmahera Islands." *Encyclopedia Britannica*. Accessed 2015. http://www.britannica.com/place/Halmahera.

Hancock, Dennis. "What Does a Round Bale Weigh?" *Forages, Southern Farmer*. September 2012. http://magissues.farm progress.com/stf/SF09Sep12/stf050.pdf.

Hayes, Frank P. Collective letters home during World War II. 1943–45.

———. "My Autobiography, Filer High School, Filer, Idaho." 1940.

Haynes, Michael. "Counting Soviet Deaths in the Great Patriotic War: Comment." *Europe-Asia Studies* 55, no. 2 (2003): 300–09.

"Hemet, California." *City of Hemet*. Accessed 2015. http://www
.cityofhemet.org/.

Hendrie, Andrew. *Flying Cats: The Catalina Aircraft of World War II*. Annapolis: Naval Institute Press, 1988.

Hickman, Kennedy. "Ace." *About Education*. Accessed 2015. http://militaryhistory.about.com/od/glossaryofmilitaryterms /g/ace.htm.

————. "Admiral Isoroku Yamamoto." *ThoughtCo*. Accessed 2015. http://militaryhistory.about.com/od/naval/p/Yamamoto.htm.

Historical Aviation Preservation Film Unit. *Consolidated PBY-5a Catalina*. Video (February 17, 2014). http://wn.com/pby_5 _catalina.

"History of the Magic Valley." *AndersonCamp.com*. Accessed 2015. http://www.andersoncamp.com/info-and-amenities/his tory-of-the-magic-valley/.

Hoyt, Edwin P. *Yamamoto: The Man Who Planned Pearl Harbor*. New York: McGraw-Hill, 1990.

Hut, P.M. "Allowing Turf Battles To Impact The Project Team— Project Management Mistake #13." In *The Project Management Hut*. September 24, 2008. http://www.pmhut.com/all owing-turf-battles-to-impact-the-project-team-project-management-mistake-13.

"Inflation Calculator." *Dollar Times*. Accessed 2015. http://www
.dollartimes.com/calculators/inflation.htm.

Jarnagin, James L. (Captain, Second Emergency Rescue Squadron, Commanding [Philippines]). Letter to Fay Fern Jensen. October 10, 1945.

Jones, Mark. *WW2: Consolidated PBY Catalina Flying Boat*. Video (February 6, 2015). http://www.youtube.com/watch?v= UITXR_Pzh-c.

Kasel, Carole and Ron (Bud's niece and niece's husband). Interviews by author. 2015–16.

Keesler Field Headquarters. "Identification Card and Visitors Pass (Fay P. Jensen)." Issued March 22, 1945.

Kelley, Theodore F. (Captain, U.S. Air Corps). "Non-Battle Casualty Report, U.S. Army Air Force." October 15, 1945.

Kenney, George C. (General, U.S. Army Air Force, Commanding). "General Order No. 1951." September 10, 1945.

———. Letter to Fay Fern Jensen. September 14, 1945.

Kim, Minsoo. *[FSX] PBY Catalina Startup*. Video (February 10, 2013). http://www.youtube.com/watch?v=gXsGEtI8AbA.

Korematsu v. U.S., 323 U.S. 211 (1944); 584 F.Supp. 1406 (N.D. Cal. 1984).

Leonard, Larry (brother of Flight Officer John "Jack" Leonard). Interviews by author. 2015–16.

Lewis, W. David and Newton, Wesley Phillips. *Delta: The History of an Airline*. Athens: University of Georgia Press, 1979.

Lindberg, Charles. *Wartime Journals*. New York: Harcourt Brace Jovanovich, 1970.

Lippincott, Lieutenant Colonel Benjamin E. *From Fiji Through The Philippines With The Thirteenth Air Force*. San Angelo: Newsfoto Publishing Co., 1948.

Lowenstein, Murray H. *Passover Haggadah*. Richmond: 1991.

MacArthur, Douglas A. (General, U.S. Army Forces, Pacific, Commander-in-Chief). Letter to Fay Fern Jensen. October 31, 1945.

———. "Thayer Award Speech, 'Duty, Honor, Country,' to the U.S. Military Academy, West Point." West Point, May 12, 1962. http://www.au.af.mil/AU/AWC/AWCGATE/au-24/au 24-352mac.htm.

Manchester, William. *American Caesar: Douglas MacArthur 1880–1964*. Boston: Dell Publishing, 1978.

———. *The Last Lion: Winston Spencer Churchill Alone 1932–1940*. Boston: Little Brown and Co., 1988.

"Manhattan Project." *U.S. Department of Energy, Office of Management*. Accessed 2015. http://energy.gov/management/office-management/operational-management/history/manhattan-project.

Manning, Thomas A. *History of Air Education and Training Command, 1942–2002.* Randolph Air Force Base, Texas: AETC, 2005.

Matthews, Michel. "Hidden History of the Magic Valley." *The Times-News* (Twin Falls, ID), 2015.

Mattice, W.A. "The Weather of 1941 in the United States." *Weather Bureau, Washington, DC* (1942).

McCoy, H.L. (Director of Insurance, Veterans Administration, New York, NY). Letter to Fay Fern Jensen. December 28, 1945.

McDermid, A. Elliott (Superintendent, Filer Rural High School). Invitation letter to Bud's family. May 26, 1947.

Merced Army Air Field. "Aviation Cadet Class 44-B, U.S. Army Air Force." In *Flight Lines*. 1943.

Messenger, Robert. "The Luckiest General." *Wall Street Journal* (New York, NY), July 2–3, 2016, C7.

"Military Aviation on Oahu, 1944." *Hawaii Aviation, State of Hawaii.* Accessed 2015. http://aviation.hawaii.gov/world-war-ii/military-aviation-on-oahu-1944/.

Miller, Merle. *Plain Speaking: An Oral Biography of Harry S. Truman.* New York: Berkley Publishing Corporation, 1974.

Miscamble, Wilson D. "Obama, Truman and Hiroshima." *Wall Street Journal* (New York, NY), May 12, 2016, A15.

———. *The Most Controversial Decision: Truman, the Atomic Bombs, and the Defeat of Japan.* Cambridge: Cambridge University Press, 2011.

Moberg, First Lieutenant Donald R. and Roult, Staff Sergeant Robert E., Office of the Operations Officer (APO #719), U.S. Army Air Force. "Second Emergency Rescue Squadron, Squadron History 1 September 1945 to 30 September 1945, Inclusive." September 1945.

Mokyr, Joel. "Great Famine, Irish History." *Encyclopedia Britannica.* Accessed 2015. http://www.britannica.com/event/Irish-Potato-Famine.

Moran, Captain J.R. (DDS, U.S. Army Dental Corps). "Dental Records of Lieutenant Frank P. Hayes." August 23, 1944.

"Morotai Island." *Encyclopedia Britannica*. February 9, 2016. http://www.britannica.com/place/Morotai-island-Indonesia.

"Mountain Home Air Force Base, History." *Mountain Home Air Force Base, U.S. Air Force*. Accessed 2015. http://www.mountainhome.af.mil/library/factsheets/factsheet.asp?id=4316.

Munoz, Carlo. "The Philippines re-opens military bases to US forces." *The Hill*. July 6, 2012.

"National Services Life Insurance Act." 54 Stat. 1008 (1942).

"November 17, 1944, Just Another Day for 2nd Emergency Rescue Squadron." *World War II Today*. Accessed 2015. http://ww2today.com/17-november-1944-just-another-day-for-2nd-emergency-rescue-squadron.

O'Reilly, Bill and Dugard, Martin. *Killing Patton: The Strange Death of World War II's Most Audacious General*. New York: Henry Holt and Co., 2014.

———. *Killing the Rising Sun: How America Vanquished World War II Japan*. New York: Henry Holt and Co., 2016.

Office of the Operations Officer (APO #719), U.S. Army Air Force. "Second Emergency Rescue Squadron, Mission Reports" (various). June–August 1945. (Courtesy of the U.S. Air Force Historical Support Office.)

"Old-Fashioned Navigation." *Microsoft*. September 30, 2008. http://www.microsoft.com/Products/Games/FSInsider/freeflight/Pages/OldFashionedNavigation.aspx.

Patton, General George S. "Speech to the U.S. Third Army." England, June 5, 1944.

PCAviator. Accessed 2015. http://pcaviator.com.

Pescador, Katrina, Aldrich, Mark and San Diego Air and Space Museum. *Consolidated Aircraft Corporation (Images of America: California)*. Mt. Pleasant: Arcadia Publishing, 2008.

Philby family Bible. (Courtesy of Michael and Dot Greene, Twin Falls, Idaho.)

Poissant, William A. "National Service Life Insurance: Its Administration and Experience." *Transactions of Society of Actuaries* 2, no. 3 (1950): 11–29.

Putnam County, Illinois. Accessed 2015. http://www.co.putnam.il.us/.

"Quick Facts" (various). *United States Census Bureau.* Accessed 2015. http://www.census.gov/quickfacts.

Radowski, Mike. "Selman Army Airfield." *USAF-NAV-History.com.* Accessed 2015. http://usaf-nav-history.com/selman.html.

Rawlings, Nate. "The Warrior Ethos: Why We Leave No One Behind." *Time.* May 12, 2012.

"Readjustment Benefits Act." Pub.L. 89–358; 80 Stat. 12 (March 3, 1966).

Reed, Robert H. (General, U.S. Air Force, Retired; Former Chief of Staff, Supreme Headquarters Allied Powers Europe [NATO]). E-mail message to author. July 14, 2016.

Reinhold, Arnold. "Gibson Girl, Own Work, CC BY-SA 3.0." April 19, 2009. http://commons.wikimedia.org/w/index.php?curid=6605294.

Robertson, Colonel W.A. (Commandant and Base Commander, Santa Ana Army Air Base, Santa Ana, CA). Letter to Fay Fern Jensen. June 24, 1943.

Sanhedrin, Mishnah. "4:9; Yerushalmi Talmud." In *Tractate Sanhedrin*, 37a.

Santayana, George. *Reason in Common Sense: The Life of Reason Volume 1.* United States: Dover Publications, 1980.

Scarborough, William E. *"PBY Catalina—Walk Around No. 5."* Carrolton: Squadron/Signal Publications Inc., 1995.

Schiff, Barry. "Ryan PT-22: Not Just Another Pretty Face." *AOPA.org.* June 1, 2008. http://www.aopa.org/news-and-media/all-news/2008/june/01/ryan-pt-22-not-just-another-pretty-face.

Scott, Walter (World War II PBY pilot and PBY instructor, U.S. Navy). Interview by author. September 15, 2016.

Sears, David. *Pacific Air: How Fearless Flyboys, Peerless Aircraft, and Fast Flattops Conquered the Skies in the War with Japan.* Cambridge: Da Capo Press, 2011.

"Second Emergency Rescue Squadron, Squadron History." *PBYRescue.com.* Accessed 2015. http://pbyrescue.com.

Serling, Robert J. *From the Captain to the Colonel: An Informal History of Eastern Airlines.* New York: The Dial Press, 1980.

"Servicemen's Readjustment Act." Pub.L. 783–46; 58 Stat. 284m (June 22, 1944).

Shaw, Frederick J. *Locating Air Force Base Sites: History's Legacy* (CreateSpace Independent Publishing Platform, 2012).

Sim, David. "VE Day 70th anniversary: A look at Germany's surrender in 1945 and the end of World War II." *International Business Times.* May 6, 2015. http://www.ibtimes.co.uk/ve-day-70th-anniversary-look-germanys-surrender-1945ww2-graphic-images-1499979.

Simms, Stacy-Ann B. (Chief Warrant Officer 4, U.S. Army; Chief, Awards and Decorations Branch). Letter to the Honorable Senator Mike Crapo (Idaho). July 8, 2016.

———. "Memorandum for Service Member's Record: Awards and Decorations for Hayes, Frank P. 0-768-089 1st Lt." July 8, 2016.

"Site FLOR8. Aircraft—'The House under the Sea': PBY-5 Catalina BuNo. 08136, Plane Side No. 44-P-8." *Archaehistoria.* Accessed 2015. http://www.archaehistoria.org/solomon-islands-archaeology/21-wwii-archaeological-sites-of-the-florida-islands/51-site-flor8-aircraft-the-house-under-the-sea-pby-5-catalina-buno-08136-plane-side-no-44-p-83.

"Specifications, The Consolidated PBY 5A." *The Catalina Preservation Society.* Accessed 2015. http://pbycatalina.com /specifications/.

Stoss, Matthew. "War Stories." *GW Magazine.* Summer 2016.

"Stuttgart Army Air Field." *Encyclopedia of Arkansas History and Culture.* Accessed 2015. http://www.encyclopediaofark ansashistoryandculture.

"Stuttgart, Arkansas." *Stuttgart Chamber of Commerce*. Accessed 2015. http://www.stuttgartarkansas.org/.

Teegarden, James (Chief Warrant Officer 4 and UH-60 Black-hawk instructor pilot, U.S. Army Aviation Center of Excellence, Fort Rucker, Alabama; Director, http://pbyrescue.com). Interviews by author. 2015–16.

———. Collective archive of the Second Emergency Rescue Squadron. *PBYRescue.com*. Accessed 2015–16. http://pbyrescue.com.

"The Catalinas." *Qantas Airlines*. Accessed 2015. http://www.qantas.com/travel/airlines/history-catalinas/global/en.

"The Doolittle Tokyo Raiders." *DoolittleRaider.com*. Accessed 2015. http://www.doolittleraider.com.

"The Great Famine of 1847." *Donegal Town Website*. Accessed 2015. http://www.donegaltown.ie/Donegal-Town-History/The-Great-Famine/.

"The MacArthur Memorial." *MacArthurMemorial.org*. Accessed 2015. http://www.macarthurmemorial.org.

The Manhattan Engineer District. "The Atomic Bombings of Hiroshima and Nagasaki." *AtomicArchieve.com*. June 29, 1946. http://www.atomicarchive.com/Docs/MED/index.shtml.

The National World War II Museum, New Orleans. Accessed 2015. http://www.nationalww2museum.org.

Thrash, Charles (Colonel, U.S. Air Force, Retired). E-mail message to author. June 1, 2016.

"Tinian Island." *Atomic Heritage Foundation*. May 1, 2016. http://www.atomicheritage.org/location/tinian-island.

"Tojo Hideki, Prime Minister of Japan." *Encyclopedia Britannica*. Accessed 2015. http://www.britannica.com/biography/Tojo-Hideki.

Tryckare, Tre. *The Lore of Flight*. Gothenburg: Cagner & Co., 1970.

Twain, Mark. *The Innocents Abroad*. New York: American Publishing Co., 1899.

"Twin Falls County, Idaho." *State of Idaho*. Accessed 2015. http://www.idaho.gov/aboutidaho/county/twin-falls.

U.S. Air Force Historical Agency. "U.S. Air Force Historical Study No. 95—Air Sea Rescue 1941–1952." 1953. http://www.afhra.af.mil/studies/numberedusafhistoricalstudies51-100.asp.

U.S. Army Advanced Flying School, Douglas, Arizona. *Class Book*. 1943.

U.S. Army Air Force. "Form 54 Personal Effects (First Lieutenant Frank P. Hayes)." November 1945.

———. "Form 371 Missing Crewman (First Lieutenant Frank P. Hayes, Second Lieutenant John F. Leonard and Private First Class Wayne H. Peoples)." March 19, 1948.

———. "Form I-380 Personal Identification (First Lieutenant Frank P. Hayes)." September 23, 1948.

———. "General Order, Thirteenth Air Force, Second Emergency Rescue Squadron" (various). 1944–45.

———. "Missing Air Crew Report, Aircraft A-10A, #44-34-52, 10 October 1945, Panay Philippines." April 25, 1949.

———. "Personal Affairs Statement, Frank P. Hayes, Second Lieutenant, U.S. Army Air Force." 1945.

———. "Squadron Order, Thirteenth Air Force, Second Emergency Rescue Squadron" (various). 1944–45.

U.S. Army, Headquarters, Philippines Command. "Transmittal of Non-Recoverability Case, Board of Review, Case No. 293.9." July 18, 1949.

U.S. Congress. "Air Mail Act of 1934." 1934.

U.S. War Department. "State of Idaho, World War II Honor List of Dead and Missing." June 1946.

Wagner, William. *Reuben Fleet and the Story of Consolidated Aircraft*. Sacramento: Aero Publishers, Inc., 1976.

"War Declared." *Idaho Evening Times* (Twin Falls, ID), December 8, 1941.

"Welcome to Douglas, Arizona." *City of Douglas*. Accessed 2015. http://www.douglasaz.org/.

"Westward Expansion." *Digital Atlas of Idaho, Idaho State University.* Accessed 2015. http://imnh.isu.edu/digitalatlas /geog/explore/expand.pdf.

"William 'Billy' Mitchell: An Air Power Visionary." *HistoryNet.* Accessed 2015. http://www.historynet.com/william-billy-mitchell-an-air-power-visionary.htm.

World War II Foundation. Accessed 2015. http://www.wwii foundation.org.

Wynter Woodbury (Bud's grand-niece). E-mail messages to author. May 2016.

Yates, Ron (Twin Falls area historian). E-mail messages to author. March–June 2016.

About the Authors

Henry Lowenstein, Ph.D., a native of Danville and Richmond, Virginia, is professor of management and law and former dean of the Wall College of Business at Coastal Carolina University, Conway, South Carolina. Previously he was dean of business and public administration at California State University Bakersfield and chair of the California State Universities Association of Business Deans. Dr. Lowenstein has written many academic articles on law and public policy. He has been a consultant to federal, state and local governments and has served in executive management and board positions in the oil, financial services and furniture industries. He served under the Ford Administration in the Executive Office of the President of the United States and has numerous awards for public service and for academics. Dr. Lowenstein received his Ph.D. in Labor and Industrial Relations from the University of Illinois at Urbana—Champaign, his MBA in Transportation from The George Washington University and his B.S. in Business Administration and Economics from Virginia Commonwealth University.

Carla Faye Grabert-Lowenstein, Esq., a native of Twin Falls, Idaho and niece of First Lieutenant Frank Philby "Bud" Hayes, is an attorney in independent law practice in Conway, South Carolina. She is a member of the bars of California, South Carolina, District of Columbia, the U.S. Fourth Circuit Court of Appeals and the U.S. Supreme Court. She was, for over twenty-two years, Senior Deputy District Attorney for Kern County, California.

Today she serves as appointed counsel for State of South Carolina Department of Social Security cases and as appointed defense counsel for the U.S. District Court—District of South Carolina. Carla received her J.D. degree from Whittier College School of Law (California), attended Willamette University Graduate School of Management and received her B.S. in Political Science from the University of Idaho.

63383661R00170

Made in the USA
Middletown, DE
26 August 2019